moving to microsoft windows vista

Visual QuickProject Guide

by John Rizzo

Visual QuickProject Guide

Moving to Microsoft Windows Vista

John Rizzo

Peachpit Press

1249 Eighth Street
Berkeley, CA 94710
510/524-2178
800/283-9444
510/524-2221 (fax)

Find us on the Web at: www.peachpit.com
To report errors, please send a note to errata@peachpit.com
Peachpit Press is a division of Pearson Education

Project Editor: Rebecca Freed
Production Editor: Becky Winter
Proofreader: Karyn Johnson
Compositor: Myrna Vladic
Indexer: Rebecca Plunkett
Interior design: Elizabeth Castro
Cover design: Peachpit Press, Aren Howell
Cover photo credit: iStockPhoto.com

ISBN-13: 978-0-321-49120-6 ISBN-10: 0-321-49120-3

9 8 7 6 5 4 3 2 1

Printed and bound in the United States of America

contents

4. explore windows vista 33

5. personalize the desktop 47

6. take charge of the start menu 59

7. take charge of the taskbar 73

8. navigate folder windows 85

contents

introduction

The Visual QuickProject Guide you're reading offers a unique way to learn new skills. Instead of boring you with long text descriptions, this book uses color screen shots with clear, concise, step-by-step instructions to show you how to complete a specific project in a matter of minutes.

The short projects in this book move you from an older version of Windows to Windows Vista. If you're installing Vista on a PC you already have, you'll clean it up, back it up, upgrade its hardware, and install the Windows Vista software. If you need to buy a new PC that can handle Vista, you'll learn what to shop for and migrate your files and settings from your old computer.

You'll then dive into Vista itself, discovering how it differs from previous Windows versions. You'll learn to use brand-new features, including integrated search, enhanced security, and the handy little programs called gadgets.

Moving to Vista also means making it your own. You'll get to know the most useful of Vista's many personalization features. Once you know how configuration works in Vista, you can go on to explore the other customization options available.

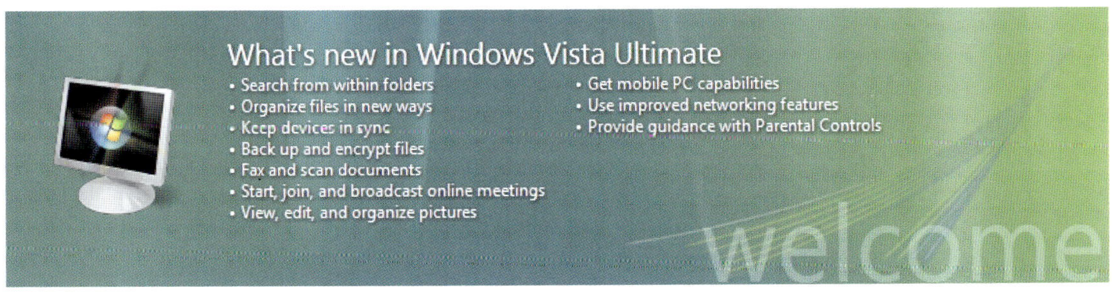

what you'll learn

Determine what your computer requires to upgrade to Windows Vista.

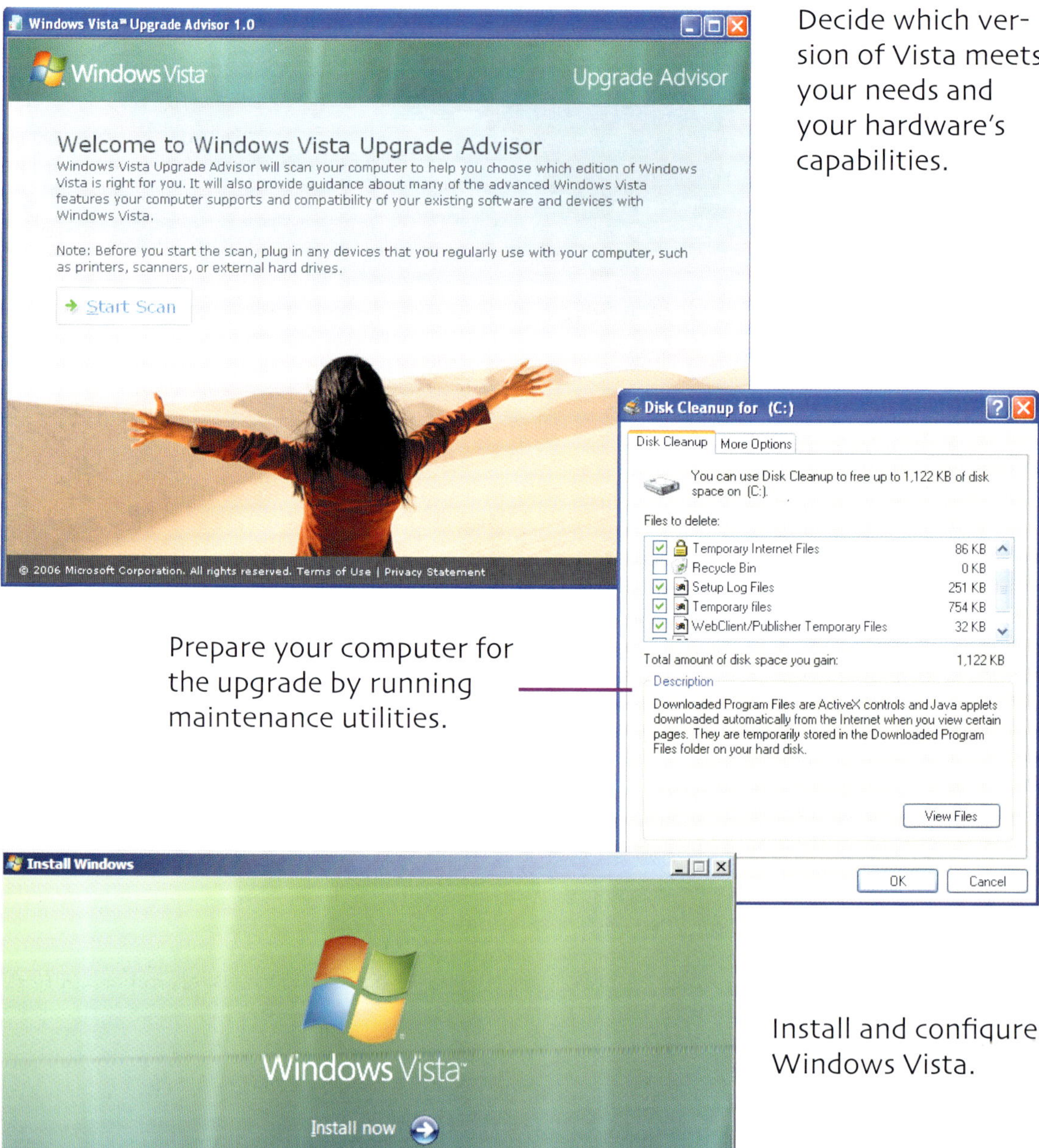

Decide which version of Vista meets your needs and your hardware's capabilities.

Prepare your computer for the upgrade by running maintenance utilities.

Install and configure Windows Vista.

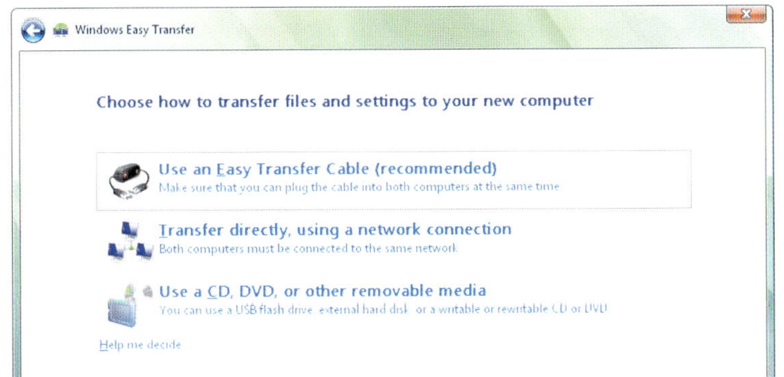

Transfer files, e-mail, application settings, bookmarks, and other data to Windows Vista from an older computer.

Use and customize the Vista Start menu.

Add programs to the Start menu.

Change the size and number of program icons.

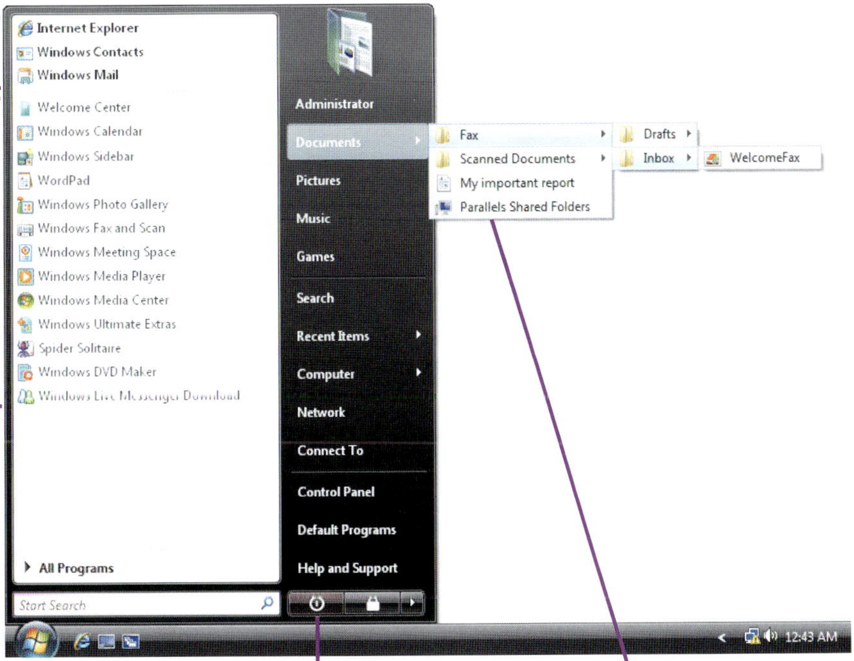

Make the Power button work as it does in Windows XP.

Convert links to menus.

what you'll learn (cont.)

Move the taskbar around or make it disappear.

Add your own programs to the Quick Launch area of the taskbar.

Add your folders to the taskbar for easy access.

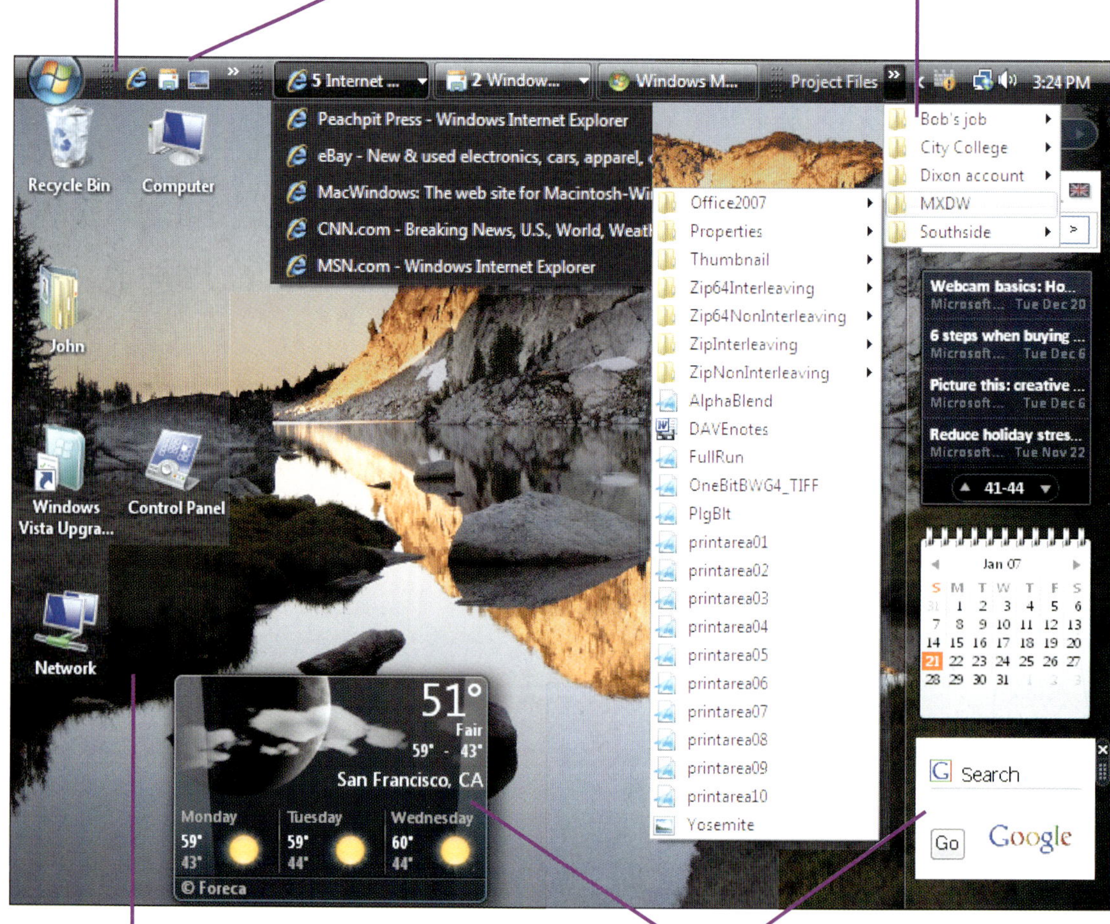

Redecorate the Desktop with art from Vista or your own photos, and change or resize the icons.

Use and modify the Vista Sidebar and gadgets.

Navigate with the new address bar.

Locate and move files using the new Explorer built into every folder window.

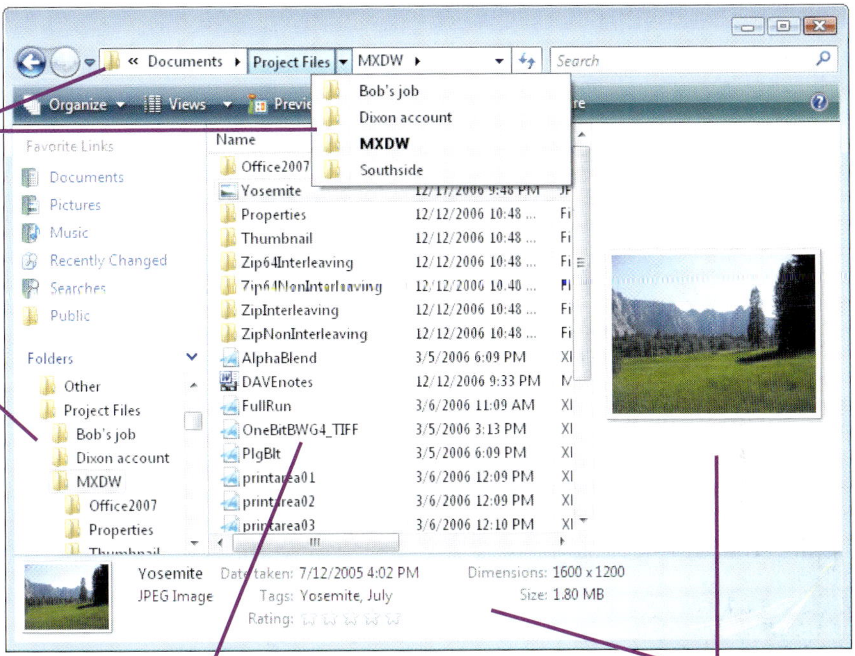

Modify the views of files.

Show and hide the different panes for previewing and editing files.

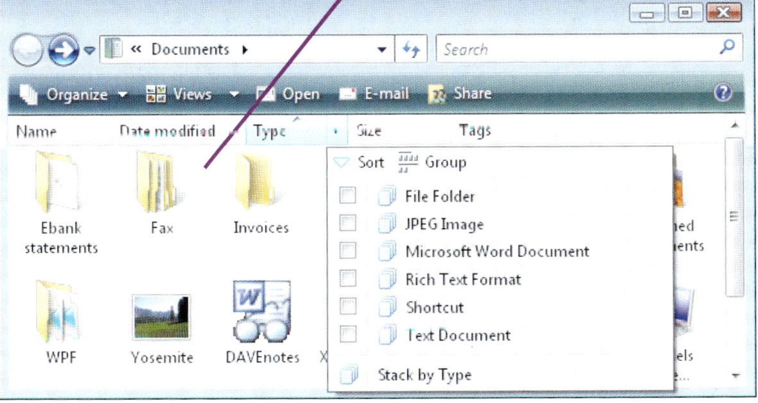

Group, sort, and search for files and folders.

Keep your computer secure.

how this book works

The title of each section explains what is covered on that page.

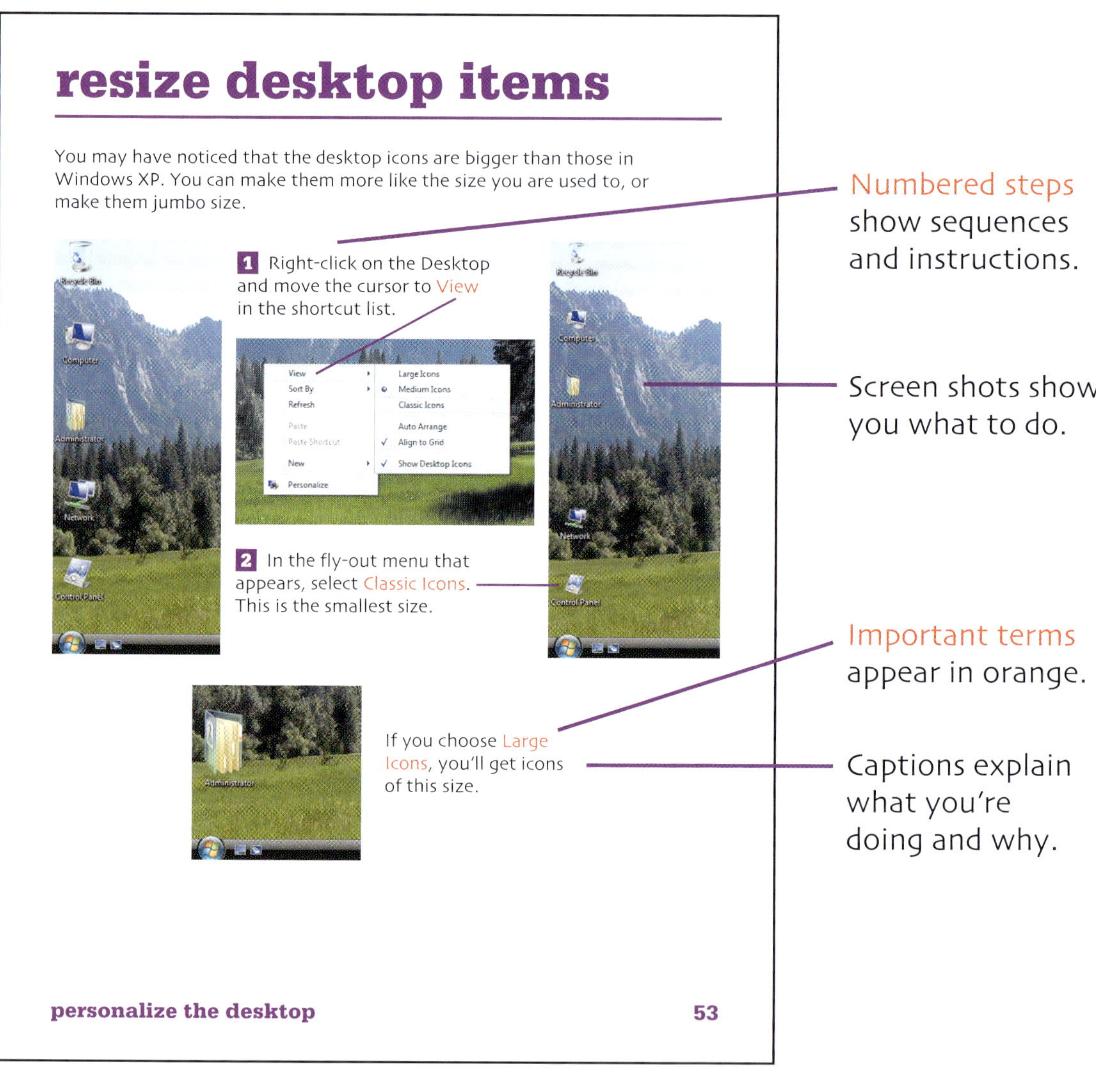

resize desktop items

You may have noticed that the desktop icons are bigger than those in Windows XP. You can make them more like the size you are used to, or make them jumbo size.

1 Right-click on the Desktop and move the cursor to View in the shortcut list.

2 In the fly-out menu that appears, select Classic Icons. This is the smallest size.

If you choose Large Icons, you'll get icons of this size.

personalize the desktop 53

The extra bits section at the end of each chapter contains additional tips and tricks that you might like to know—but that aren't absolutely necessary for completing the upgrade and using Windows Vista.

The heading for each group of tips matches the section title.

The page number next to the heading makes it easy to refer back to the main content.

extra bits

start easy transfer p. 24

- Another way to open Easy Transfer in Windows Vista is to open the Welcome Center and double-click Transfer files and settings.

choose transfer method p. 25

- Having trouble deciding which transfer method to use? Consider how much each type of storage media holds.
- CDs hold 600 MB or 700 MB of data.
- DVDs come in two capacities: Standard DVDs hold 4.7 GB of data; double-density discs hold 8.5 GB.
- A USB flash drive can hold as much as 4 GB in a package about the size of your thumb.
- USB external hard drives can hold up to several hundred gigabytes, which is useful for moving large volumes of data. A network is also good for big file moves, as is the Easy Transfer Cable.

32 move files & settings from another PC

the next step

While this Visual QuickProject Guide will walk you through getting started with Windows Vista, there's much more to learn about this operating system.

If you want to dive into even more details of using and configuring Windows Vista, try Microsoft Windows Vista: Visual QuickStart Guide, also published by Peachpit Press, as an in-depth, handy reference.

The Desktop

Using the Quick Launch Toolbar

Quick Launch begins with four Microsoft-supplied buttons (**Figure 2.43**). You can add buttons for instant one-click access to favorite files and folders or delete buttons that you don't need.

Figure 2.43 (Left to right) The Show Desktop button hides all windows; click it again to restore them to their original positions (keyboard shortcut: Windows logo key+D). The Switch Between Windows button changes the active window (keyboard shortcut: Windows logo key+Tab or Alt+Tab). The next two buttons launch Internet Explorer (Chapter 14) and Windows Media Player (Chapter 10)

To add a button to Quick Launch:

- Locate the item (icon) that you want to add, drag it over the toolbar, and then drop it where you want it to appear (**Figure 2.44**).

  or

  Locate the icon in the Start menu, right-click it, and then click Add to Quick Launch (**Figure 2.45**).

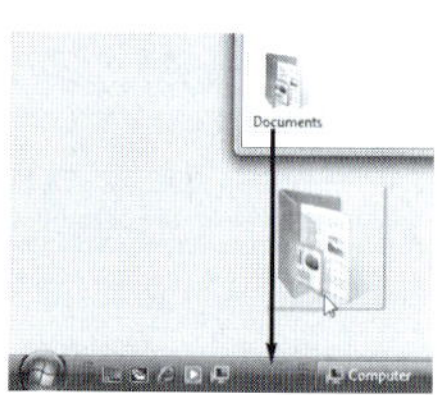

Figure 2.44 When you drag over the Quick Launch toolbar, an I-beam will appear to show where the item will land when you drop it.

✔ **Tips**

- You can add almost anything to the Quick Launch toolbar: a program, file, folder, disk, web address (URL), hardware device, Control Panel program, and so on.
- Drag buttons within the toolbar to reorder them.
- Hold down Shift when you right-click a file in a folder window, and Add to Quick Launch will appear in the shortcut menu.
- If, instead of buttons that you've added, you see the chevron button (»), it means that the hidden buttons won't fit on the toolbar. You can click the chevron to reveal the hidden buttons or—better—preserve one-click access by resizing the toolbar. To do that, right-click an empty area of the taskbar and make sure the taskbar is unlocked; then drag Quick Launch's ribbed sizing handle (refer to Figure 2.43) to the right until you see all your buttons.

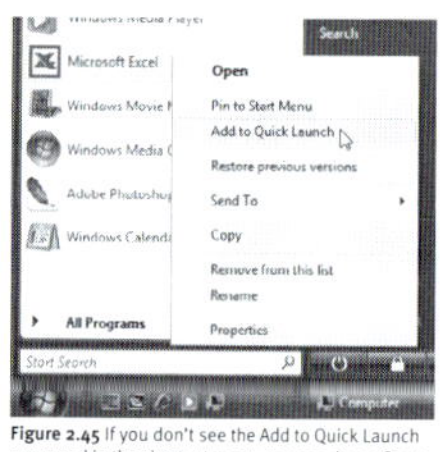

Figure 2.45 If you don't see the Add to Quick Launch command in the shortcut menu, you can drag a Start-menu icon directly to the Quick Launch toolbar.

Using the Quick Launch Toolbar

87

The Windows Vista Visual QuickStart Guide features clear examples, concise, step-by-step instructions, hundreds of illustrations, and lots of helpful tips that will help you become a master of Windows Vista.

1. prepare to upgrade

Windows Vista is so appealing that you probably just want to jump in as soon as you can. Before you take the Vista plunge, spend a little time on some preliminaries. Whether you are installing Vista on your existing computer or buying a brand-new machine, you need some background information so you can upgrade successfully.

Before you buy Vista or any hardware, you should know which version of Vista you want to get, and what hardware it will require.

In this chapter, you'll consider which version of Vista is right for you, check to see if your current or future PC is ready, and do some preventive maintenance before making the big move to Vista.

choose a vista version

There are four versions of Windows Vista available to individuals. Each has a different set of features and different hardware requirements. Since you pay more for Vista versions with more features, make sure that the version you buy fits both your expectations and your hardware budget.

These are the versions available to you, in order of increasing price and sophistication:

- Home Basic: This is the most stripped-down version of Windows Vista. It's a complete operating system that will run most of your programs but lacks the glitziest features of Vista.

  Missing from Home Basic is the Aero user interface theme and its associated features. With the Aero theme, the Start menu and most windows have a translucent look—you can see right through them to what's sitting behind them.

  Aero also has features such as taskbar thumbnail images, which previews contents of a minimized file. (Chapter 4 has more about Aero.) Instead of Aero, the Vista Home Basic edition provides a theme called Windows Vista Basic. If you want Aero, you'll need to get one of the other versions of Vista.

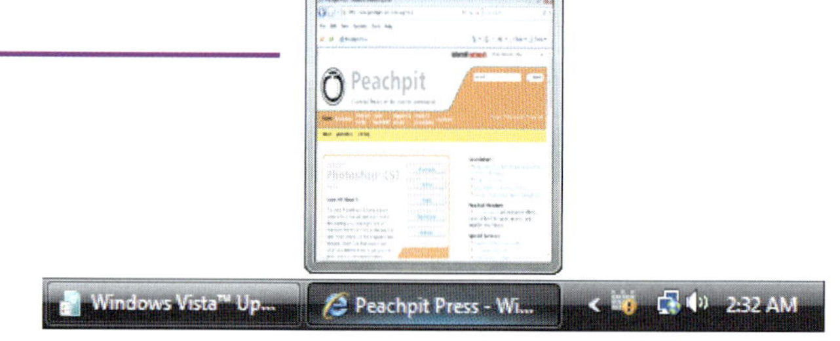

- Home Premium: In addition to the Aero theme, this version includes the Windows Media Center, which can play movies and music and, if your computer has the right hardware, record TV shows and play them back. Vista Home Premium is compatible with high-definition cable TV. Home Premium (as well as Business and Ultimate) also comes with the Windows Mobility Center, for configuring notebook settings in one place.

- Business: Windows Vista Business does not come with the Windows Media Center; instead it offers advanced backup and diagnostic software, the Network Center for connectivity, and Remote Desktop remote control software. (You may also hear about a Business Enterprise version that is for large customers.)
- Ultimate: The top of the line of Vista versions, Ultimate has all the features of both Home Premium and Business, plus the ability to encrypt data on your drive for security. Of course, you need adequate hardware to run these advanced features. On the next page you'll read about these Vista versions' varying hardware requirements.

For more information about the different versions of Vista, go to Microsoft's Web site at www.microsoft.com/windowsvista/getready/editions.

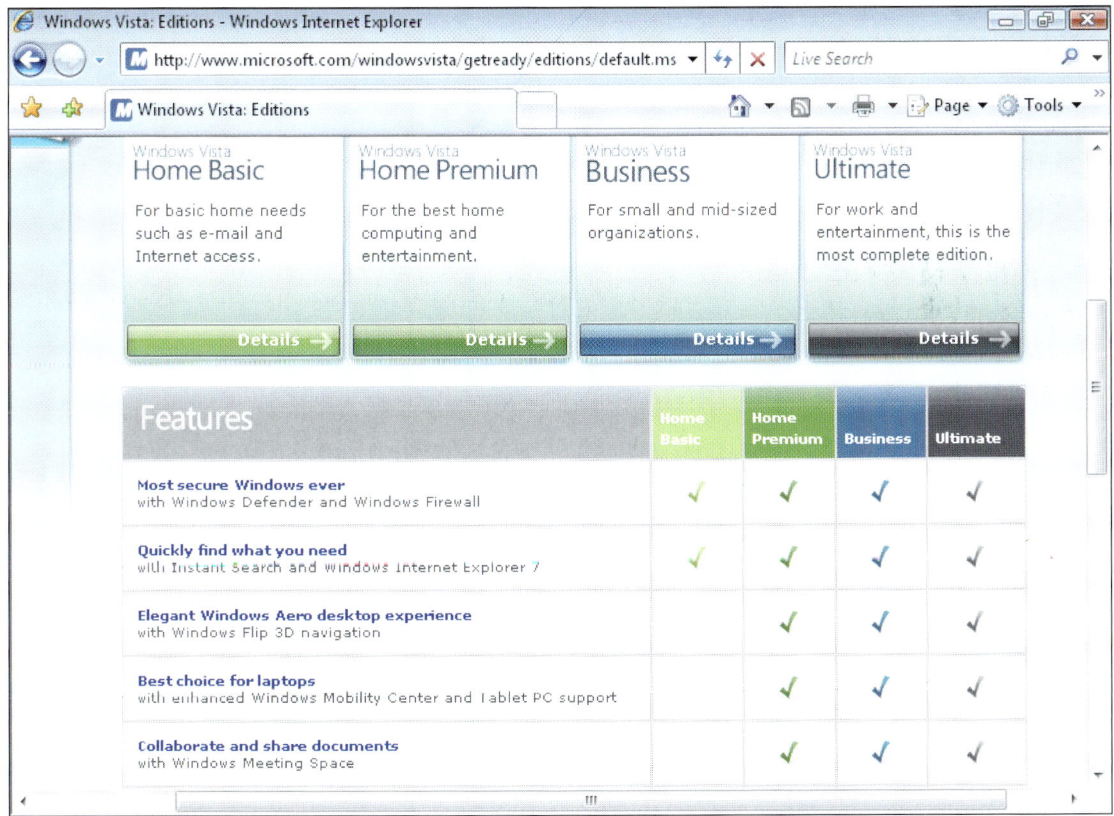

check your system

Before you buy a new PC with Windows Vista, or install Vista on your old computer, check whether the hardware can run the Vista edition you want. Vista has significantly stricter hardware requirements than previous versions of Windows, so you need to be aware of them even when buying a new computer. Here is what you need:

- Processor (aka CPU): Must run at the equivalent of 800 MHz or faster for the basic Vista experience. For the Aero theme, the processor needs to run at the equivalent of 1 GHz or faster.
- Hard drive: You need a 40 GB or bigger hard drive with at least 15 GB of free space.
- RAM: Windows Vista will technically run in 512 MB of RAM, but for any version other than Home Basic, you'll need 1 GB of RAM.
- Graphics card: This is the stickler that will keep a lot of laptops from running Vista or the Aero theme.

  For the Home Basic edition, you need a graphics card that supports DirectX 9.

  For the full Vista experience, the graphics card also needs to support WDDM (Windows Display Driver Model) drivers and Pixel Shader 2.0. It must be able to display at 32 bits per pixel and needs at least 128 MB of graphics memory. And for resolutions higher than 1920 by 1200 pixels, the graphics card needs 256 MB of graphics memory.
- DVD drive, built-in or external USB: The standard Windows Vista installation disc is a DVD-ROM (although Microsoft refers to it as a CD). You can get Vista on CDs, but it's a special order. You'll also find that in the coming years, it will become more difficult to find software on CD.

This is a lot of tech jargon to absorb. Don't worry about it. Consider this a shopping list of must-haves.

Remember that even if you pay for Vista Ultimate, if you don't have this hardware, you won't see the Aero interface or be able to use some of its multimedia features with smooth performance.

Now let's see if your Windows XP machine has enough hard drive space, processor power, and RAM to install Windows Vista.

1 Open My Computer from the Start menu or Desktop.

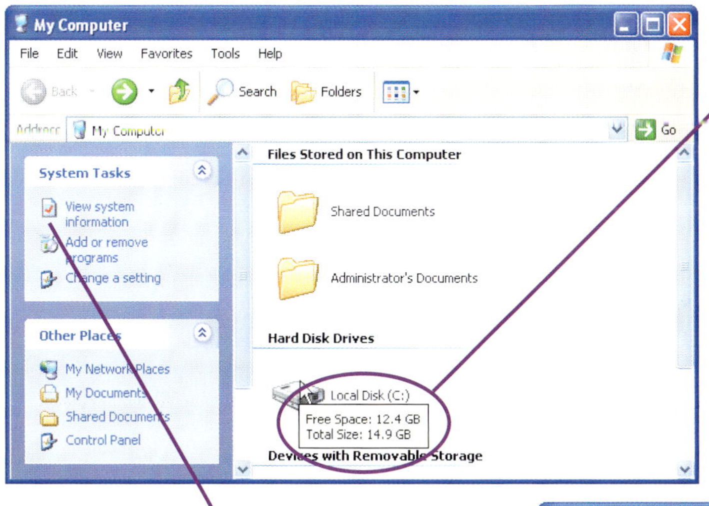

2 Move the cursor over the hard drive icon. A note will appear telling you the drive size and the free space.

This computer does not have the required 15 GB free space or 40 GB total space.

3 Click View system information in the left column of the My Computer window. The System Properties dialog opens to display the processor speed and the amount of RAM.

This computer does meet the processor requirement for the higher-end versions of Vista.

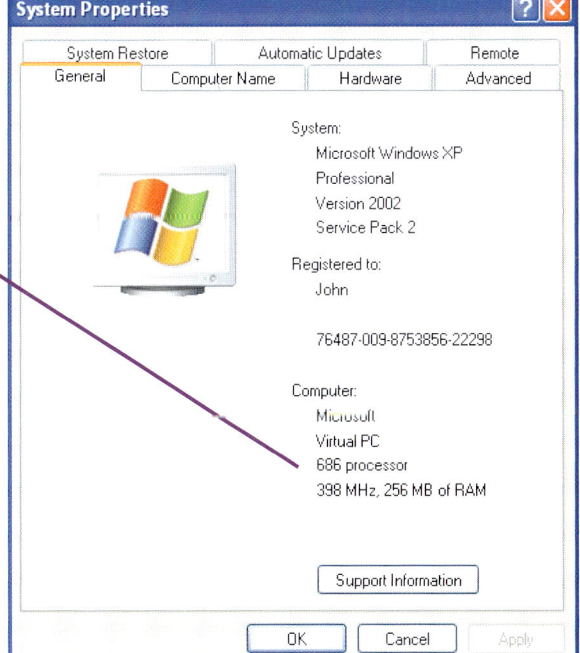

find graphics card info

Windows XP will also give you information about your graphics card, but you have to dig a little to get it.

1 Open My Computer from the Start menu or Desktop.

2 Click View system information in the left column of the My Computer window.

3 The System Properties dialog opens. Click the Hardware tab.

4 Click the Device Manager button.

5 The Device Manager window appears. Double-click the Display adapters icon.

The model of your graphics card appears here. Unfortunately, it doesn't tell you how much graphics memory you have. If you don't know, you can run Microsoft's Windows Vista Upgrade Advisor (see next page).

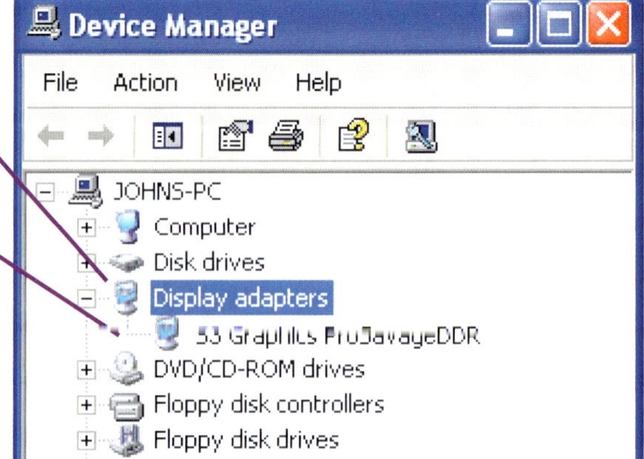

run upgrade advisor

Microsoft's free Windows Vista Upgrade Advisor is software that you run on your old Windows XP computer. It doesn't tell you how much graphics memory you have, but it does tell you if your graphics card and other hardware meet the requirements for Windows Vista. It also scans your computer and lets you know if you need to install device drivers. Upgrade Advisor also recommends which version of Windows Vista to buy and provides suggestions about what, if any, hardware updates may be necessary.

Upgrade Advisor presents the results in a more understandable, less technical manner than the dialog boxes of Windows XP. The drawback is that it will take some time to download and install the software. You can download Windows Vista Upgrade Advisor from this Web address: www.microsoft.com/windowsvista/upgradeadvisor/.

To run Upgrade Advisor on Windows XP, do the following:

1 Connect to the PC any peripheral devices that you plan to use with Windows Vista.

2 Launch Windows Vista Upgrade Advisor from the Start menu's All Programs area.

3 Click Start Scan in the welcome window that appears. The software will scan your computer for a few minutes.

run upgrade advisor (cont.)

Upgrade Advisor issues a report when it finishes scanning your computer.

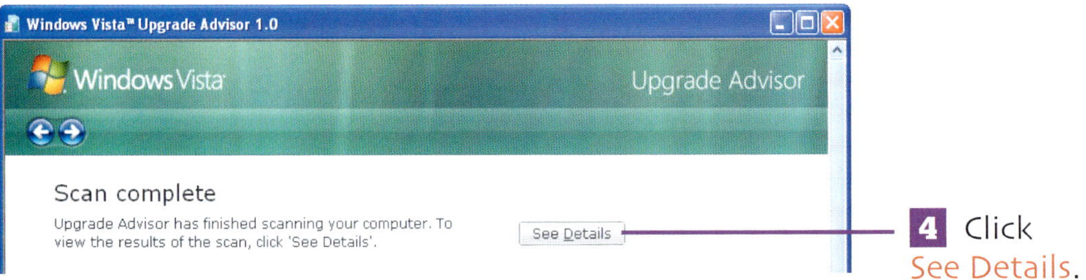

4 Click See Details.

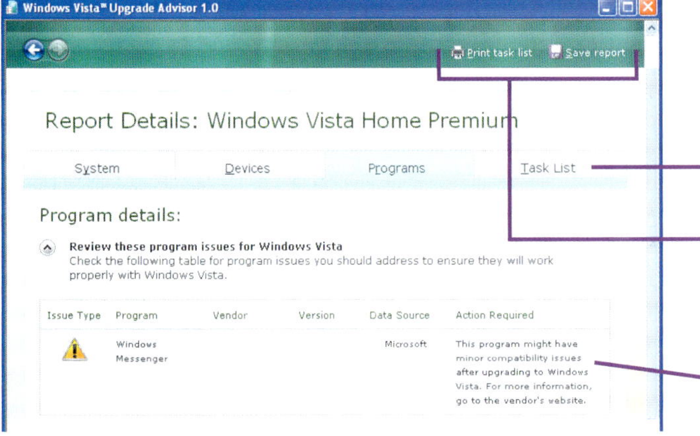

Upgrade Advisor presents a multipage report that lists compatibility issues with your hardware and software. The Task List summarizes what you should upgrade.

These two icons let you print the task list and save the entire report.

Here it found an application that may have problems running in Vista.

This part of the report shows that the Aero theme will not run. You can click this link to go to a Web page for a list of cards that will run Aero.

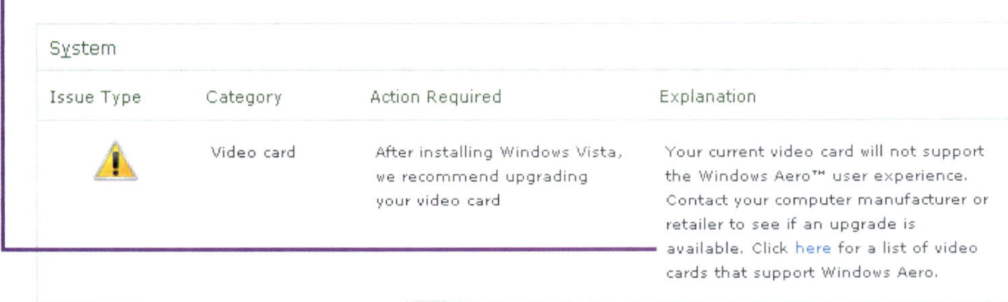

System

Issue Type	Category	Action Required	Explanation
⚠	Video card	After installing Windows Vista, we recommend upgrading your video card	Your current video card will not support the Windows Aero™ user experience. Contact your computer manufacturer or retailer to see if an upgrade is available. Click here for a list of video cards that support Windows Aero.

The graphics card in this computer is adequate to run Windows Vista Home. It also could run Vista Business—if you didn't mind using the Windows Vista Basic theme instead of Aero.

buy a new PC for vista

It may not be worth the cost or trouble to upgrade a computer to Vista, and upgrading may not even be an option with some computers. For instance, some notebooks can't be upgraded to the degree that Vista requires. On the other hand, a brand-new, bargain-basement computer also may not have what it takes to run Vista.

Be careful when shopping for a new PC. You'll see two labels for computers that can run Vista: Windows Vista Capable and Windows Vista Premium Ready.

Not all PCs labeled Windows Vista Capable can run all the features of Vista. Vista Capable PCs are guaranteed to run Windows Home Basic, but they may not support the features of higher versions, such as the full Aero interface or the Windows Media Center. For that, you need a Vista Premium Ready PC and a copy of Vista Home Premium or Vista Ultimate.

clean up the hard drive

Before installing Windows Vista or moving your data from an old XP system to a new Vista computer, it's a good idea to run some of the hard drive utilities of Windows XP to make sure the transition goes as smoothly as possible. You should also back up important data in case disaster—like a power failure—strikes in the middle of your installation.

Your maintenance tasks include automatically deleting old unwanted files, running error-checking and defragmentation programs, and backing up your data. This is all done from the Disk Properties dialog.

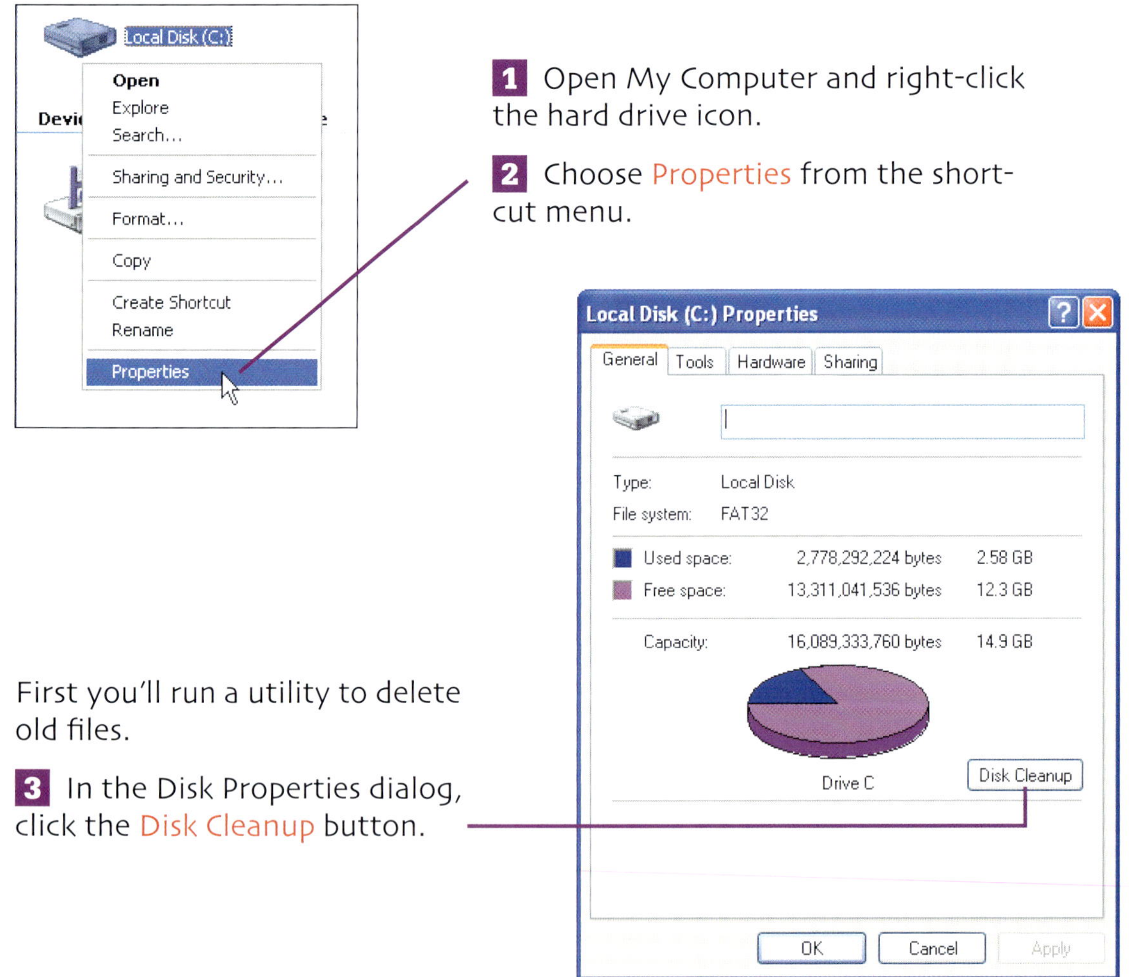

1 Open My Computer and right-click the hard drive icon.

2 Choose Properties from the shortcut menu.

First you'll run a utility to delete old files.

3 In the Disk Properties dialog, click the Disk Cleanup button.

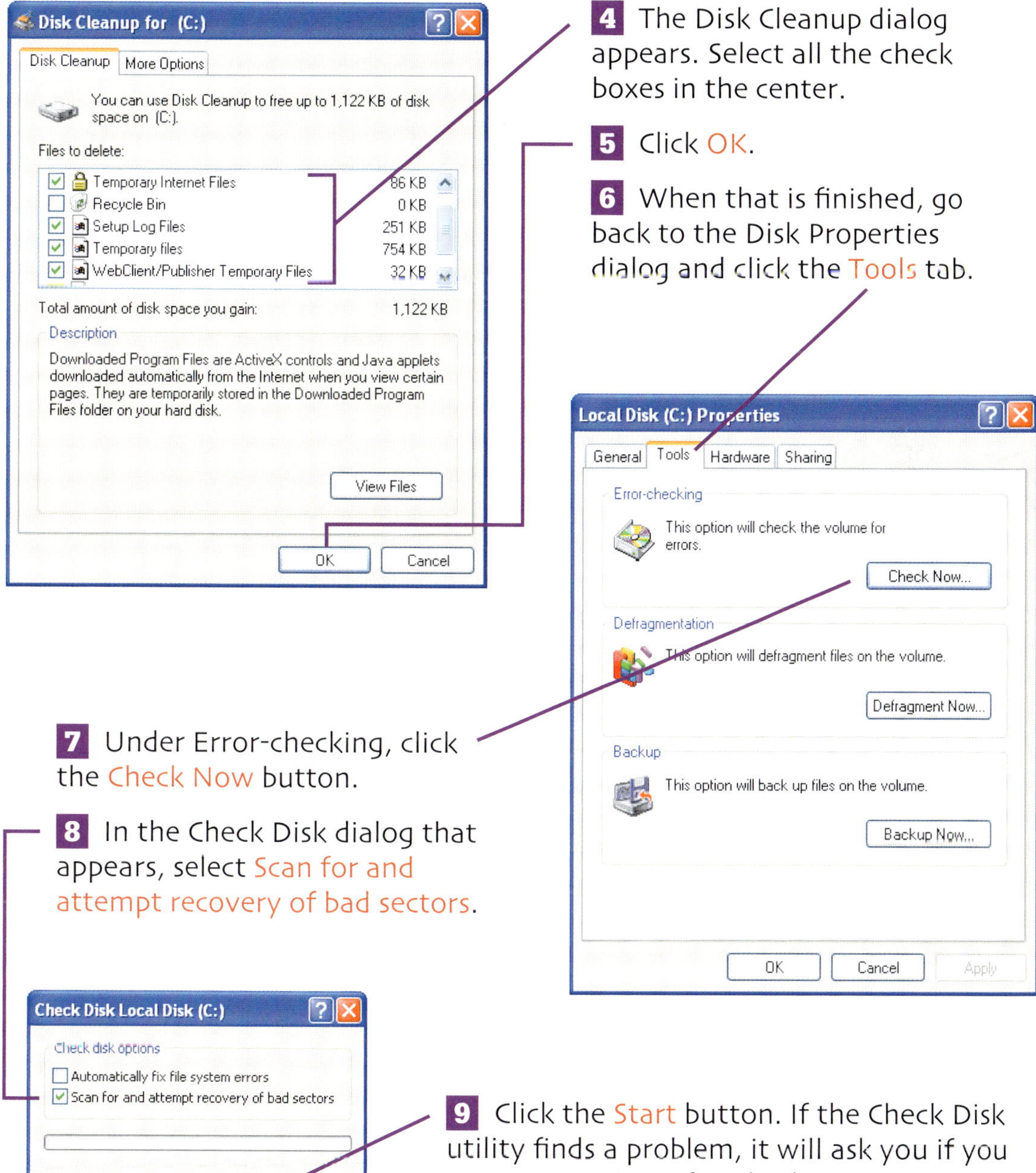

4 The Disk Cleanup dialog appears. Select all the check boxes in the center.

5 Click OK.

6 When that is finished, go back to the Disk Properties dialog and click the Tools tab.

7 Under Error-checking, click the Check Now button.

8 In the Check Disk dialog that appears, select Scan for and attempt recovery of bad sectors.

9 Click the Start button. If the Check Disk utility finds a problem, it will ask you if you want to repair it. If so, back up your important data first. Then go back and run Check Disk again.

defrag the hard drive

Now it's time to defragment (or defrag) the hard drive. You'll back up your data after that.

1 Back in the Disk Properties dialog, under Defragmentation, click the Defragment Now button.

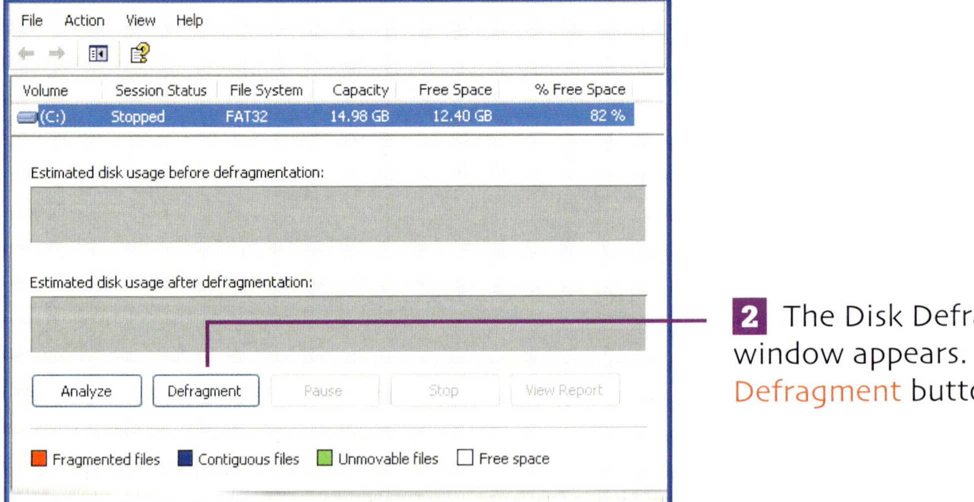

2 The Disk Defragmenter window appears. Click the Defragment button.

back up your data

If you use Windows XP Professional, the Windows Backup utility is preinstalled. For Windows XP Home Edition, you'll have to install it from your Windows XP disc if you haven't already. Once it's installed, follow these steps.

1 Make sure your backup medium is connected to your computer. This can be an external hard drive or flash drive plugged into the USB port, a CD or DVD disc in the optical drive, or a network drive.

2 Go back to the Disk Properties dialog and click the Backup Now button.

3 The Backup or Restore Wizard appears. Click through the screens until you get to the What to Back Up dialog. Click My documents and settings.

4 Click Next.

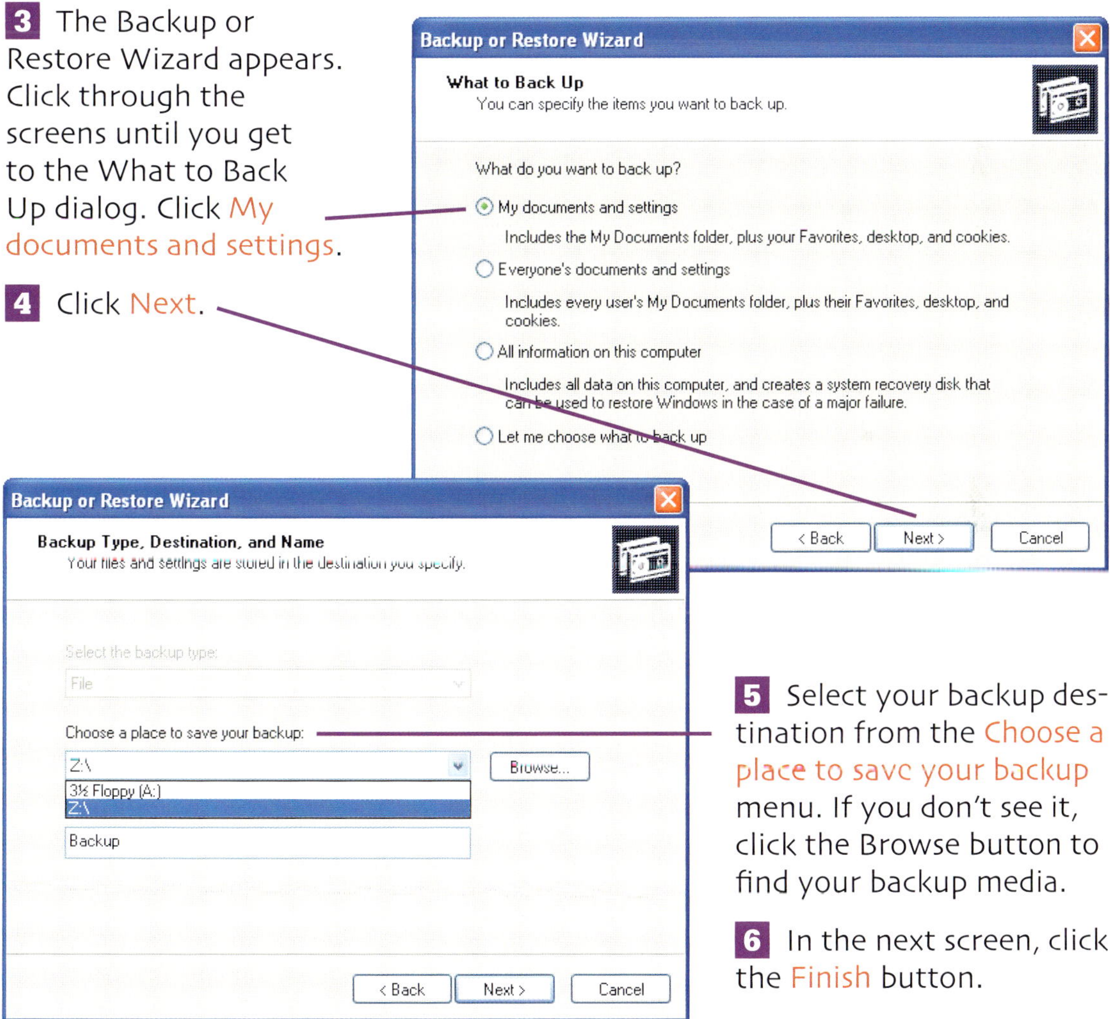

5 Select your backup destination from the Choose a place to save your backup menu. If you don't see it, click the Browse button to find your backup media.

6 In the next screen, click the Finish button.

extra bits

check your system p. 4

- Vista hardware requirements may seem strict, but even owners of Apple computers can run Windows Vista, using some special software. Mac users running Vista can follow the information in this chapter and, in fact, in the whole book.
- The hardware requirements for running Windows Vista on a Mac are the same as those for any computer. The CPU must be an Intel processor, which means Macs older than a few years are incompatible with Vista.
- Mac users have several Vista-enabling software choices. Mac OS X 10.5 Leopard comes with Boot Camp, which lets you reboot a Mac into Windows XP or Windows Vista. For Mac OS X 10.4 Tiger, you can download Boot Camp for free at www.apple.com/bootcamp.
- For running Windows and Mac OS X at the same time, you can buy a copy of Parallels Desktop (www.parallels.com) or VMware (www.vmware.com).
- Parallels and VMware also have versions for standard Windows-based computers. Microsoft also has one called Virtual PC. These programs let you run Windows XP and Windows Vista both on the same computer and at the same time. Now that's ultimate Windows.

run upgrade advisor p. 7

- The Windows Vista Upgrade Advisor isn't always correct. When it can't locate installed Vista drivers, it may tell you that some peripheral devices won't work. But devices such as printers sometimes do work without new Vista drivers, even though Upgrade Advisor might say otherwise.
- If you'd like a second opinion, try the AMD/ATI Vista Readiness Assessment Tool. It's a Web-based tool that downloads a program to your computer. It can provide more details than Microsoft's Upgrade Advisor. To use it, point your browser to: http://ati.amd.com/technology/windowsvista/AreYouVistaReady.html.

2. install windows vista

Windows Vista comes preloaded on many brand-new PCs. If you already have a computer with Windows Vista installed, you can go directly to Chapter 3, "Move Files & Settings from Another PC."

If you want to upgrade your computer from an older version of Windows, read on. You'll need a Windows Vista installation disc and at least 15 GB of free hard disk space on your PC.

To get started, insert the Windows Vista DVD. After some loading of data onto the computer, the screen below appears.

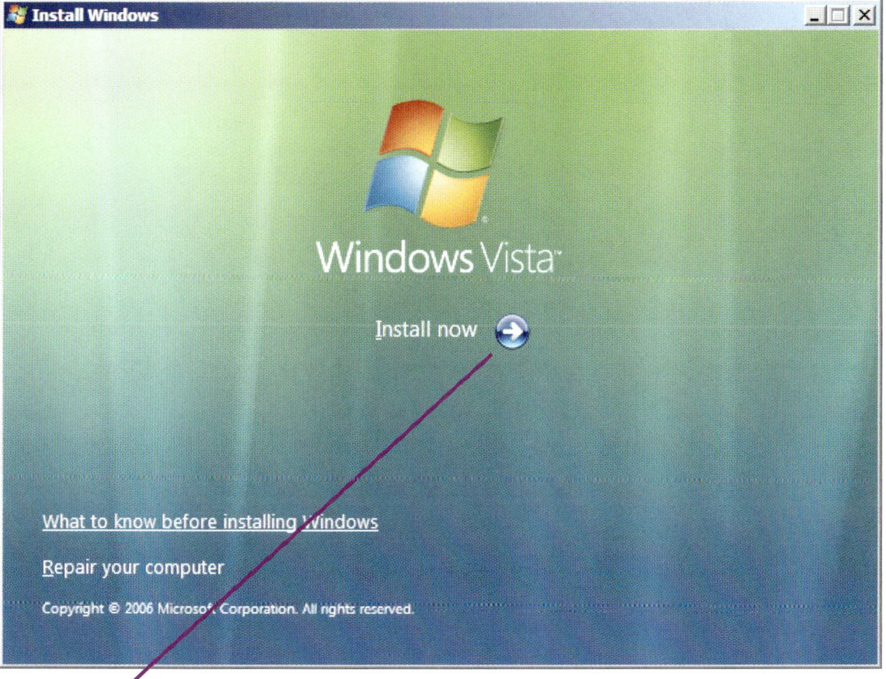

Click the Install now button and you're on your way.

begin the installation

During the installation process, Windows will restart several times, booting from the DVD and then rebooting from the computer hard disk. You'll then get a window asking you to enter the product key number that came with your copy of Windows Vista.

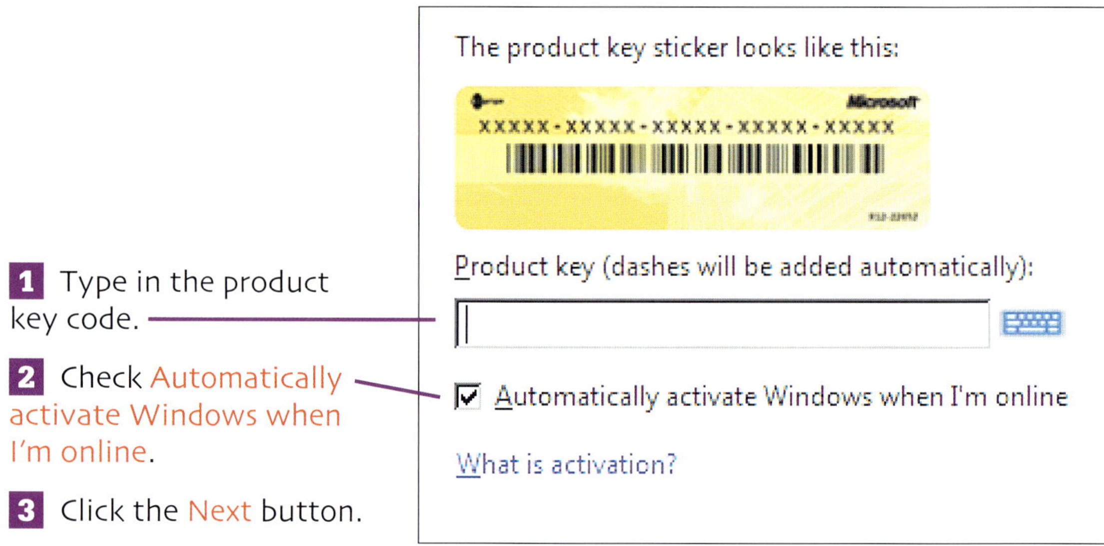

1 Type in the product key code.

2 Check Automatically activate Windows when I'm online.

3 Click the Next button.

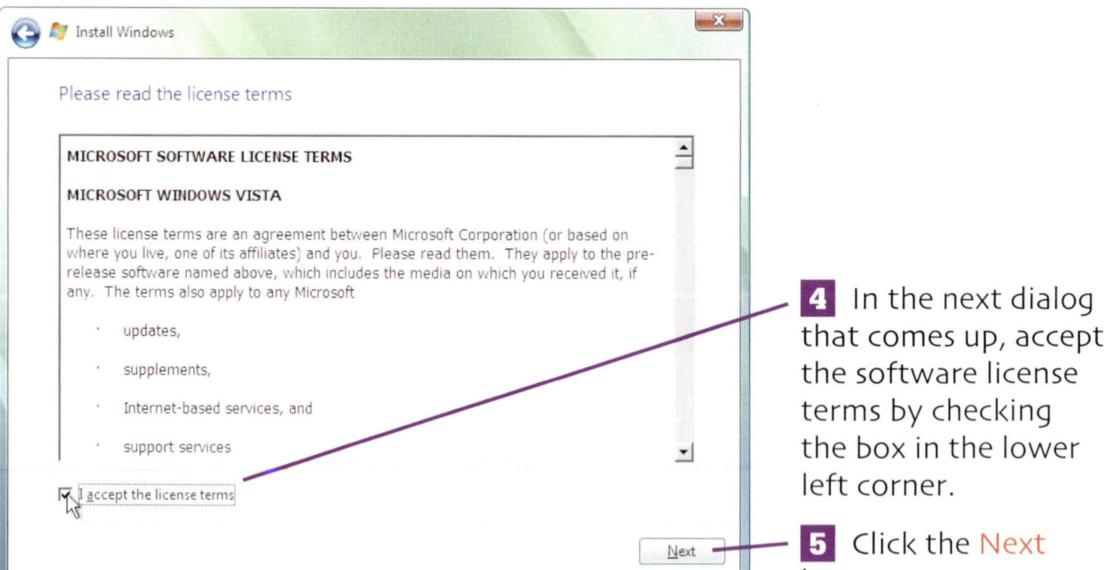

4 In the next dialog that comes up, accept the software license terms by checking the box in the lower left corner.

5 Click the Next button.

choose installation type

The next window asks you to choose between two types of installations.

Which type of installation do you want?

Upgrade
Keep your files, settings, and programs and upgrade Windows.
Be sure to back up your files before upgrading.

Custom (advanced)
Install a clean copy of Windows, select where you want to install it, or make changes to disks and partitions.
This option does not keep your files, settings, and programs.

Help me decide

The Upgrade and Custom installation options are almost the same. Both will erase your old operating system on the hard drive while installing Windows Vista. The difference is that Upgrade saves your files, settings, and applications and reinstalls them after installing Vista.

The Custom option is useful for upgrading a new PC that came with Windows XP, or a PC that it's OK to completely erase. The Custom installation method also gives you some additional options.

Click one of the installation types to continue.

configure drive options

If you clicked Custom, this window will appear. Here you can make some changes to the drives attached to your computer.

The Where do you want to install Windows dialog will list the hard drives connected to your computer. If you have more than one drive or partition, click the drive where you want to install Windows Vista.

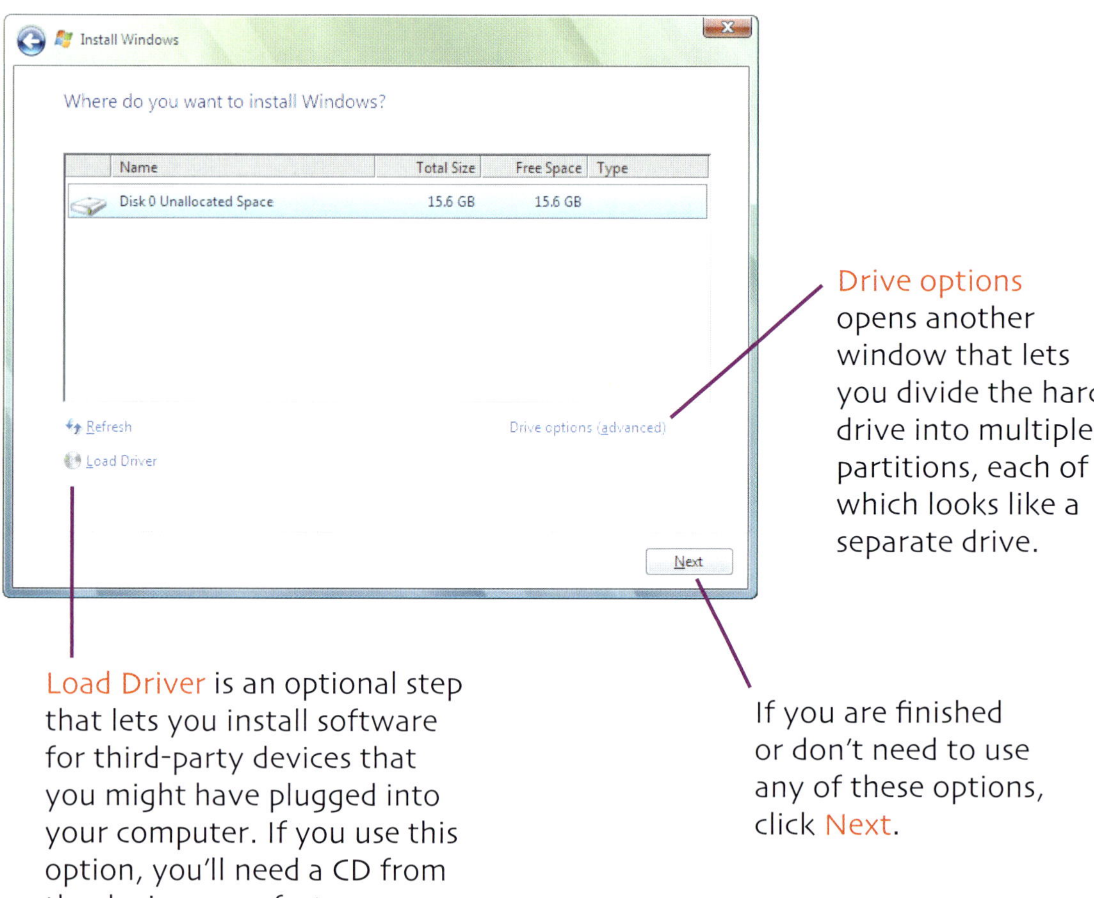

Drive options opens another window that lets you divide the hard drive into multiple partitions, each of which looks like a separate drive.

Load Driver is an optional step that lets you install software for third-party devices that you might have plugged into your computer. If you use this option, you'll need a CD from the device manufacturer.

If you are finished or don't need to use any of these options, click Next.

name user & computer

The installer will restart your computer again and display several messages. The next window that appears asks you to create a user name and password.

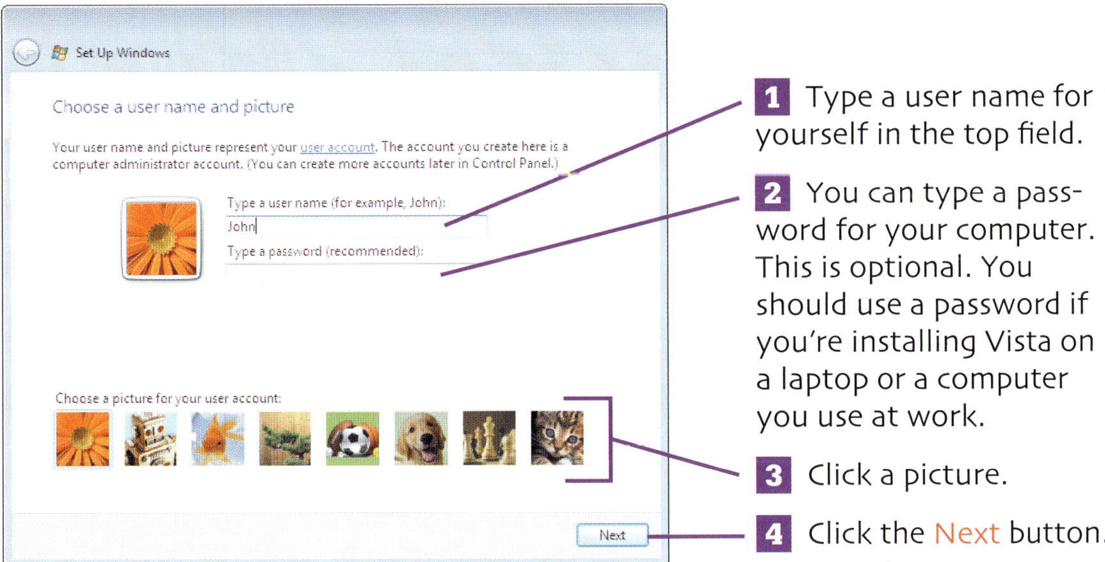

1 Type a user name for yourself in the top field.

2 You can type a password for your computer. This is optional. You should use a password if you're installing Vista on a laptop or a computer you use at work.

3 Click a picture.

4 Click the Next button.

A new window appears that asks for information to identify your computer.

5 Windows will choose a name for your computer. If you want to change it, type a new name here.

6 Click a picture to be used on the desktop. If you don't, the first picture on the left will be used. (Chapter 5 describes how to change the desktop picture, and even use your own photo.)

7 Click Next.

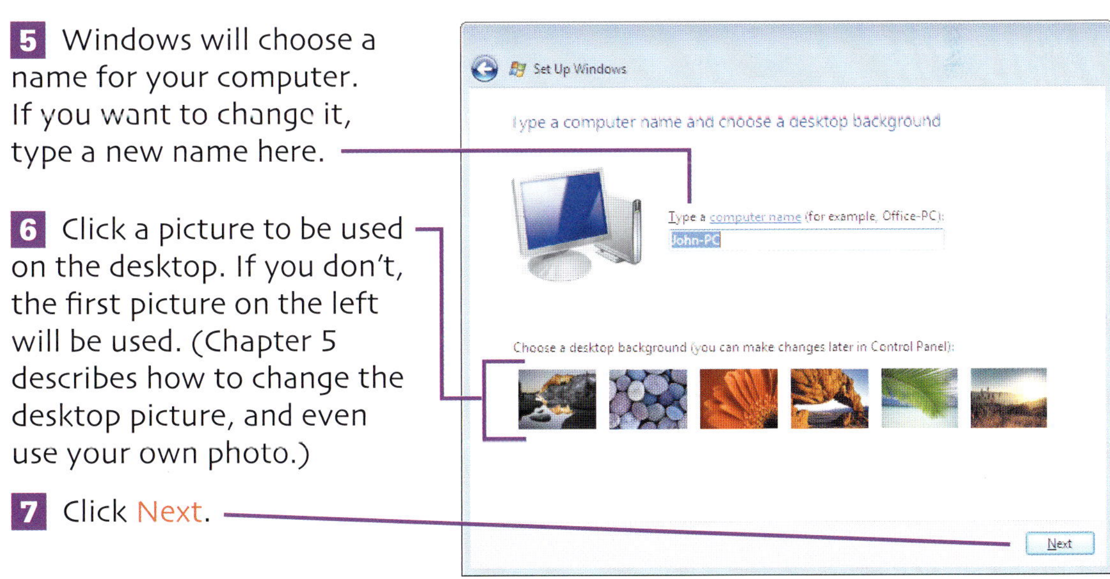

finish installing vista

The next configuration window that appears asks you to choose one of three options for software updates and security.

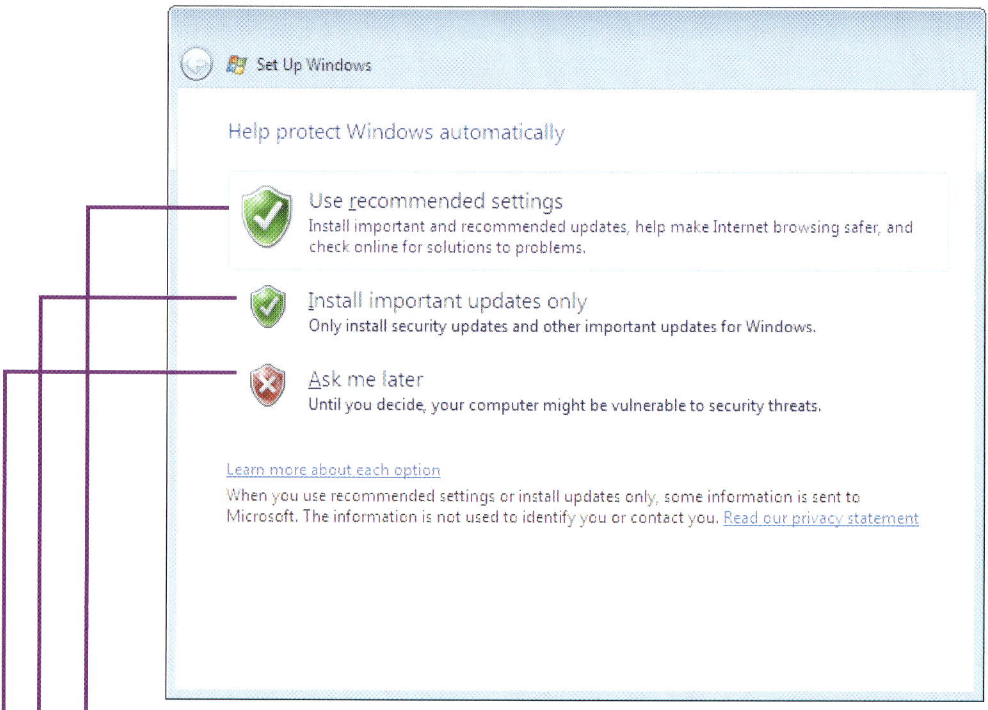

The Use recommended settings option allows Windows to check for updates on the Internet and to install them. This setting also turns on security settings for Web browsing and attempts to block harmful software such as viruses. This is the best option to choose when installing Windows Vista.

Install important updates only allows updates for Windows to be installed, but it does not turn on Internet security.

Ask me later does not allow Windows to check for any updates and does not turn on any security settings. A drawback is that you may miss periodic security updates that Microsoft creates to keep your computer safe.

Click one of the three options to continue with the installation.

Windows will ask you to check the date and time settings on your computer, and will then bring up this final setup window.

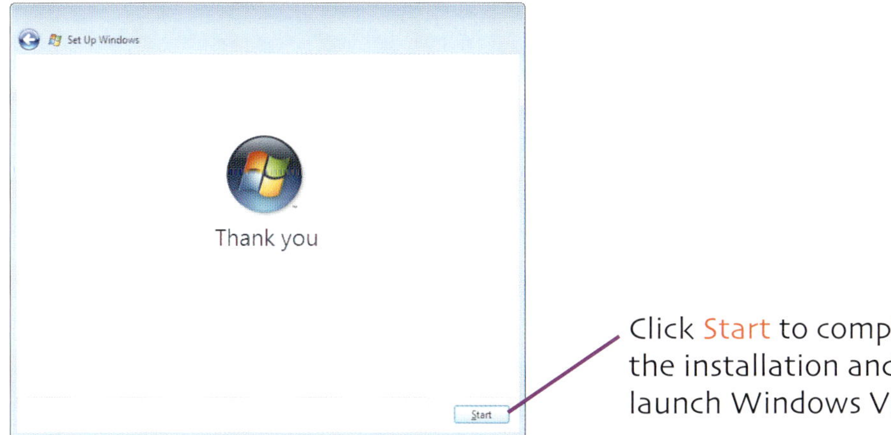

Click Start to complete the installation and launch Windows Vista.

When Windows Vista first appears, it brings you to the Welcome Center, where you can find information about your computer as well as change some of the settings.

We'll come back to the Welcome Center later in the book. For now, you have finished upgrading your computer to Windows Vista.

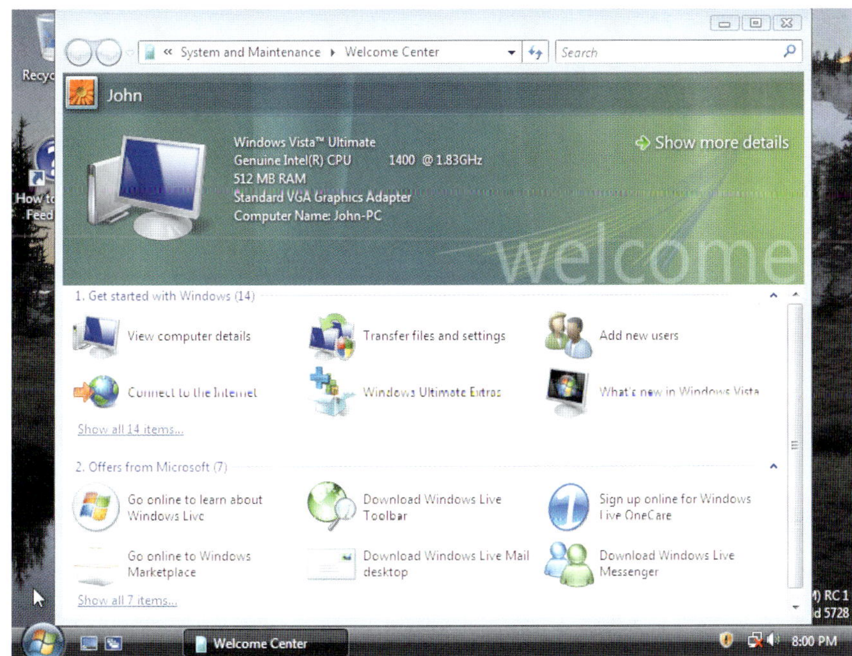

extra bits

begin the installation p. 16

- The Automatically activate Windows when I'm online option that you checked during installation causes your computer to contact Microsoft via the Internet three days after you launch Windows Vista for the first time. Windows will send Microsoft the product key to verify that you have a legal, not-counterfeit copy of Windows.
- Microsoft gives you 30 days to activate Windows Vista. If you don't, Windows will tell you how to activate by phone or by purchasing a new key online.
- If you still don't activate after 30 days, Windows will run in Reduced Functionality mode. This turns off some features, including the ability to create new files. This mode also disables Microsoft Office, rendering your computer less than functional until you activate Windows.
- If you didn't choose the option to automatically activate when you installed Windows, and you don't want to wait for Windows to get nasty, you can activate by Internet or phone. To find out how, open the Start menu, select Help and Support, and search for activate. Then click Activate Windows on this computer.

name user & computer p. 19

- You can change the user name, picture, and password that you set during installation. Go to the Start menu, choose Welcome Center, and then double-click Add new users. The dialog that appears lets you change your own information.
- In the window that appears, you can also add other users for this computer, each with their own password.

3. move files & settings from another PC

The hardest thing about moving to a new computer is getting all your settings (your bookmarks, passwords, etc.) and files onto your new computer. Windows Vista takes the work out of this with software called Easy Transfer. This utility runs on both your new Windows Vista computer and your old Windows PC. It finds your files and settings, including Internet configurations, Windows system preferences, and application settings. Easy Transfer moves these files from your old Windows XP or Windows 2000 computer to your new computer using one of the following methods:

- The Easy Transfer Cable, a special USB cable that comes with software that you install on your old computer; this is the easiest option
- A network, such as an Ethernet or a wireless network
- DVDs or CDs
- An external hard drive
- A USB flash drive

In this chapter we will use a USB flash drive as an example, but we will also point out how to use other options.

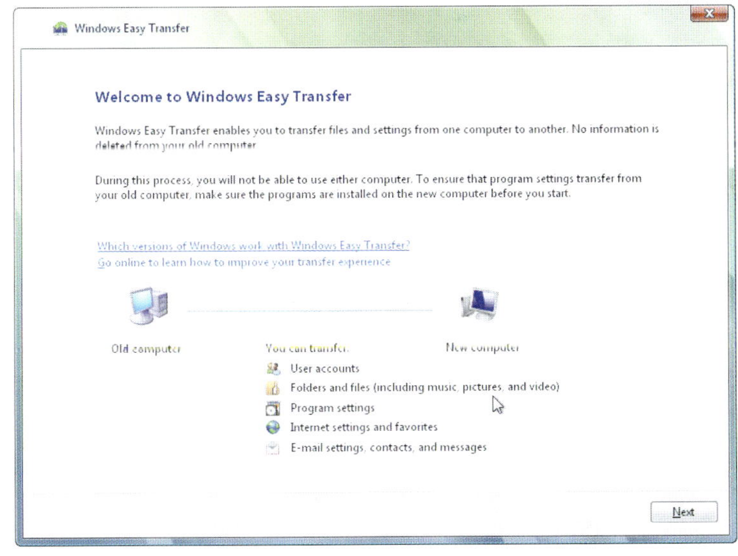

start easy transfer

If your old PC is running Windows XP or Vista, you can transfer both files and settings to your new computer. If your old computer is running Windows 2000, Easy Transfer will move only files.

You begin the transfer by starting the Easy Transfer software on the new computer.

1 Click the Start button and choose Windows Easy Transfer from the Start menu.

2 Windows asks you for permission to proceed. Click Continue.

3 Windows welcomes you to Easy Transfer. Click Next.

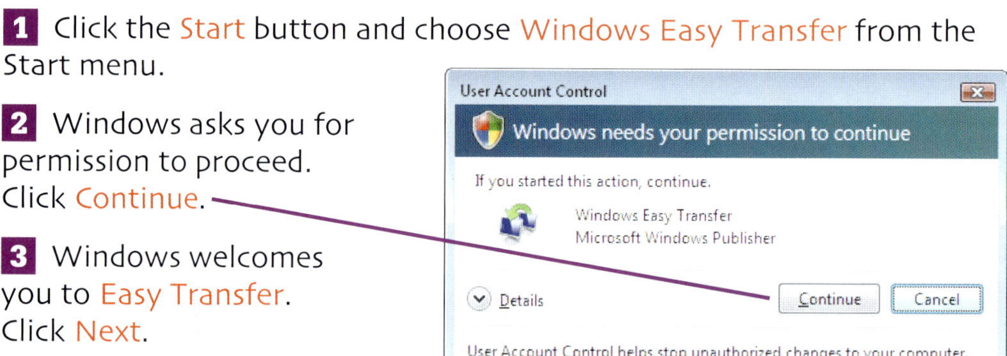

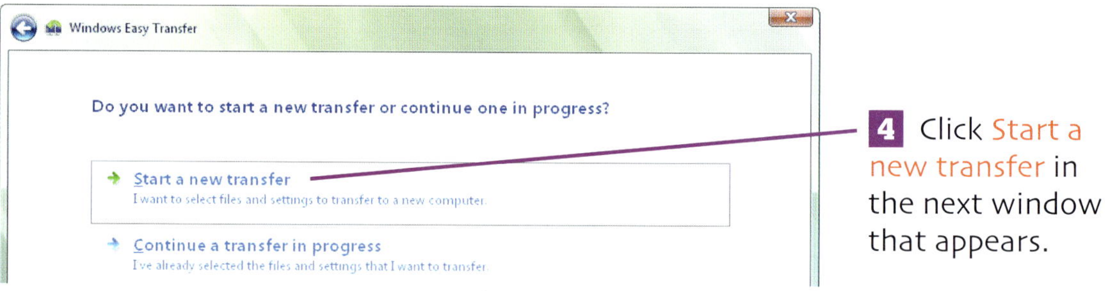

4 Click Start a new transfer in the next window that appears.

5 Easy Transfer now asks which computer you are running. Click My new computer.

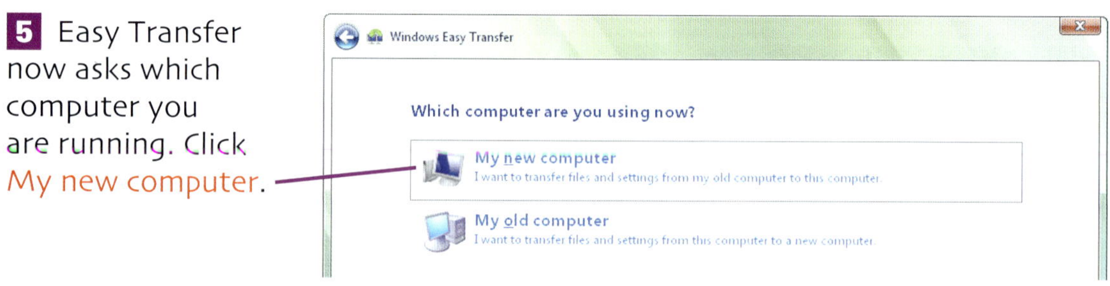

choose transfer method

The next window asks you how you want to move the data.

Using an Easy Transfer Cable is the easiest way to move your files and settings to your Windows Vista computer. They are available from various manufacturers and can be found in computer stores or online (the price was about $30 at the time Vista was released). Each cable comes with a CD of transfer software to install on the old computer. The drawback is that you might use the cable only once.

Click Yes, I have an Easy Transfer Cable if you are using this method to move your data into Windows Vista. A new screen will provide information about using the cable.

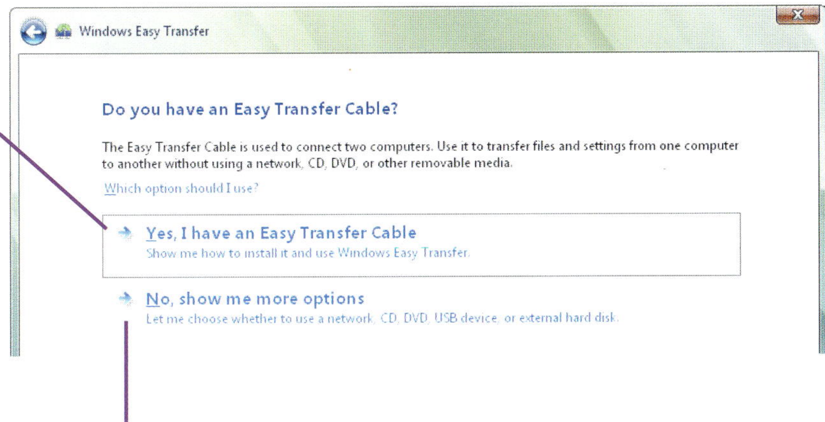

Click No, show me more options if you are moving your data using a network or storage device such as a CD or DVD, an external USB hard drive, or a USB flash drive (as in our example).

Portable storage devices like these are a good way to go if the old and new PCs are in different rooms or buildings. If you have a lot of files, you might need a lot of CDs to move them all. In this case, DVDs would be better because they hold 6 to 12 times more data than CDs.

A USB flash drive is a handy and inexpensive way to move as much as a gigabyte (10 to 20 DVDs' worth) of data between computers.

A network is the most complicated method if you don't already have one set up between the computers.

select method of transfer

If you chose No, show me more options, in the previous window, a new screen asks you if you've installed Easy Transfer on your old computer.

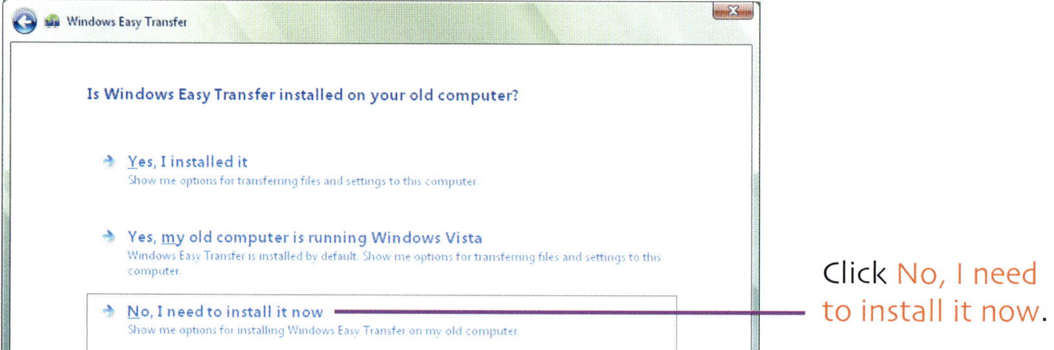

Click No, I need to install it now.

The next window asks you how you are going to install the Easy Transfer software on your old Windows XP computer. Note that the screen is not asking how you are going to move the files.

The simplest method is to use your Windows Vista installation disc to install Easy Transfer on your old Windows XP or Windows 2000 computer. Although the screen here refers to the disc as a CD, the Vista install disc is actually a DVD. The only reason not to use this method is if your old PC cannot read DVDs.

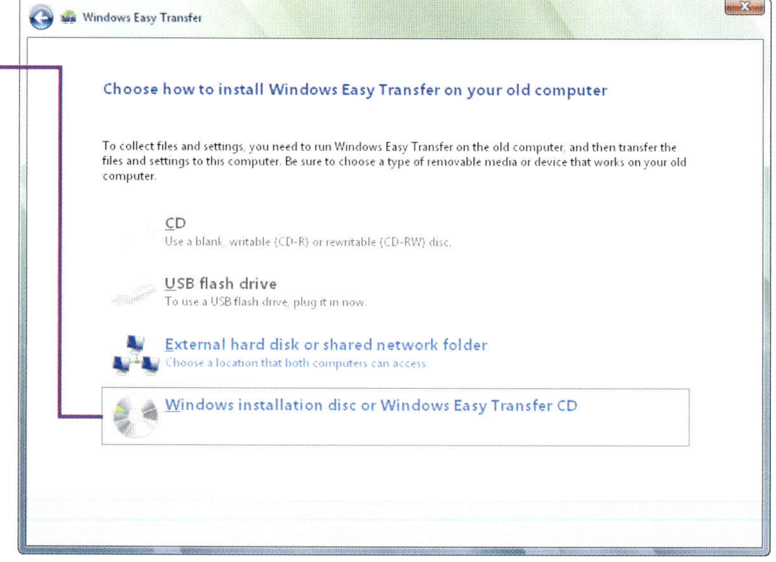

run software on old PC

You can now run Easy Transfer on your old Windows XP or Windows 2000 computer.

1 Insert your Windows Vista DVD into your old computer. The Windows Vista installation screen will appear in Windows XP.

2 Click Transfer files and settings from another computer. (Don't click Install now!)

3 Click Next in the welcome screen that appears.

copy data from old PC

The Easy Transfer software running on your old Windows XP machine will now ask you how you want to move the data to the new Windows Vista machine. In this example, we'll select USB flash memory. But you can choose another option.

If you choose Use an Easy Transfer Cable, a window will appear asking you to connect the old and new computers with the cable. The cable plugs into a USB port on each machine.

If you choose Transfer directly, using a network connection, a message may come up asking if Easy Transfer can change a firewall setting to allow the transfer over the network. Click Yes, then follow the directions in the next few screens.

If you choose Use a CD, DVD, or other removable media, a window will appear asking you to choose the type of device.

We will click USB flash drive in this example.

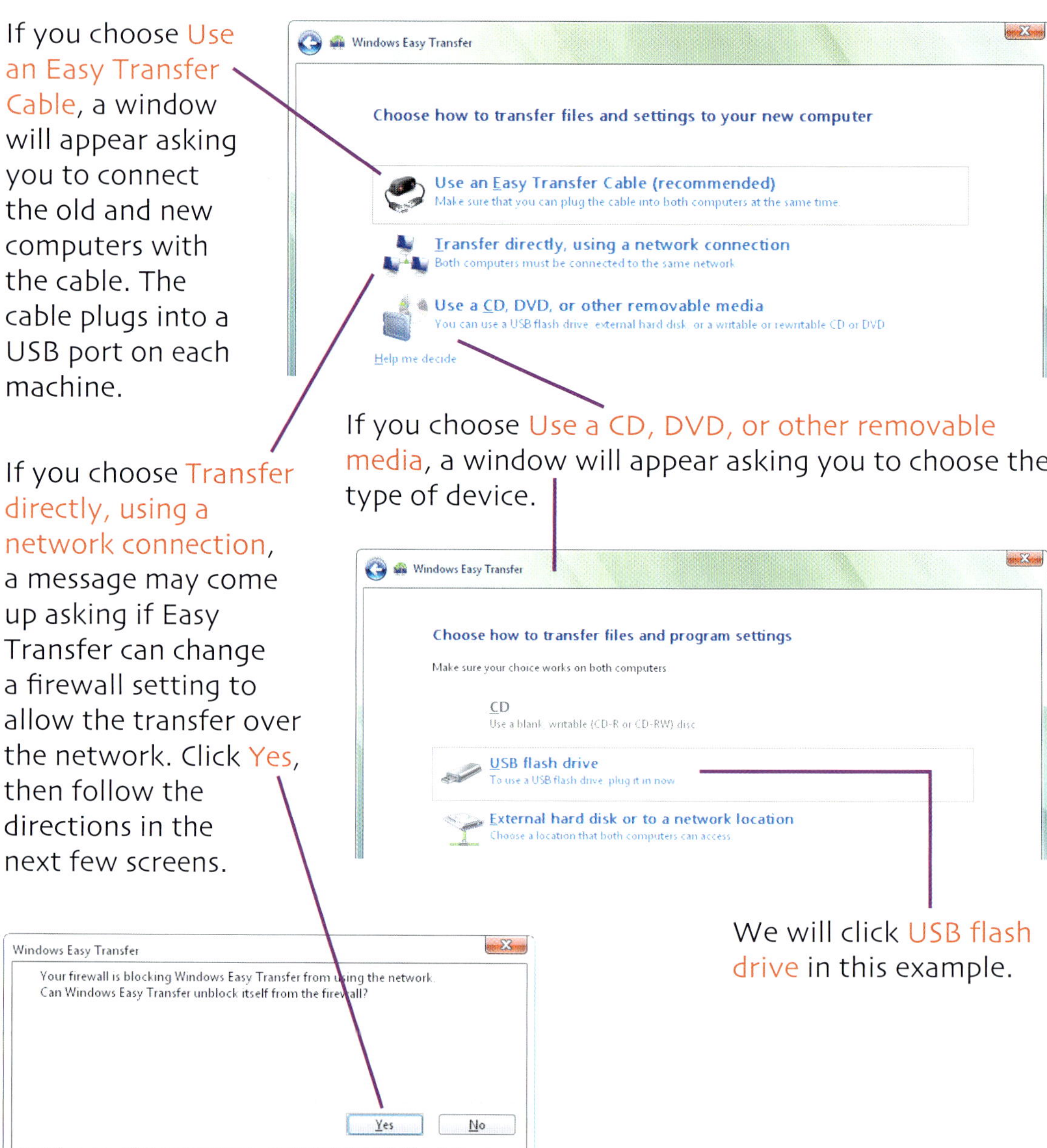

You can plug in your USB flash drive at this point. (If you previously chose to use a CD or DVD, you'd be prompted to insert a blank disc.)

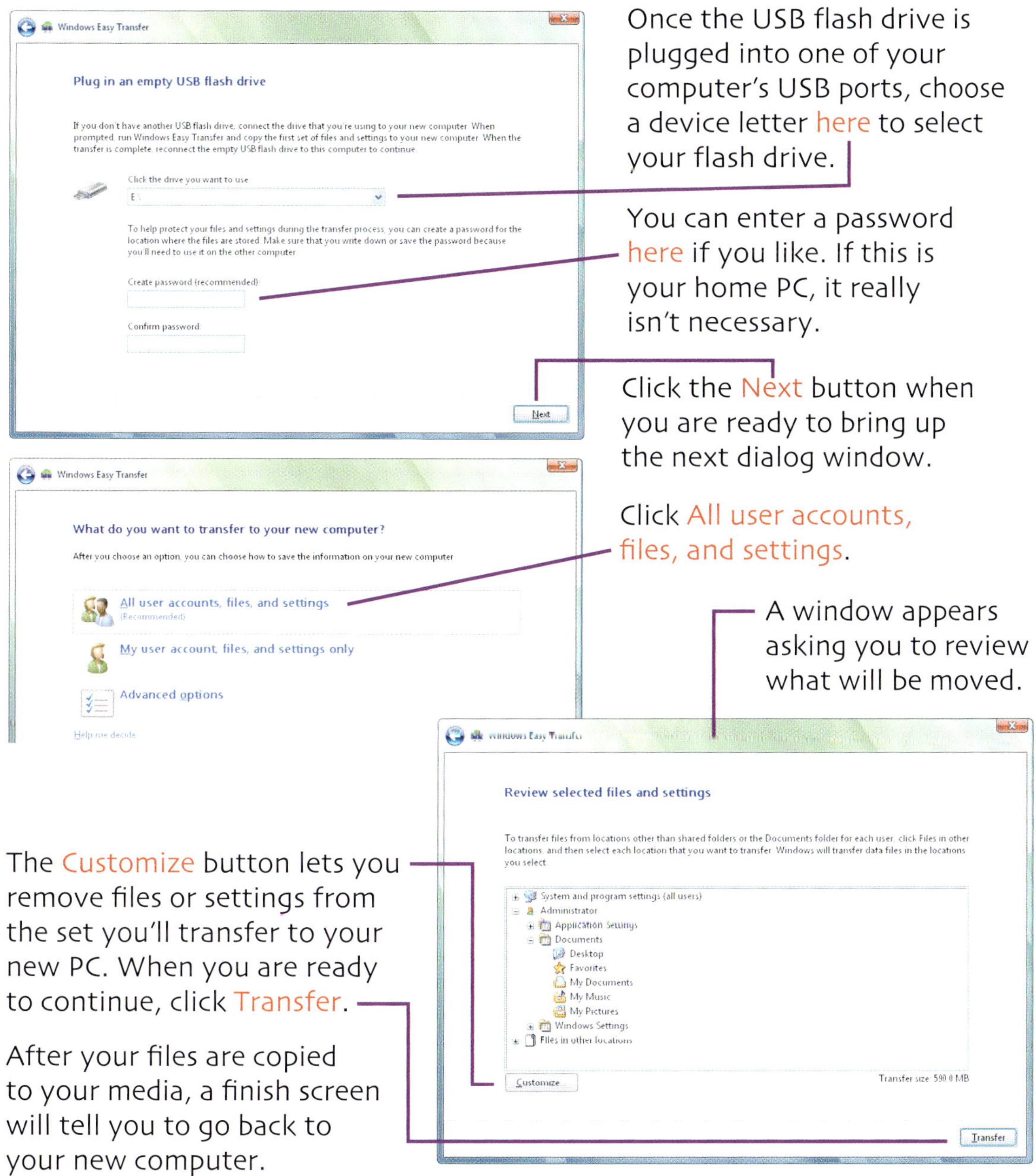

Once the USB flash drive is plugged into one of your computer's USB ports, choose a device letter here to select your flash drive.

You can enter a password here if you like. If this is your home PC, it really isn't necessary.

Click the Next button when you are ready to bring up the next dialog window.

Click All user accounts, files, and settings.

A window appears asking you to review what will be moved.

The Customize button lets you remove files or settings from the set you'll transfer to your new PC. When you are ready to continue, click Transfer.

After your files are copied to your media, a finish screen will tell you to go back to your new computer.

copy data to vista

To start the final stage of moving your data from your old PC, go back to your new Windows Vista computer with the media that you used to collect your data. Again, we are using USB flash memory as an example.

1 Plug the USB flash drive or external hard drive into your computer's USB port. Or, if you used CDs or DVDs, insert the first disc into the new computer.

2 If the Easy Transfer program isn't open or Windows doesn't launch it, go to Computer and double-click the storage device you are using to transfer data. In the window that opens, double-click the file that has a name beginning with IMG and the type Migration Store.

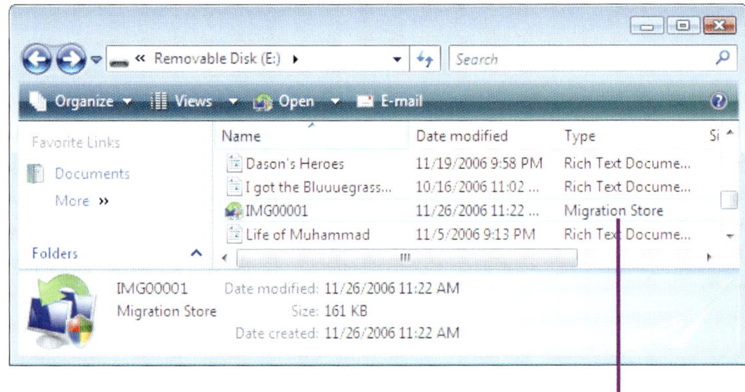

3 Windows asks your permission to proceed. Click Continue. Easy Transfer will launch.

4 Easy Transfer asks you for a user name. Click on the arrow to show the drop-down menu. Click on your name in the list and click Next.

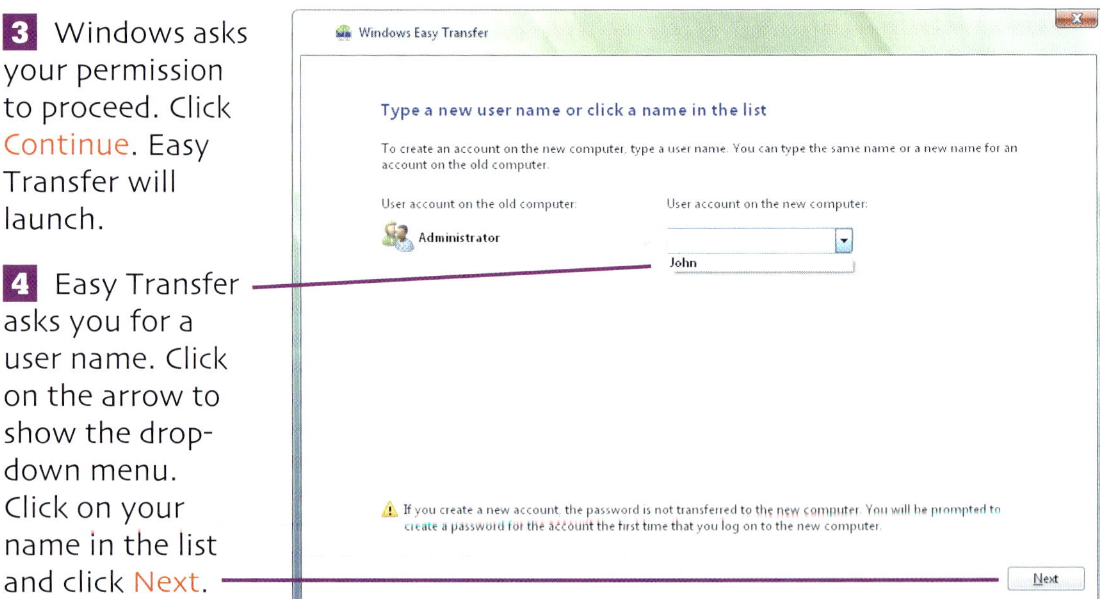

5 Easy Transfer asks you to review selected files and settings from your old PC that are now stored on your transfer media. Click the plus (+) signs to see the details.

6 Click Transfer to start copying your files and settings to Windows Vista.

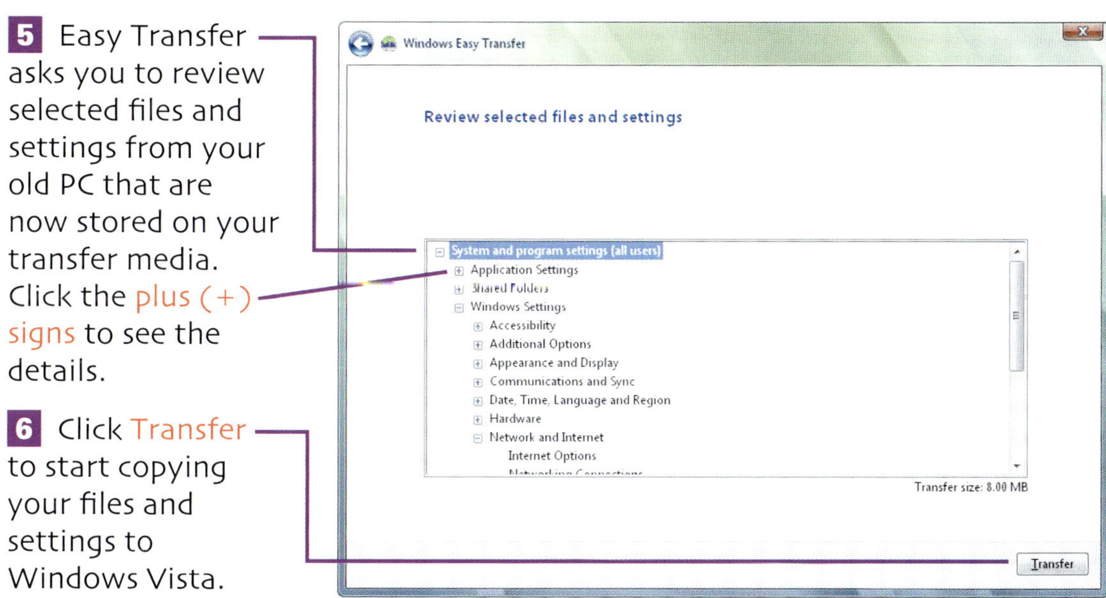

7 After the files and settings are moved to your hard drive, Easy Transfer gives you a summary of what it moved onto your Windows Vista PC. Click Close to move to the next screen.

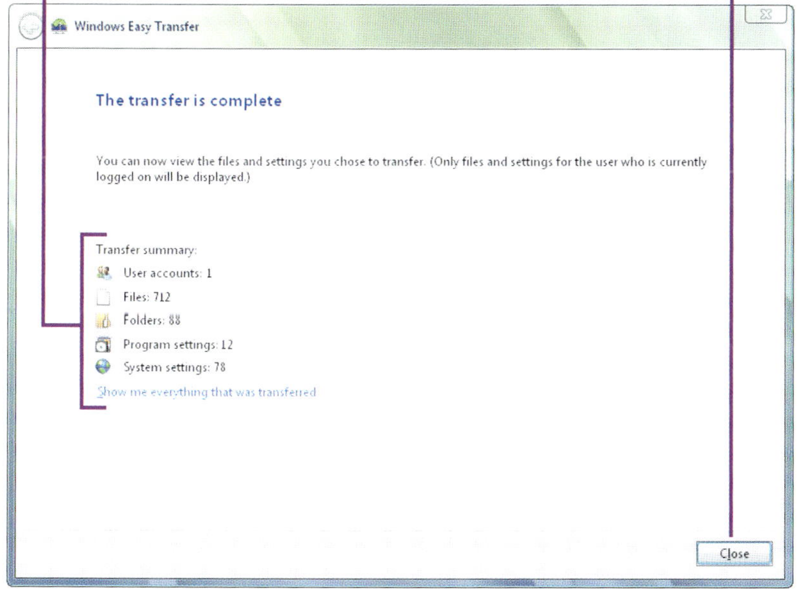

8 Easy Transfer will ask you to reboot the computer. Click Restart.

extra bits

start easy transfer p. 24

- Another way to open Easy Transfer in Windows Vista is to open the Welcome Center and double-click Transfer files and settings.

choose transfer method p. 25

- Having trouble deciding which transfer method to use? Consider how much each type of storage holds.
- CDs hold 600 MB or 700 MB of data.
- DVDs come in two capacities: Standard DVDs hold 4.7 GB of data; double-density discs hold 8.5 GB.
- A USB flash drive can hold as much as 4 GB in a package about the size of your thumb.
- USB external hard drives can hold up to several hundred gigabytes, which is useful for moving large volumes of data. A network is also good for big file moves, as is the Easy Transfer Cable.

4. explore windows vista

Now that you have Windows Vista installed, you can dig right into the great new features that it has to offer. You'll also want to personalize Vista to your own liking.

In this chapter, you'll take a tour of some of the features that you won't find in Windows XP. This includes the Aero theme and its associated features, such as Flip 3D. You'll learn how to use the miniapplications called gadgets and the flexible new search capabilities. You'll discover how to switch between themes and customize some of Vista's new features.

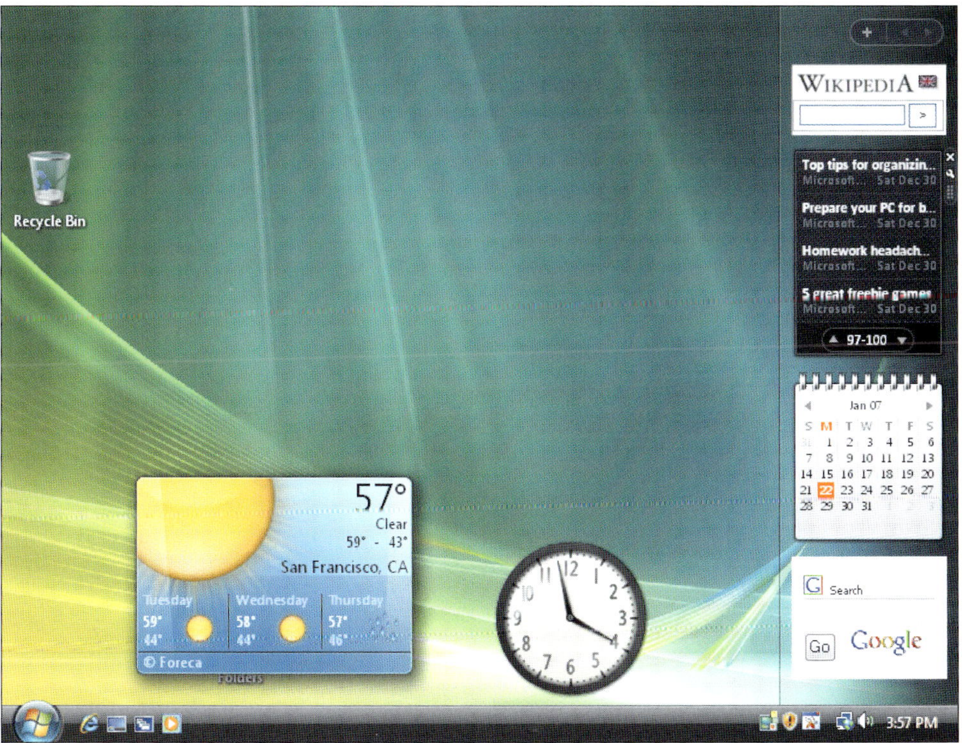

switch themes

Windows Vista includes three different themes that you can use to change the way the environment looks. As in Windows XP, switching to a different theme changes the shapes and colors of interface elements such as buttons, windows, and menus. Unlike in Windows XP, changing Vista themes can make some features unavailable. These are the three themes:

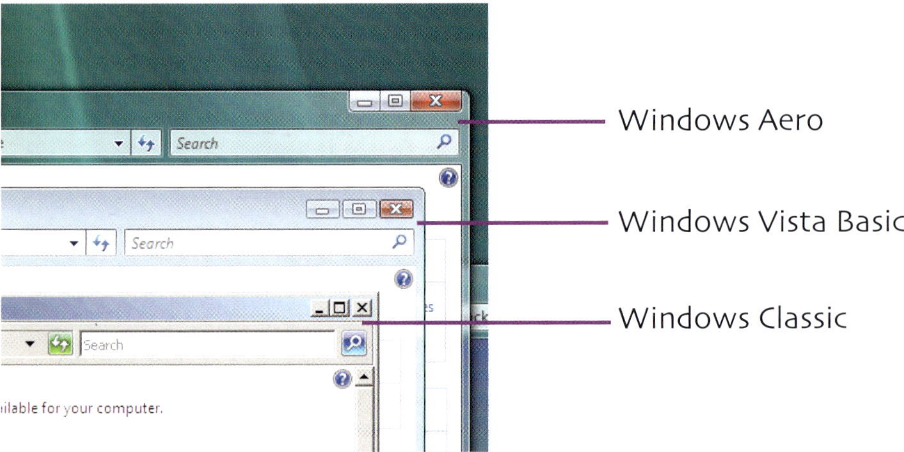

The most noticeable characteristic of the Aero theme is the transparency of its window frames and menus: You can see what's behind them.

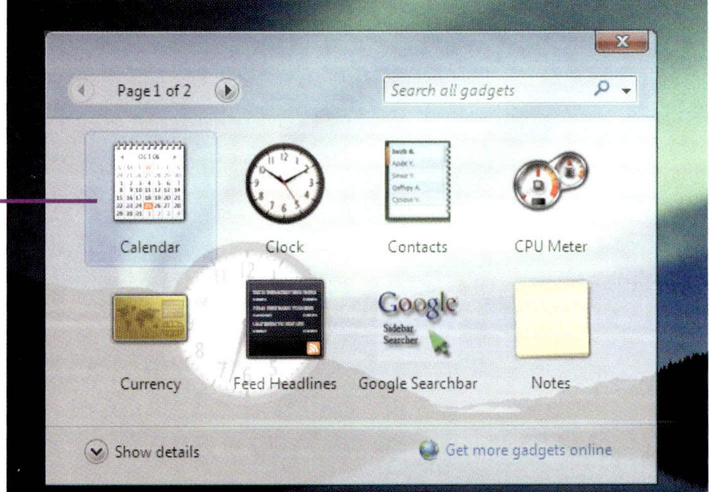

The Aero theme also has a few features that are unique to it. The Flip 3D method of switching between windows is only available when the Aero theme is turned on. (Flip and Flip 3D are described later in the chapter.)

The Windows Classic theme approximates the look of Windows versions before Windows XP. However, folder windows still have the structure and features of Windows Vista, including the new address bar and folder list.

If you don't care for Aero's transparency, you can easily switch to the Windows Vista Basic or Classic theme.

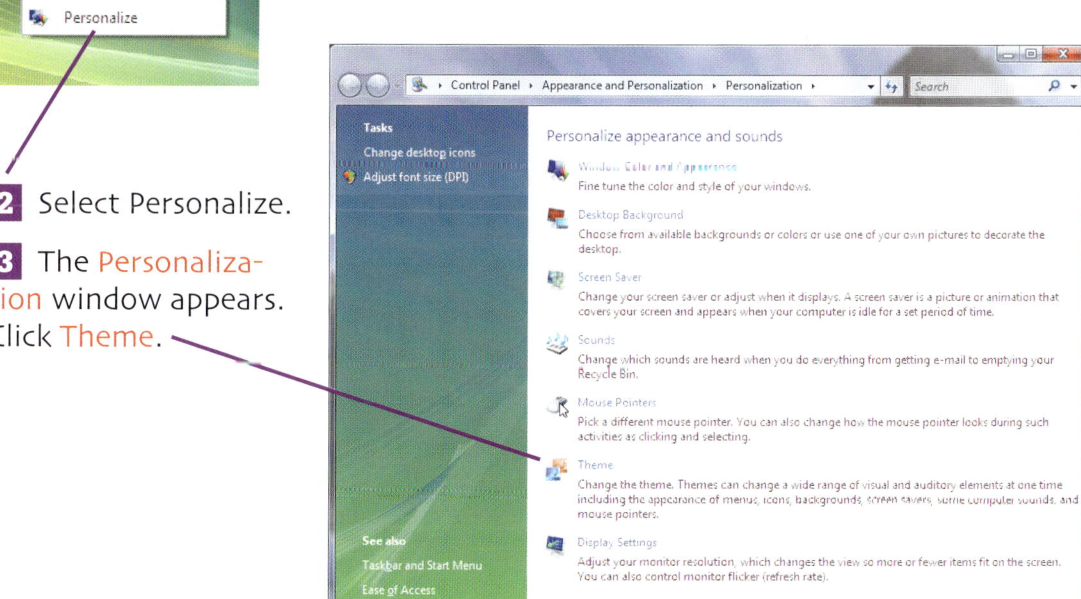

1 Right-click the desktop to bring up the shortcut menu.

2 Select Personalize.

3 The Personalization window appears. Click Theme.

switch themes (cont.)

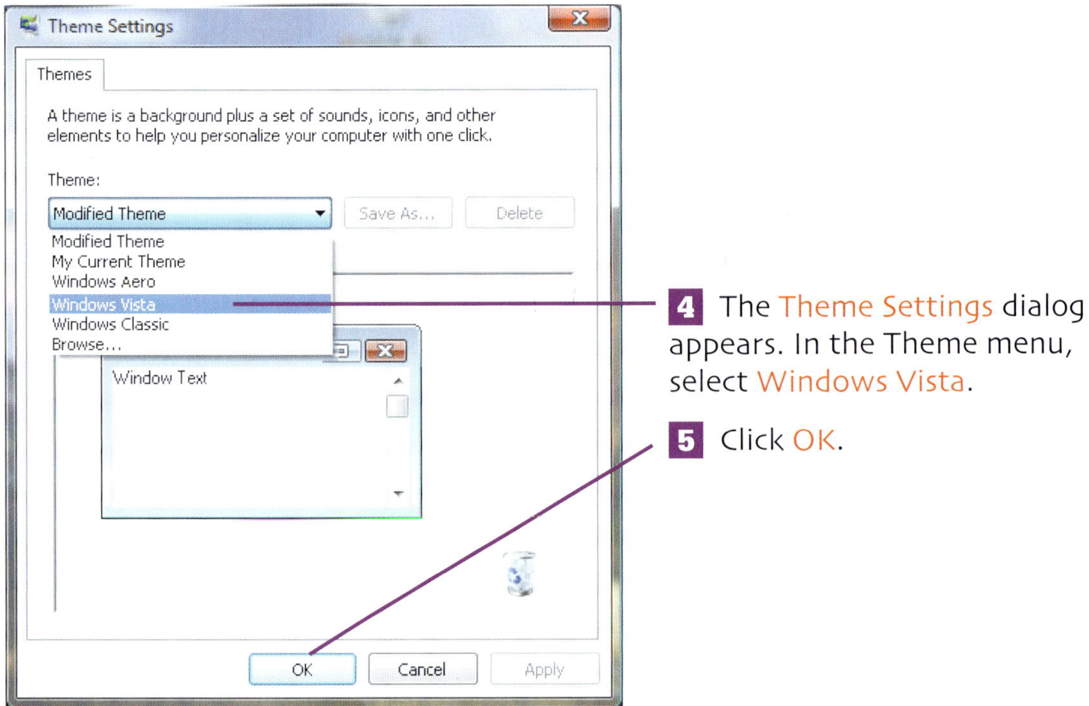

4 The Theme Settings dialog appears. In the Theme menu, select Windows Vista.

5 Click OK.

You won't be able to switch from the Windows Vista theme to the Windows Aero theme if you are running Windows Vista Home Basic, or if your computer doesn't meet the hardware requirements for Aero (see Chapter 1).

switch windows

Using the taskbar is not always a quick way to locate the window you want, particularly when you have a lot of windows open.

Vista offers a better way. Press the Alt and Tab keys, and a feature called Flip appears. It presents all of the open windows in a box. By pressing the Tab key while holding down the Alt key, you can cycle through each window, highlighting one at a time. When the window you want is highlighted, release the keys and the window will open.

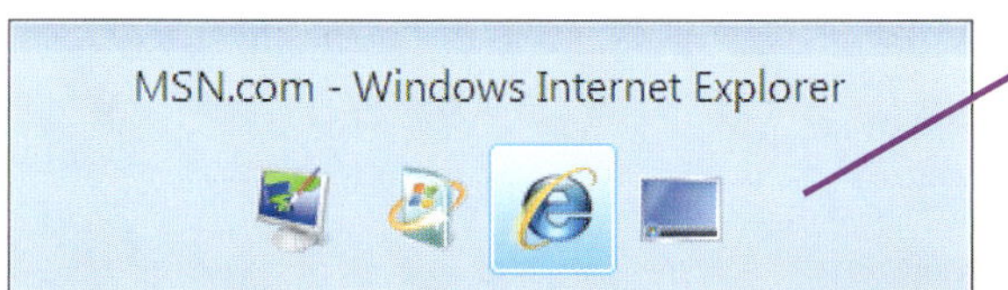

In the basic Vista theme, Flip shows you icons and window names.

In the Aero theme, Flip provides previews of the actual windows.

Aero has another trick for switching between windows. Instead of pressing the Alt-Tab key combination, press the Windows and Tab keys. This launches a feature called Flip 3D. Here, the windows line up in a 3D stack. Pressing the Tab key cycles through the windows. The Desktop appears as one of the windows. When the window you want is in the front, release the keys.

Another way to bring up Flip or Flip 3D is to click the Switch between windows icon in the Quick Launch area on the taskbar.

search for files

Finding files in Windows Vista is easier and quicker than ever. Every folder window has a search box for finding files that reside within that folder.

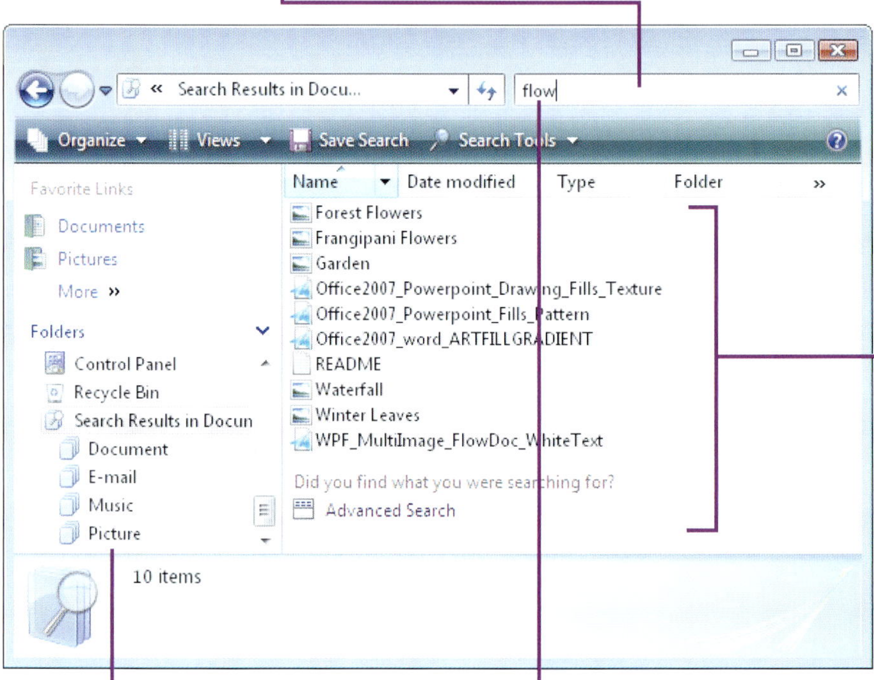

As soon as you start typing, Vista instantly returns search results right in the main pane of the folder window. Double-click a file to open it.

In this example, we are looking for photographs of flowers in our Documents folder. To do that, type the word flow in the search box. The results include files with the word flower in the filename, as well as files with flow inside the file, in the author name, or in the files' keyword tags.

You can narrow the search results with a single mouse click. In the Folders list, you can filter your results by type of file: documents, e-mail, music, or pictures. Since we are looking for photographs, click Picture.

The window now displays only the files from the search results that are pictures.

Notice now that only two of the files have the word flower in the filename. How did Vista know to display the file called Garden? To find out, click the file.

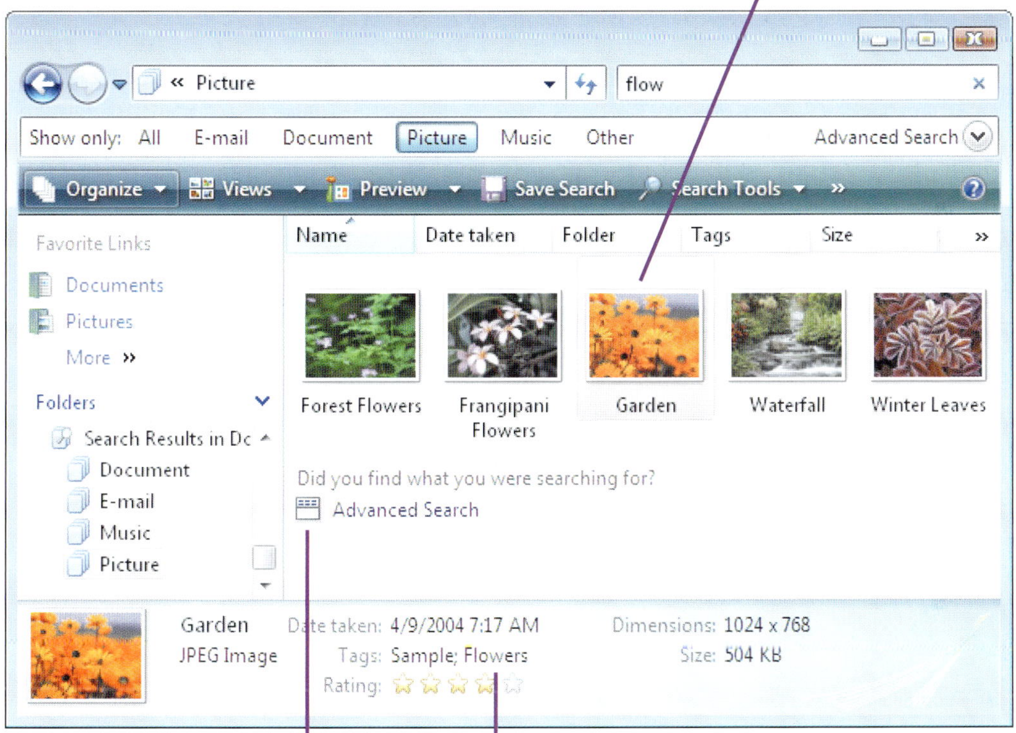

We find the answer in the Details pane. In the Tags field we see that one of the keywords is Flowers. This is why the search results included this file.

Tags are descriptive words you can add to files right here in the Details pane. (See Chapter 8 to learn how.)

You can further narrow your search by clicking Advanced Search.

search for files (cont.)

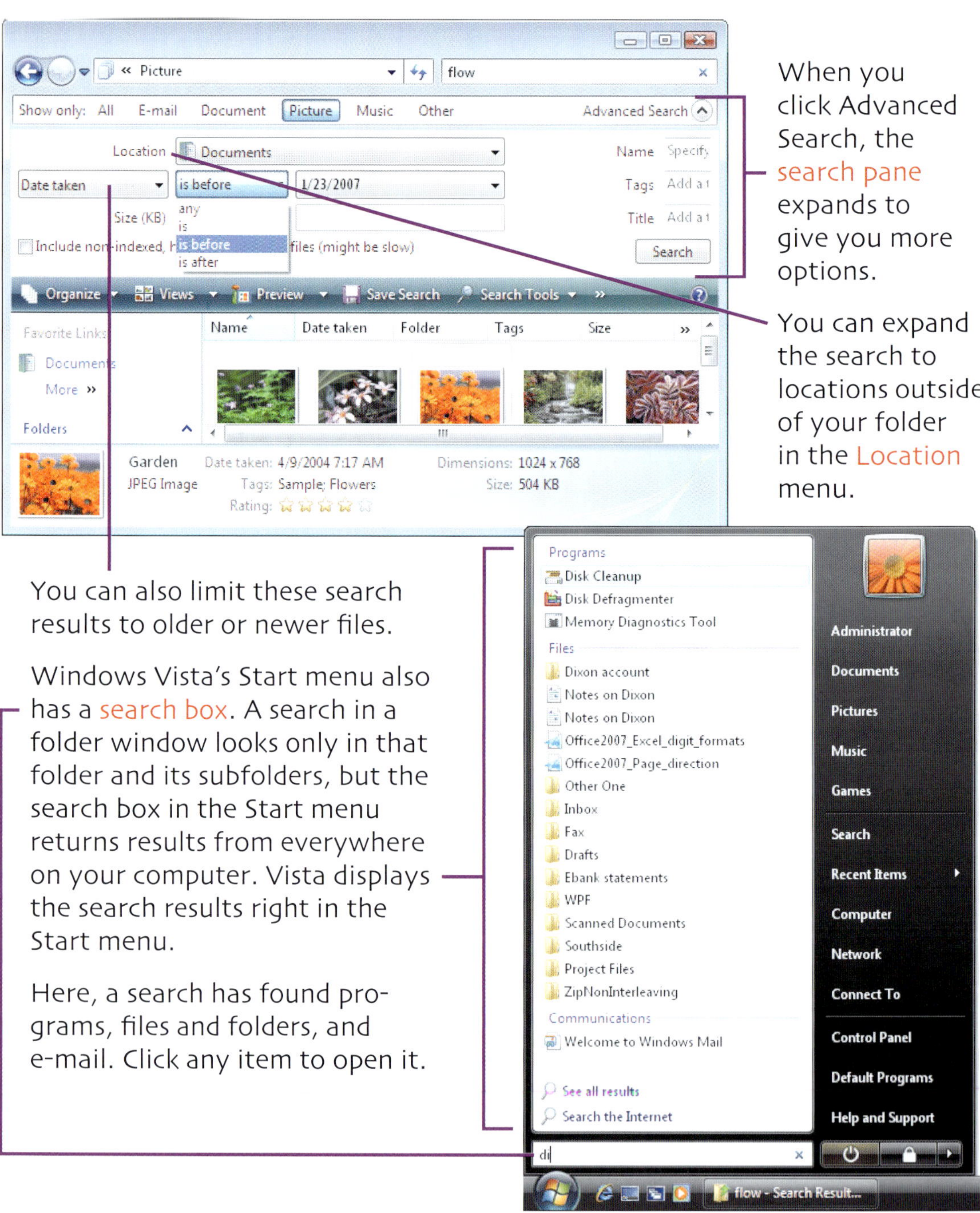

When you click Advanced Search, the search pane expands to give you more options.

You can expand the search to locations outside of your folder in the Location menu.

You can also limit these search results to older or newer files.

Windows Vista's Start menu also has a search box. A search in a folder window looks only in that folder and its subfolders, but the search box in the Start menu returns results from everywhere on your computer. Vista displays the search results right in the Start menu.

Here, a search has found programs, files and folders, and e-mail. Click any item to open it.

explore folders

You may have noticed on the preceding pages that Vista's folder windows look quite a bit different than those in previous versions of Windows. Their new features make managing files easier.

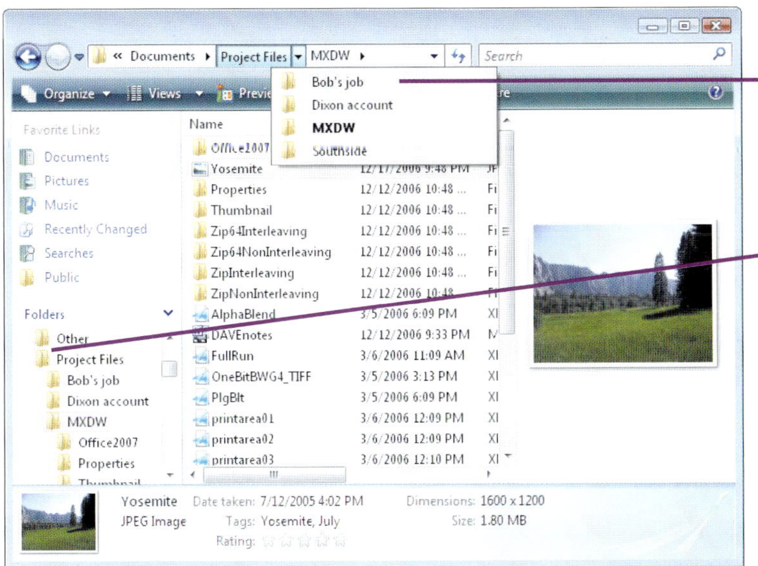

A new Address bar includes flyout menus that let you open folders anywhere in the folder path.

The folder tree of the traditional Windows Explorer is now built into every window. Click a folder to view the contents. Click to the left of a folder to expand or collapse its view.

Column heads are shown even when files aren't displayed in columns. Click a column head to sort the folder contents, even in icon view.

A new feature called Grouping organizes folder contents by name, date, or other criteria.

Chapters 8 and 9 describe how to work with folder windows in more detail.

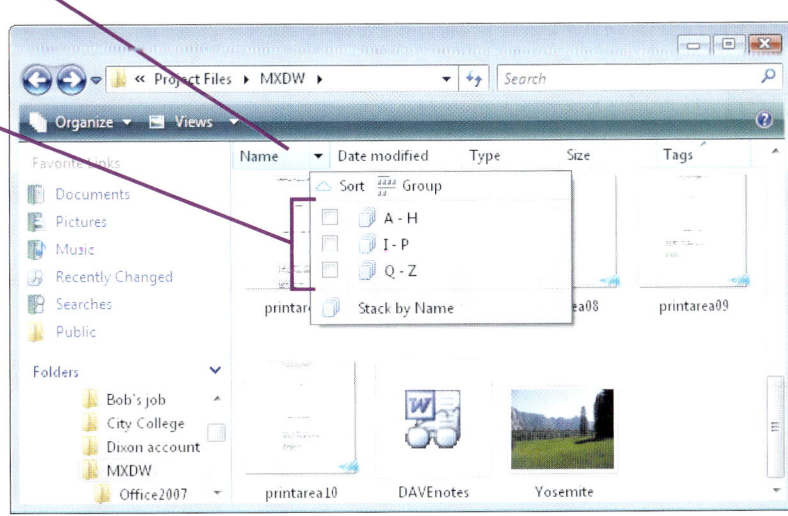

work with gadgets

Gadgets are miniapplications that each take up a small bit of screen real estate and do one thing very well. Many of them pull information from the Internet, such as the weather or news headlines.

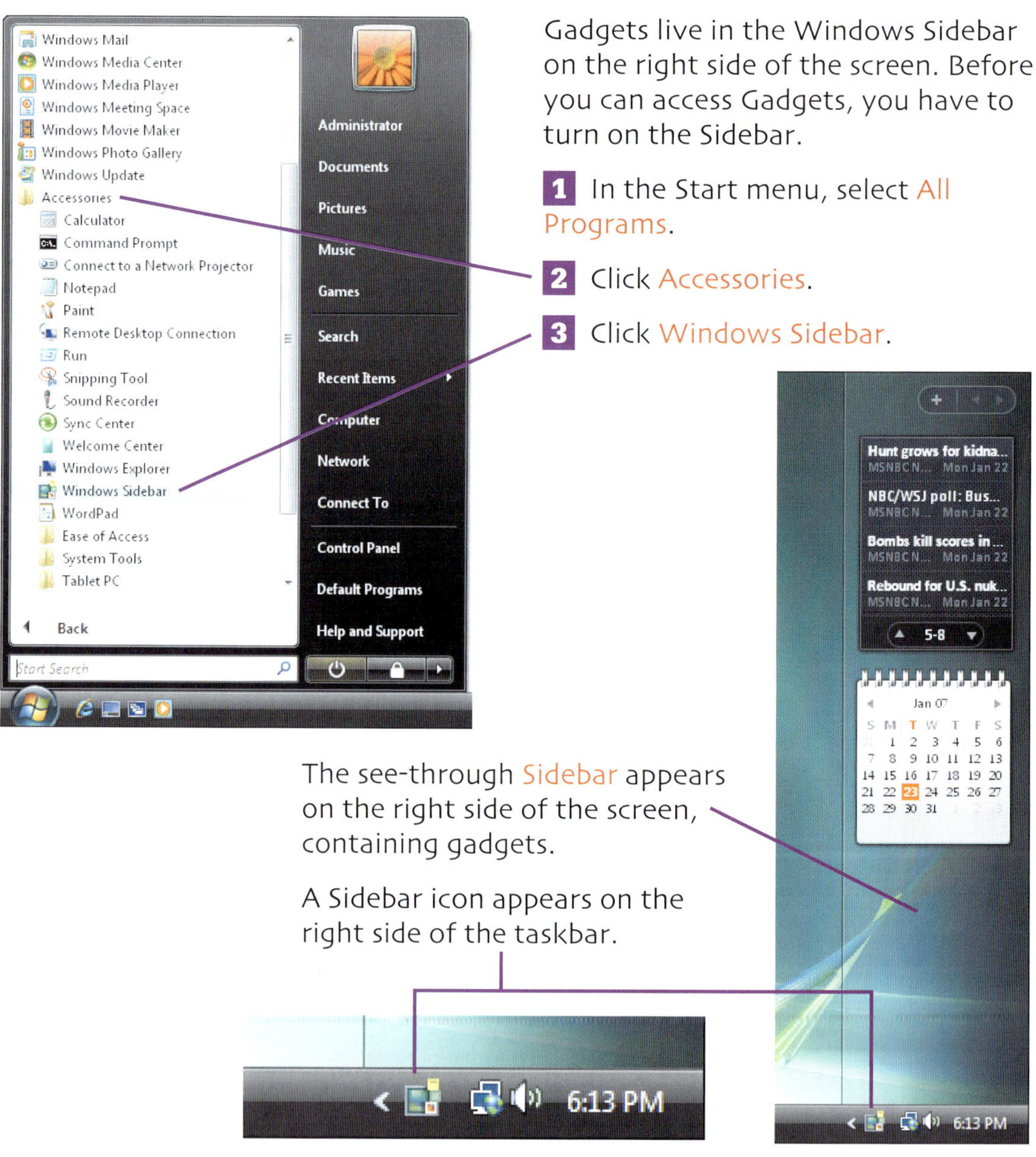

Gadgets live in the Windows Sidebar on the right side of the screen. Before you can access Gadgets, you have to turn on the Sidebar.

1. In the Start menu, select All Programs.
2. Click Accessories.
3. Click Windows Sidebar.

The see-through Sidebar appears on the right side of the screen, containing gadgets.

A Sidebar icon appears on the right side of the taskbar.

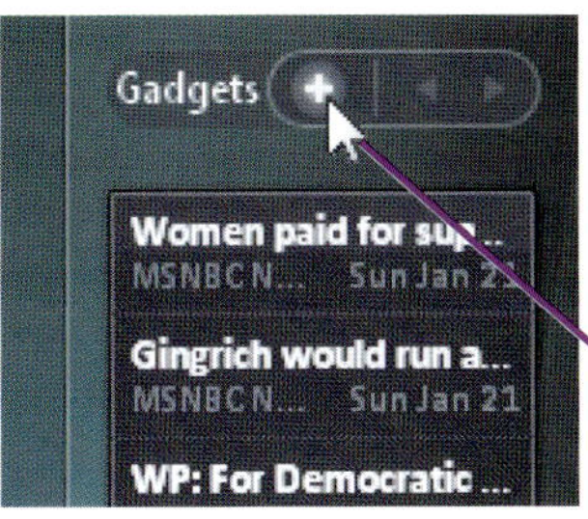

Now you'll need to customize the Sidebar so that it contains the gadgets you want.

1 Move your cursor over the plus (+) sign at the top of the Sidebar. The plus sign glows and the word Gadgets appears.

2 Click the plus sign.

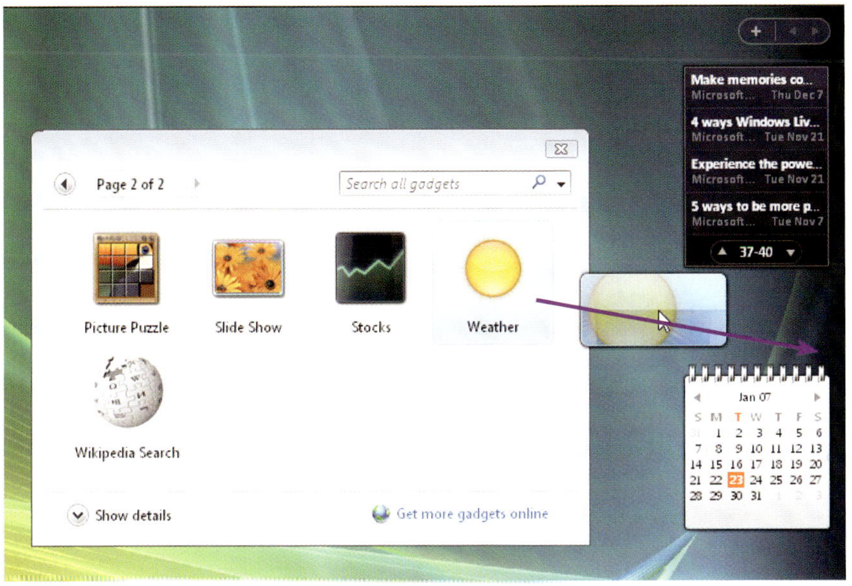

3 A palette appears with an assortment of gadgets. Drag one from the window to the Sidebar.

4 Gadgets like the Weather gadget grow larger and display more information when you drag them out of the Sidebar to the Desktop.

work with gadgets (cont.)

Some gadgets have settings that you can change. For instance, the Weather gadget lets you designate the location for which you want weather reports. To open gadget controls, move the cursor over the gadget. A small palette appears.

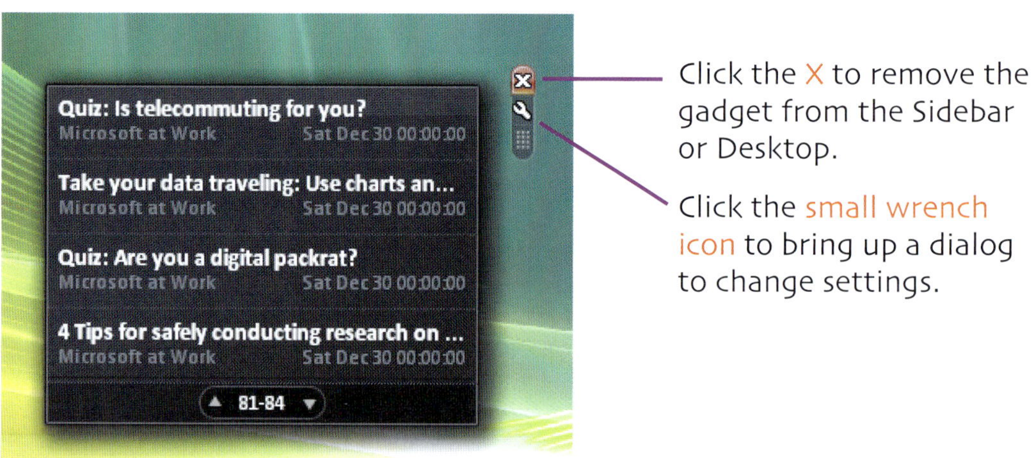

Click the X to remove the gadget from the Sidebar or Desktop.

Click the small wrench icon to bring up a dialog to change settings.

You can hide the Sidebar but leave it running. Right-click an empty space in the Sidebar and choose Close Sidebar. The Sidebar slides into the taskbar.

Gadgets on the Desktop remain when the Sidebar is hidden.

To bring the Sidebar back, click the Sidebar icon in the taskbar.

To quit the Sidebar, right-click the Sidebar icon in the taskbar. Choose Exit from the shortcut menu.

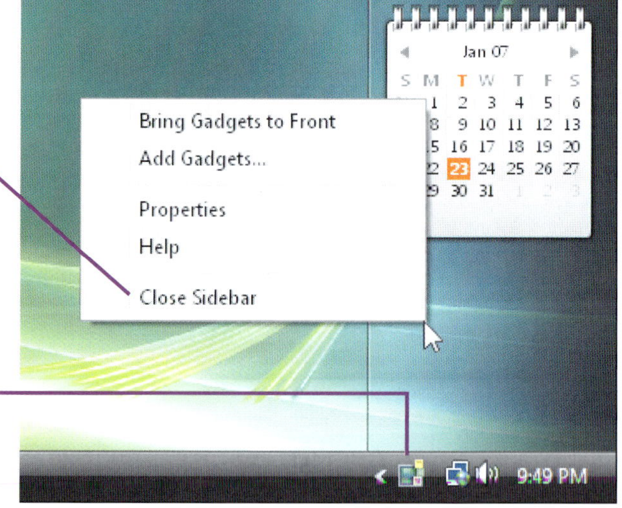

extra bits

switch themes p. 34

- Switching themes changes a whole set of elements, colors, and even sounds. You can also make less sweeping customizations than switching themes.
- In the Personalization window (right-click the Desktop and choose Personalize), choose Window Color and Appearance. Here, you can change a color scheme. Switching from the Aero color scheme to the Windows Vista Basic color scheme is another way of getting rid of Aero's transparent window frames.
- If you are trying to go from the basic Vista look to Aero, you should check in two places: The Theme Settings dialog, described on page 36, and the Window Color and Appearance dialog. Both need to be set to Aero in order to display the see-through effects.

search for files p. 38

- The speed of Windows Vista's search feature is due to the fact that it creates an index of some of the files and e-mail on your hard drive. An index is like the index in the back of this book: You could manually search through every page in this book to find a topic, but it is quicker to use the index. When you start typing in a search box, Vista consults the index.
- When you are performing an advanced search in the search pane, the Location menu has an option called Indexed Locations. This searches everywhere on your computer that has been indexed. What is not indexed are program files and various system and configuration files, which most users never need to access. If you ever do want to search for one of these files in an advanced search, choose Everywhere. This includes files that are not in the index, which means that the search will be slower.

work with gadgets p. 42

- If you're a gadgets fan, you may get tired of reaching for the Start menu every time you start the computer. Fortunately, you can tell Windows Vista to launch the Sidebar for you.
- With the Sidebar launched, right-click the Sidebar icon on the right side of the taskbar. Choose Properties from the shortcut menu. Now click the check box labeled Start Sidebar when Windows starts. The Sidebar and its gadgets will now launch whenever you turn on the computer.
- More gadgets are available for free at Microsoft's Web site. To get them, open the gadgets palette and click Get more gadgets online. Internet Explorer will take you to the download page.

5. personalize the desktop

The desktop is what appears on your monitor when you've opened Windows but don't have any programs open. In this chapter you'll learn how to change Microsoft's default desktop to make it your own.

Working with the Personalization window, you can replace the standard desktop picture with a favorite family photo, a solid color, or an abstract pattern. You can also make the desktop icons bigger or smaller, or change the size of everything on your computer screen.

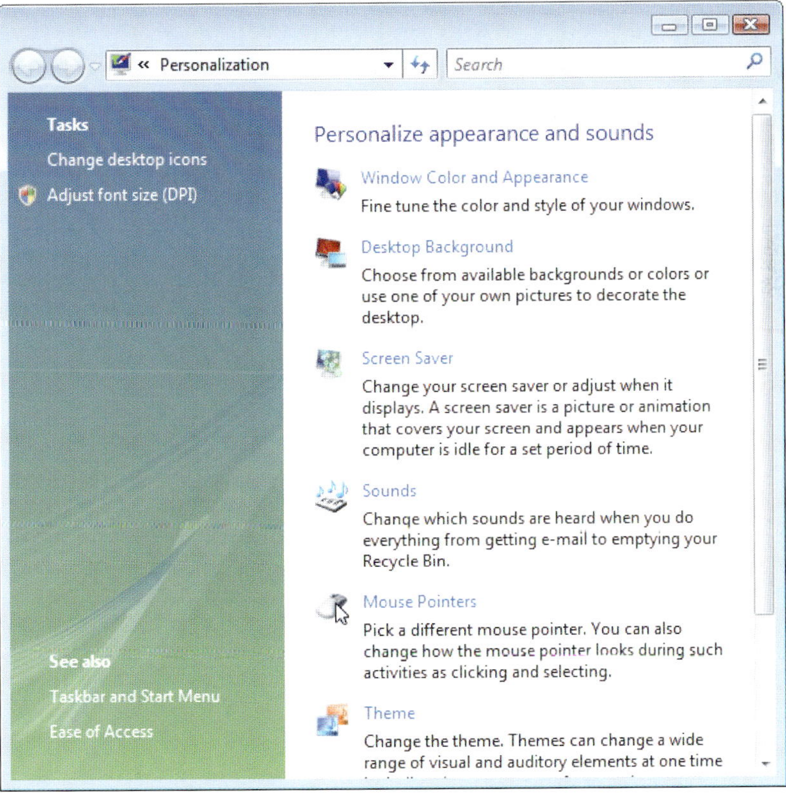

replace desktop image

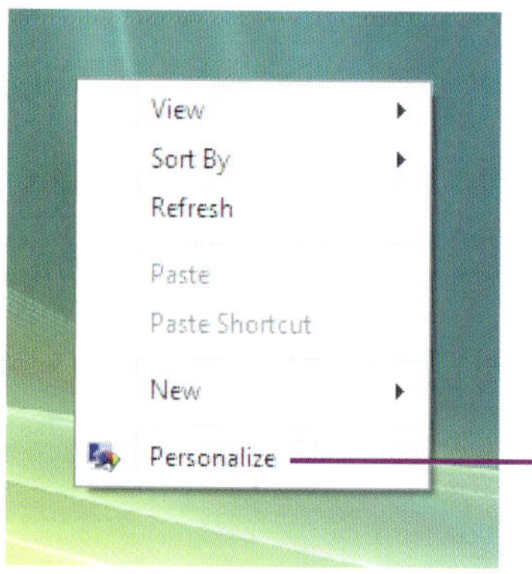

Don't like Microsoft's standard desktop image? Have a nice picture you'd rather look at? You can replace the standard desktop picture with your own digital photo (in JPEG format) from your hard drive. Use a horizontally oriented photo to have it automatically fit to the desktop.

1 Right-click on the desktop and select Personalize from the shortcut list.

2 Click the Desktop Background item.

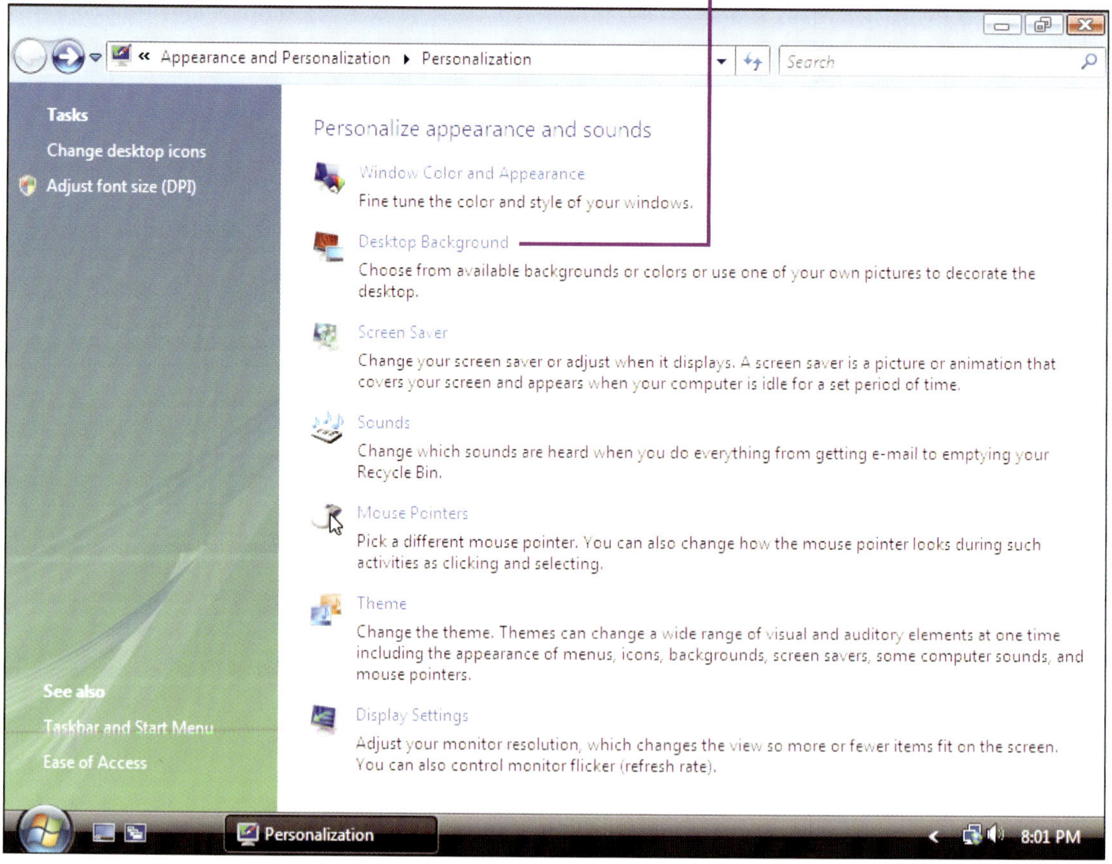

3 If your photo is in the Pictures folder, click the Picture Location drop-down menu and select Pictures.

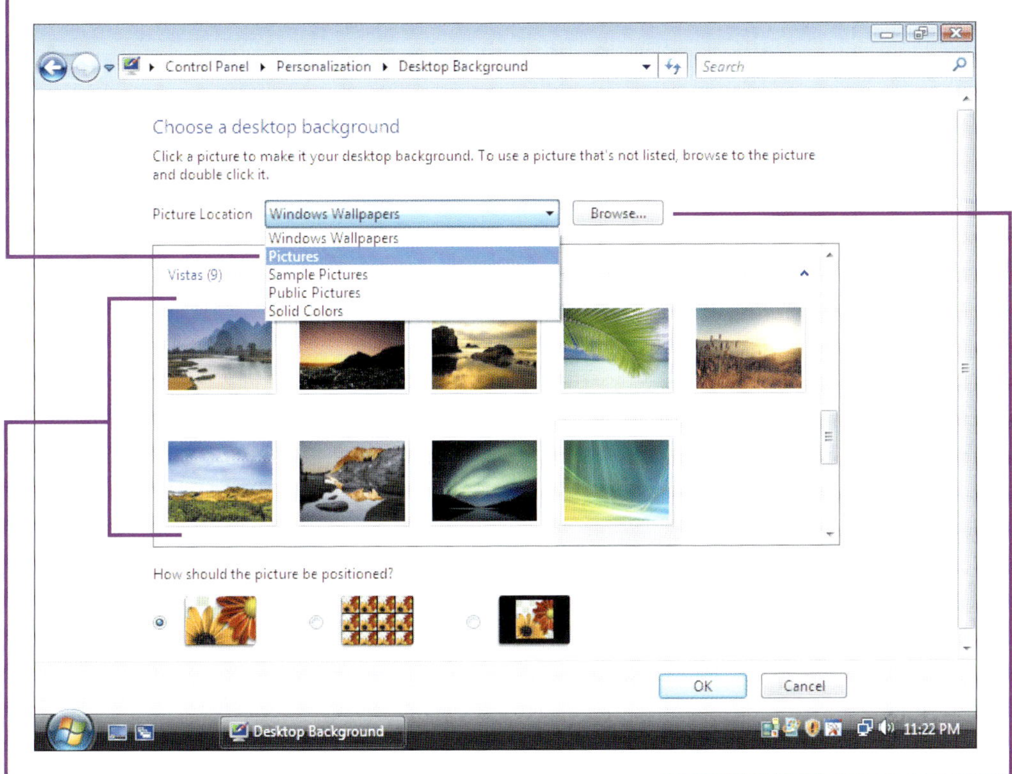

If your photo is somewhere else, click the Browse button to bring up the browser window and navigate through your folders to find the picture you'd like to use.

If you don't have your own photo, Windows Vista has many photos and patterns to choose from.

Windows Wallpapers appears in the Picture Location drop-down list when you first open Desktop Background. Here you'll find some beautiful images and stunning photos that come with Windows Vista.

4 When you find your photo (either your own or one that came with Windows), double-click it. The Desktop Background window will close. You'll see the Personalization window again, which you can close.

desktop image (cont.)

After the Personalization window closes, you'll see your photo where the standard desktop picture used to be.

Windows will shrink or stretch your photo to fit the screen if your image doesn't fit exactly. If your picture is too small, you can tell Windows to simply center the picture at full size. In our vacation picture here, we want the mountains to take up more of the screen.

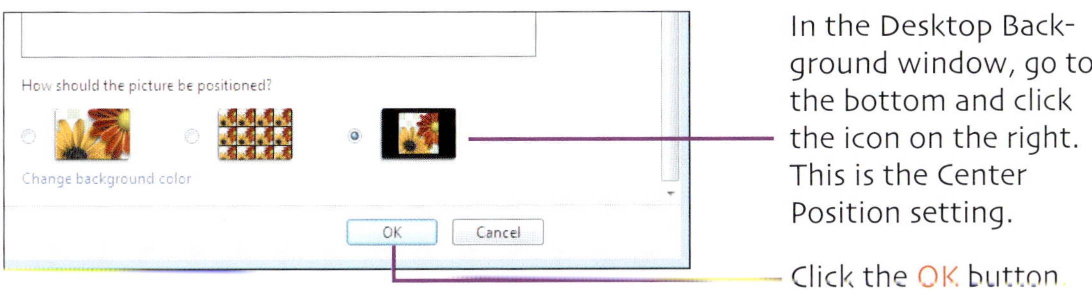

In the Desktop Background window, go to the bottom and click the icon on the right. This is the Center Position setting.

Click the OK button.

You can see that the desktop picture here is larger than on the facing page, with the outside edges cut off. In this case it's a pleasing effect, but it might not be with other photos. If you used a low-resolution photo, you might see the photo centered with the desktop background surrounding it.

change desktop icons

You may have noticed only one desktop icon—the Recycle Bin—in the previous pages. It takes just a few steps to turn on some of the other icons you've used in older versions of Windows.

1 As you did when replacing the desktop image, right-click the desktop and select Personalize to bring up the Personalization window.

2 In the column at the left under Tasks, click Change desktop icons.

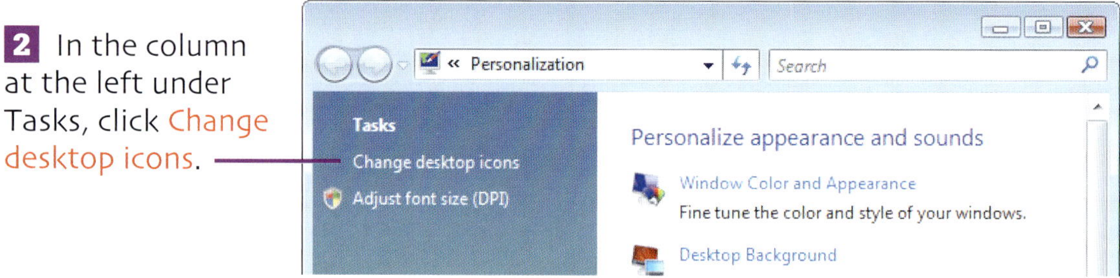

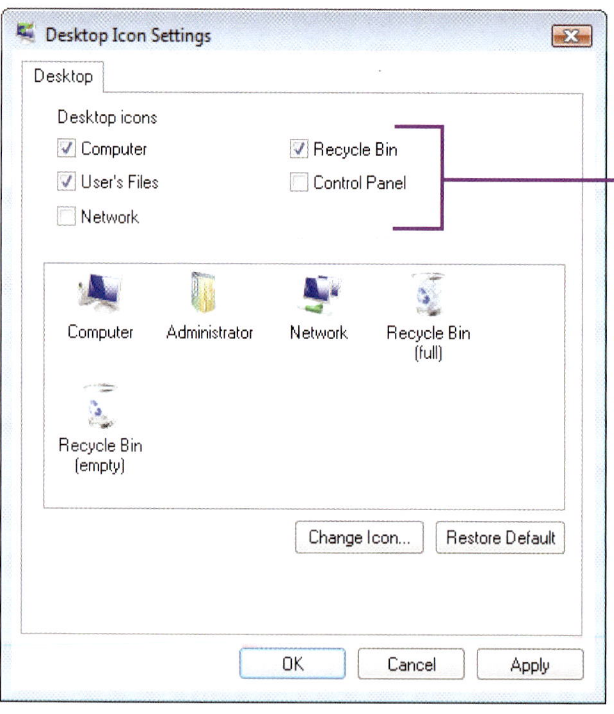

The Desktop Icon Settings dialog opens. Here, you'll see a selection of desktop icons that you can choose to display. Notice that My Computer is gone: Windows Vista calls it simply Computer. You won't find a My Documents icon here, either. Instead, there's a User's Files icon. User's Files contains common folders including Documents, Pictures, Music, and others.

3 Put a check in the box next to any of desktop icons you'd like displayed, then click OK.

resize desktop items

You may have noticed that the desktop icons are bigger than those in Windows XP. You can make them more like the size you are used to, or make them jumbo size.

1 Right-click on the desktop and select View from the shortcut list.

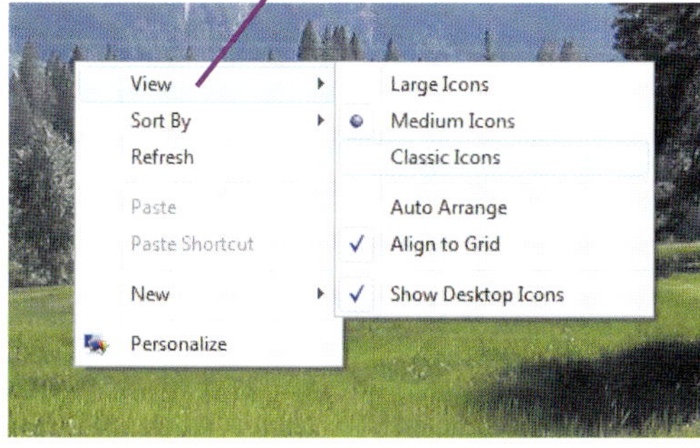

2 In the flyout menu that appears, select Classic Icons. This is the smallest size.

If you choose Large Icons, you'll get icons of this size.

change desktop size

If your desktop is getting crowded with icons and windows that you want to keep in view, shrinking all of them will help make your desktop appear less cluttered. You can do this by adjusting the display resolution.

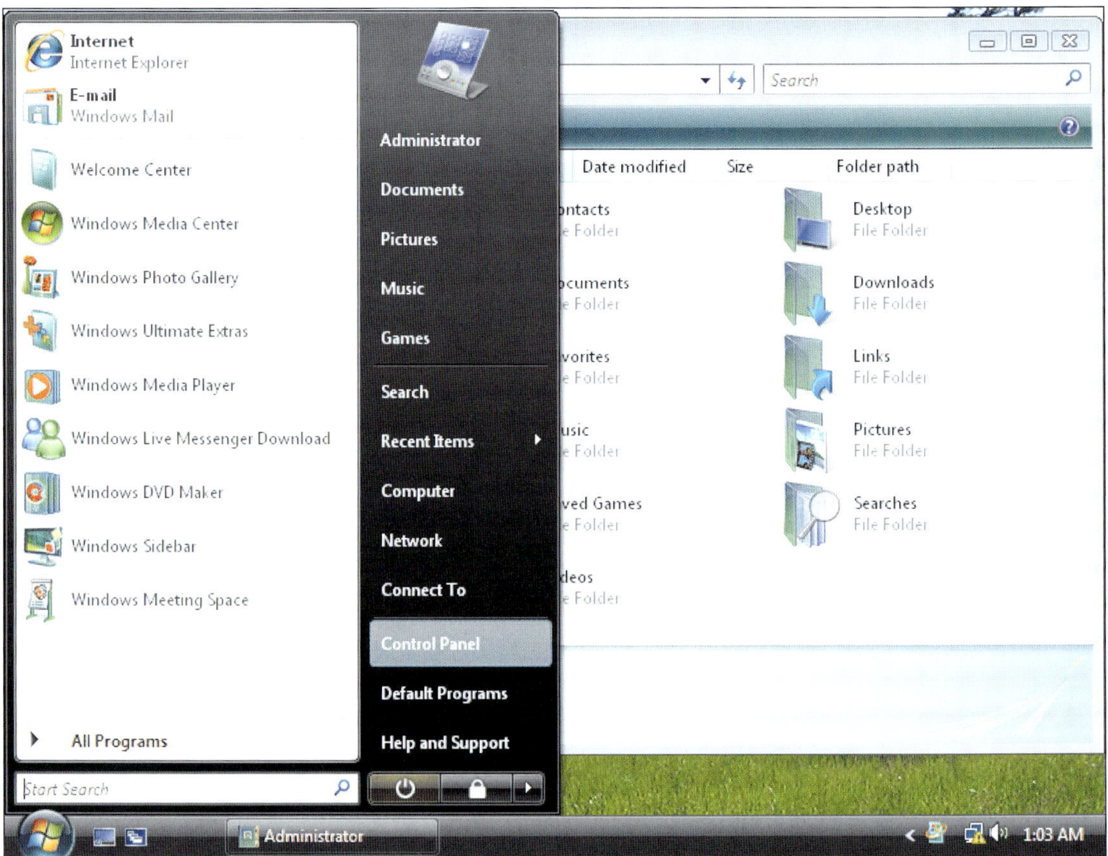

For instance, on this screen, set at 800 by 600 pixels, there isn't enough room to see all of a window when the Start menu is open.

When you increase the resolution (to 1024 by 768 pixels, in this case), everything shrinks, giving you more room on the desktop for icons, windows, and other objects.

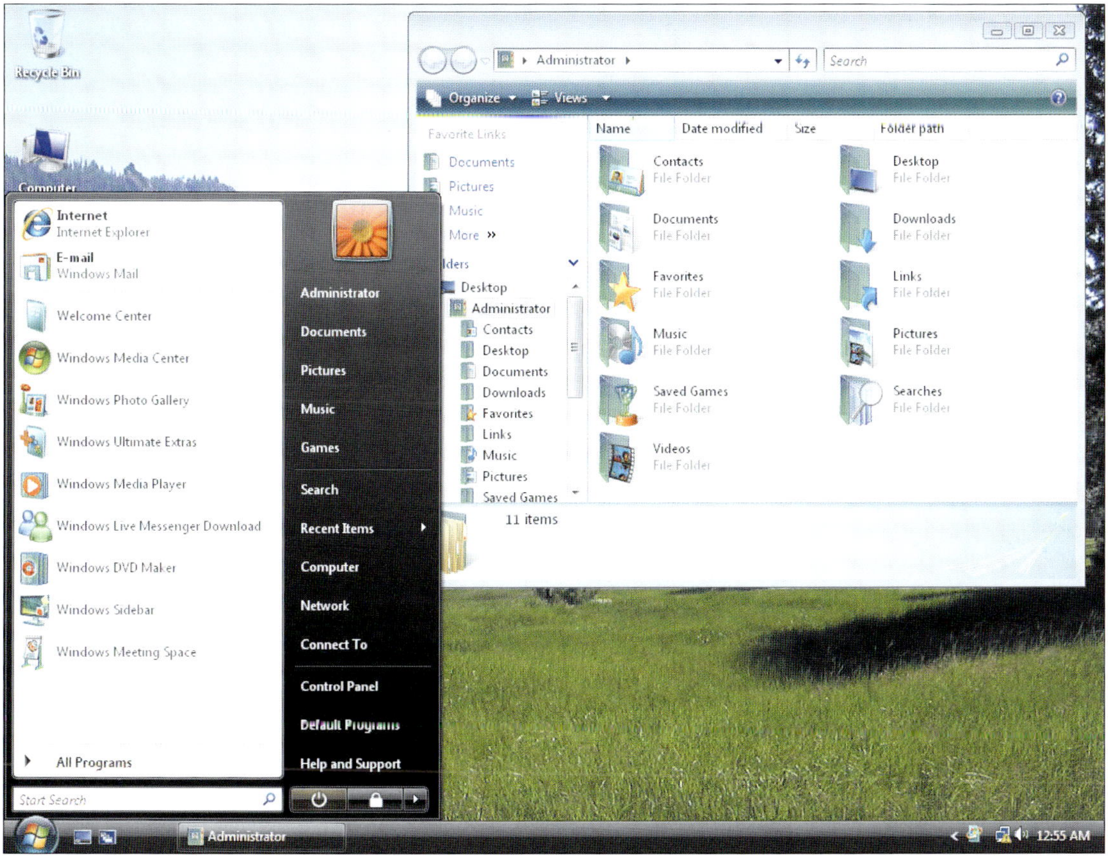

1 Right-click the desktop and select Personalize from the shortcut menu.

change desktop size (cont.)

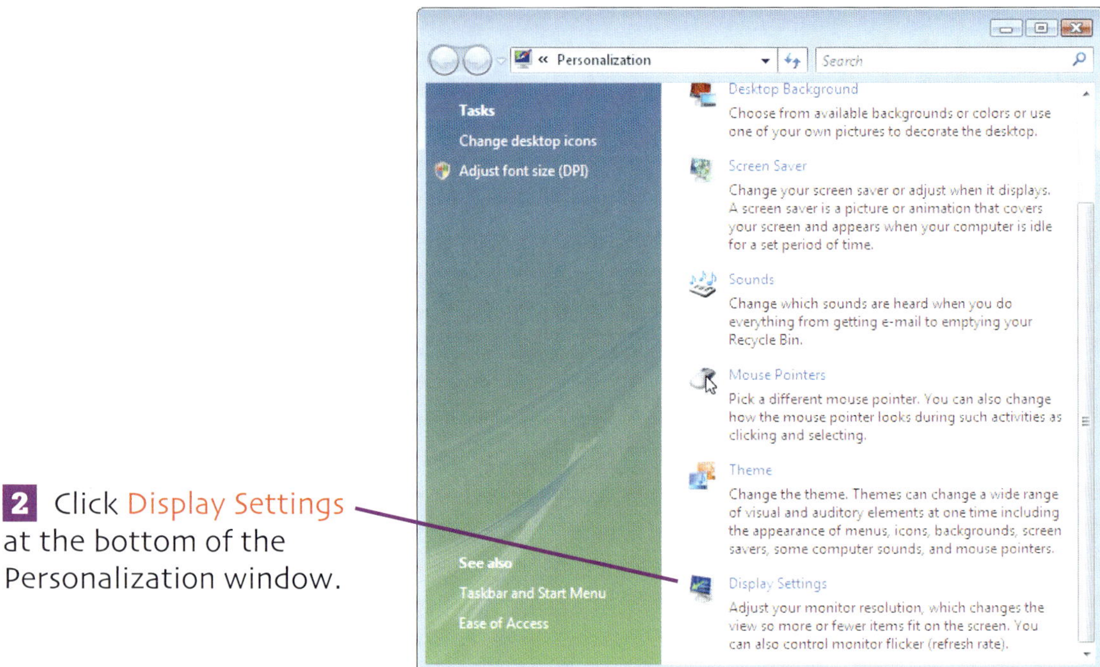

2 Click Display Settings at the bottom of the Personalization window.

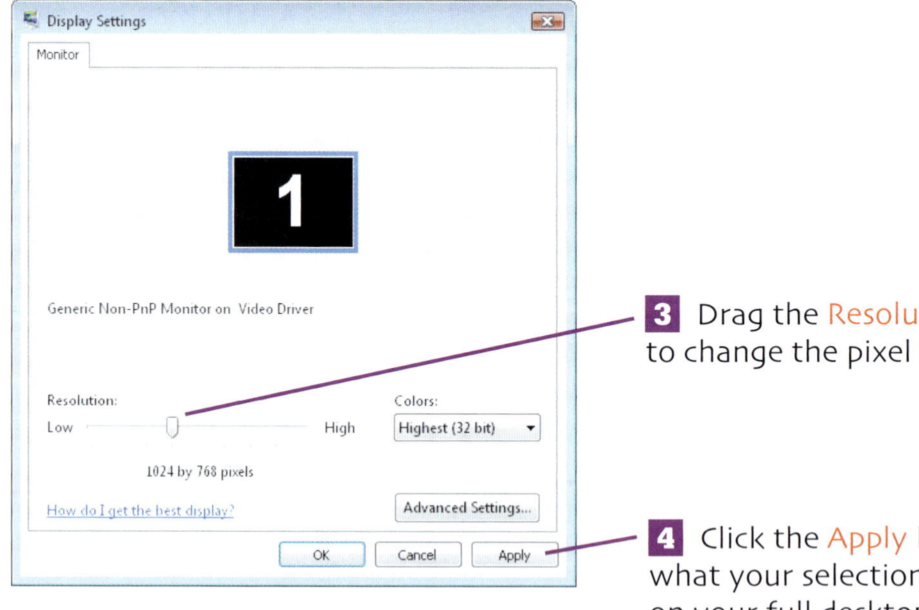

3 Drag the Resolution slider bar to change the pixel resolution.

4 Click the Apply button to see what your selection will look like on your full desktop.

5 Your desktop resolution changes, but only temporarily. A warning dialog appears, which says the display will revert to the previous setting in a few seconds. If you do nothing, your desktop will revert to the previous resolution when the countdown reaches zero seconds. By clicking the No button you'll cancel the change without waiting for the countdown.

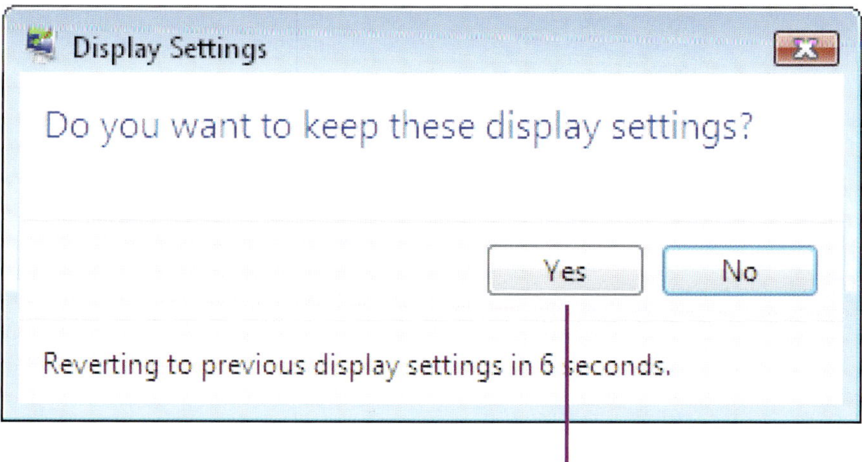

6 To accept the new resolution, click Yes before the countdown ends.

7 Click OK to close the Display Settings dialog.

extra bits

replace desktop image p. 48

- If you don't know the pixel resolution of a photo, it's easy to find out. Right-click it and choose Properties from the shortcut menu. Next, click the Details tab. The dialog will show the height and width of the photo in pixels.
- You don't need to switch to the Windows Classic theme in order to set the desktop to a solid color. Right-click the desktop and select Personalize. Click Desktop Background. In the Picture Location drop-down menu, select Solid Colors. Now double-click a color to see it on the desktop.

change desktop size p. 54

- Flat-panel displays, including those in notebook computers, have one resolution that looks sharper than others. This is the display's native resolution—and usually its default resolution. Using a nonnative resolution can make the text look a little fuzzy, so you may need to try a few options to find the best appearance. CRT monitors don't have a native resolution and look equally sharp at most pixel settings.
- Switching to a higher resolution not only makes icons smaller, but also makes text smaller. To make the text larger, right-click the desktop and select Personalize. On the left side, choose Adjust font size. Click the Larger Scale button.

6. take charge of the start menu

The Start menu is the chief method of getting to your programs and files. The Start menu in Windows Vista behaves differently from the Start menu in Windows XP. Like Windows XP, Vista provides a number of ways to customize the Start menu to better suit your needs.

The left side of the Start menu contains icons representing programs. The icons at the top left are always present. The lower left area lists programs you've recently used. In this chapter, you'll customize the icons displayed here.

All Programs displays a list of all the programs installed on your computer.

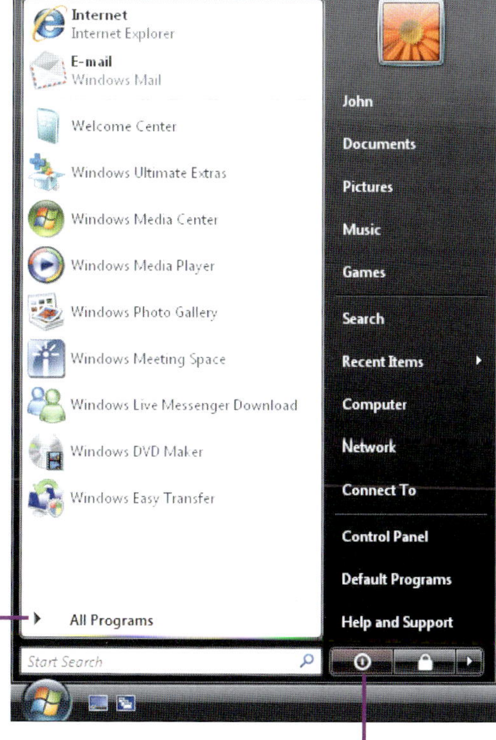

The right side of the Start menu gives you access to your files, settings, the Help system, and other features of Windows Vista. In this chapter, you'll convert some of these links into menus. You'll also remove and add items to the Start menu.

The Turn Off Computer button of Windows XP is gone. Instead, the Windows Vista power button puts Windows into sleep mode. In this chapter, you'll change this into a shutdown button.

display more programs

The icons on the left side of the Start menu represent recently used programs. Click one, and the program opens. Wouldn't it be great to list even more programs here? You can, by telling Windows how many program icons to display and by shrinking the size of the icons.

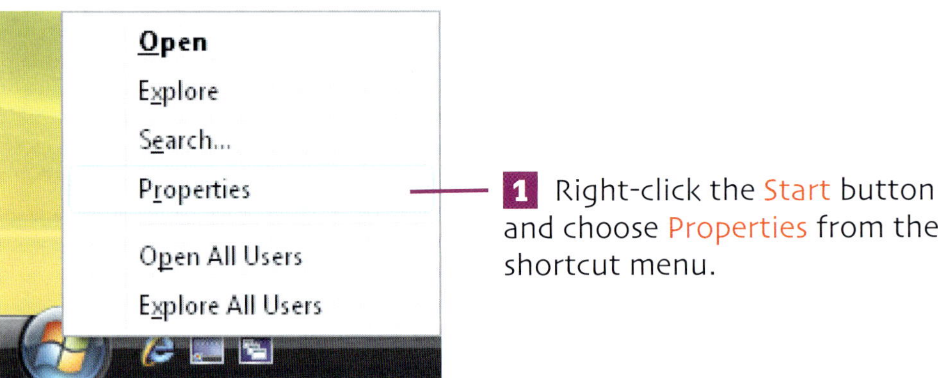

1 Right-click the Start button and choose Properties from the shortcut menu.

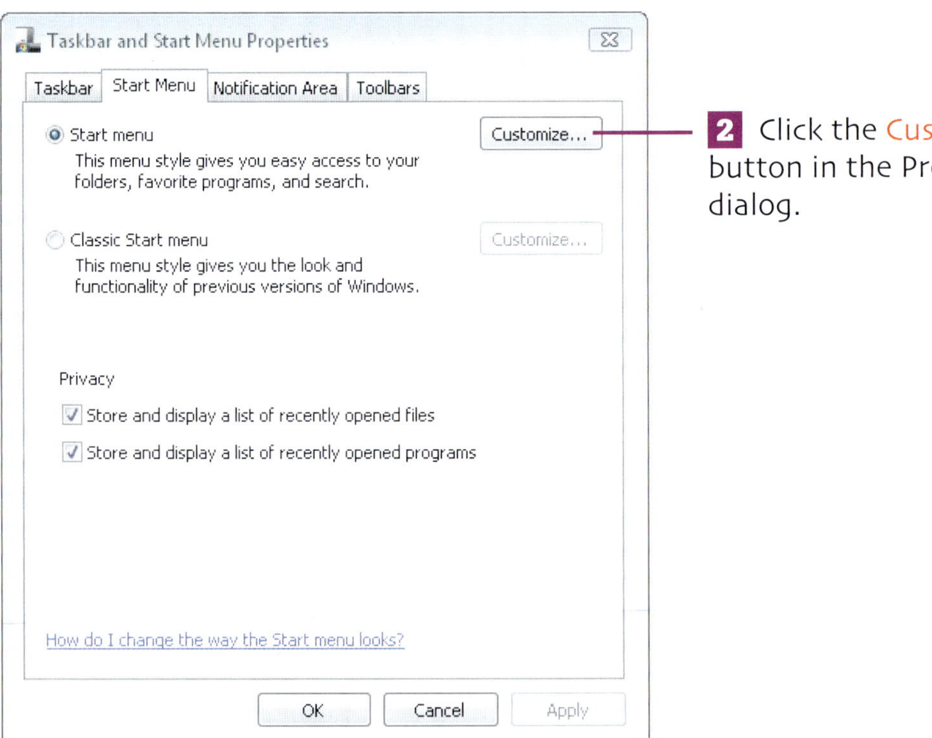

2 Click the Customize button in the Properties dialog.

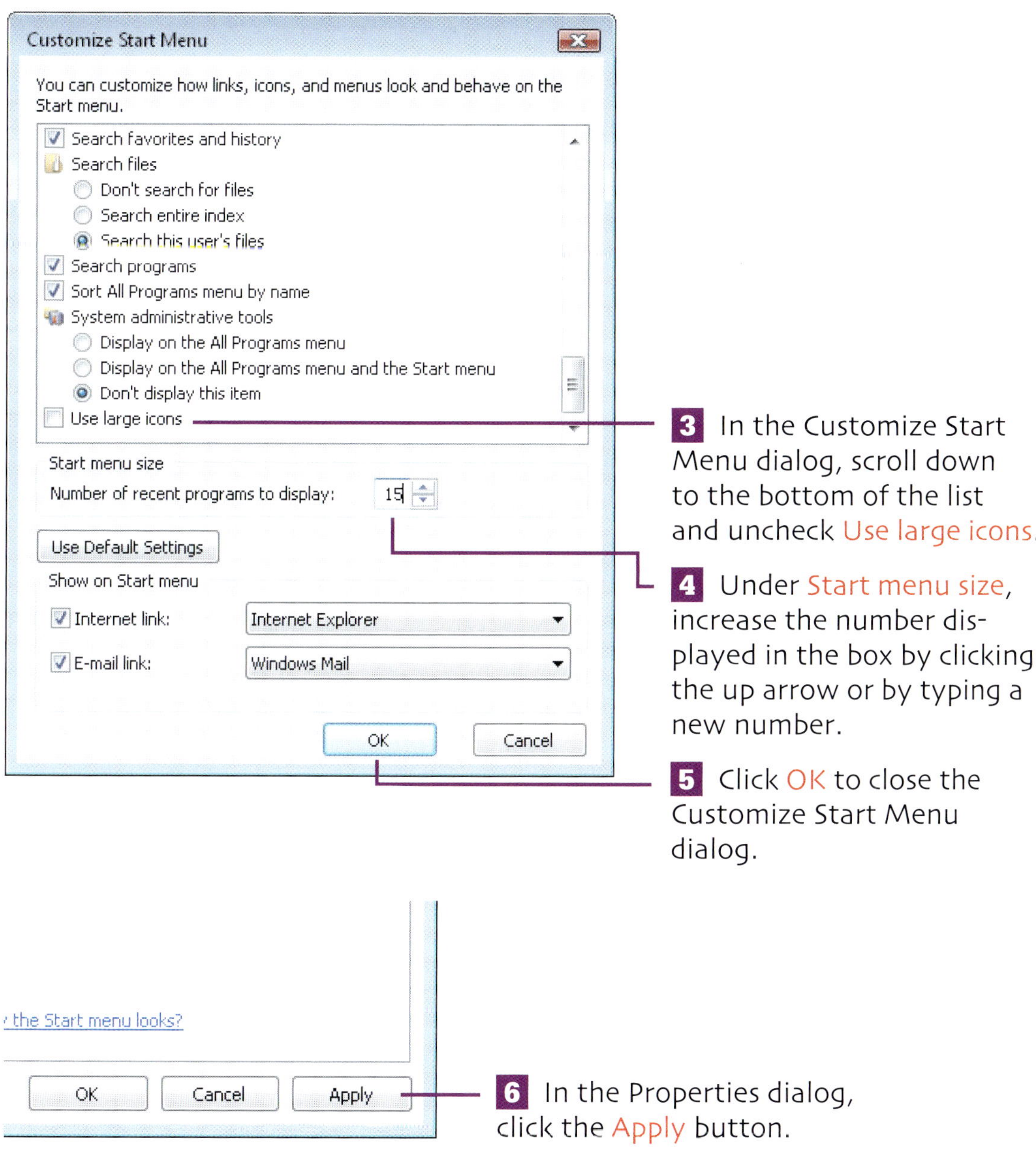

3 In the Customize Start Menu dialog, scroll down to the bottom of the list and uncheck Use large icons.

4 Under Start menu size, increase the number displayed in the box by clicking the up arrow or by typing a new number.

5 Click OK to close the Customize Start Menu dialog.

6 In the Properties dialog, click the Apply button.

more programs (cont.)

7 Go back to the Start menu to see the results of your changes. You'll see that there are now more icons displayed than before, and the icons have shrunk to the size of the icons in the All Programs view.

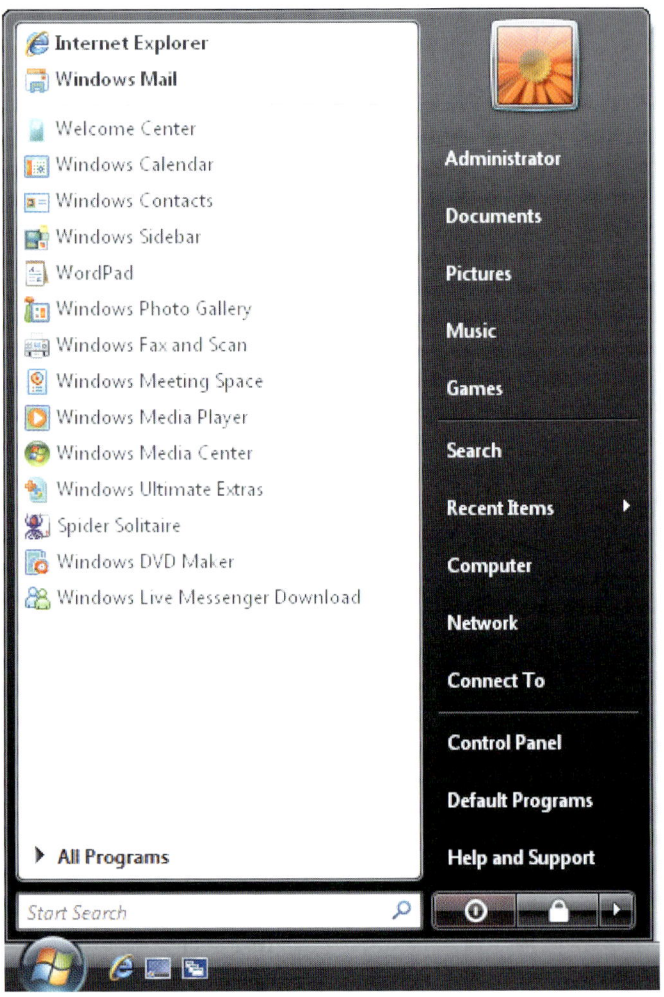

8 If you are satisfied with the results, click OK in the Properties dialog to close it.

convert links to menus

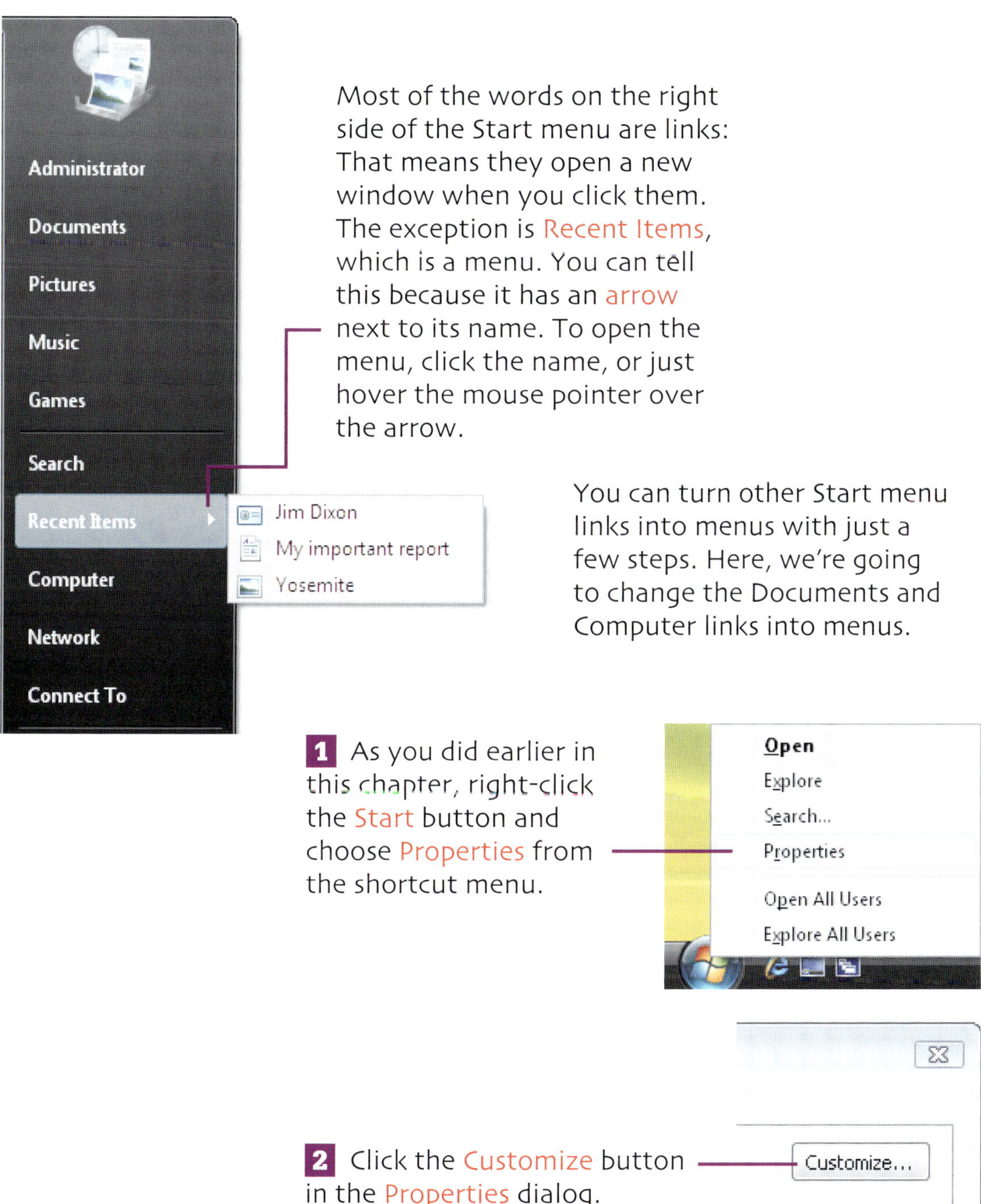

Most of the words on the right side of the Start menu are links: That means they open a new window when you click them. The exception is Recent Items, which is a menu. You can tell this because it has an arrow next to its name. To open the menu, click the name, or just hover the mouse pointer over the arrow.

You can turn other Start menu links into menus with just a few steps. Here, we're going to change the Documents and Computer links into menus.

1 As you did earlier in this chapter, right-click the Start button and choose Properties from the shortcut menu.

2 Click the Customize button in the Properties dialog.

convert links (cont.)

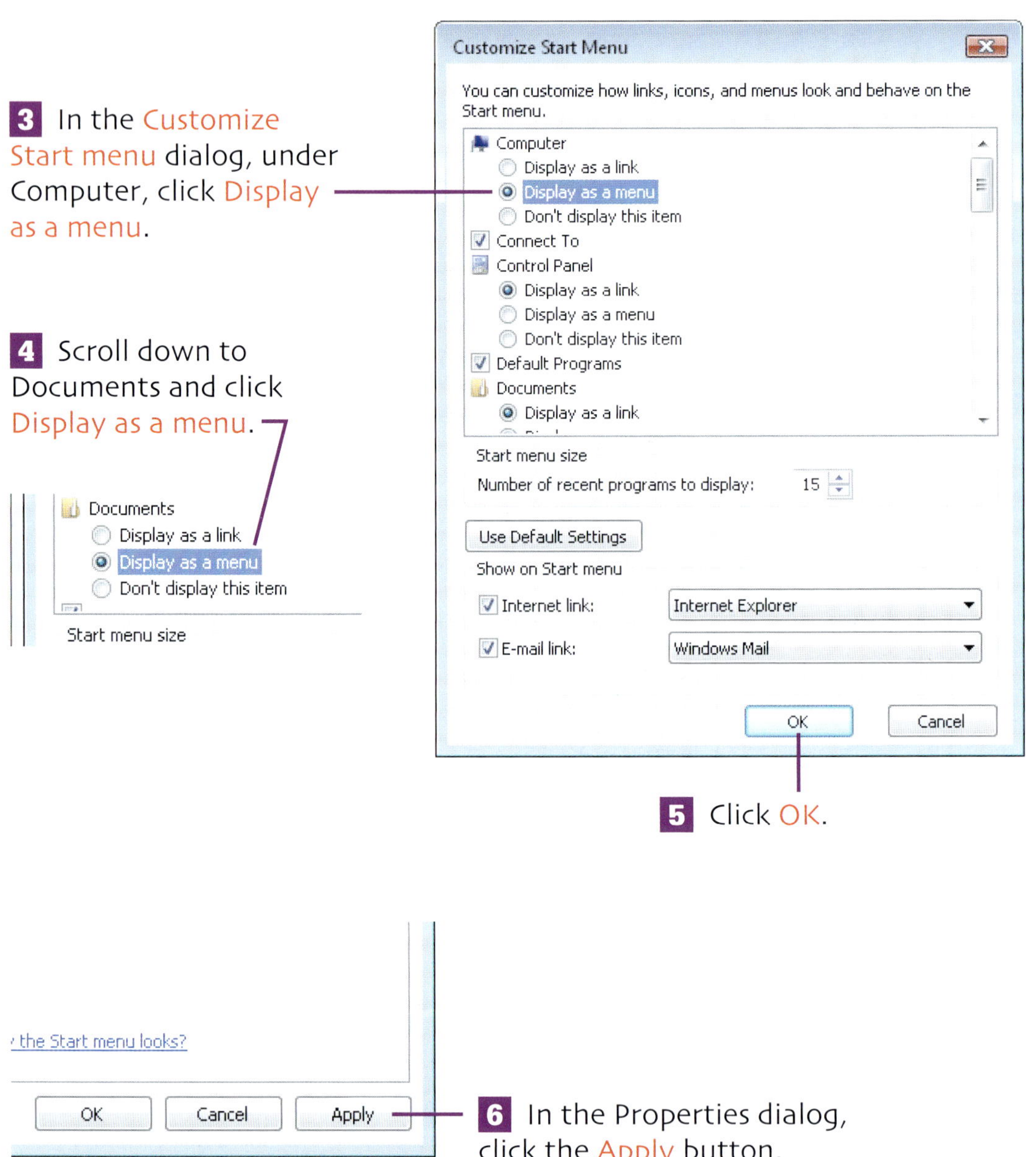

3 In the Customize Start menu dialog, under Computer, click Display as a menu.

4 Scroll down to Documents and click Display as a menu.

5 Click OK.

6 In the Properties dialog, click the Apply button.

7 Go back to the Start menu to see the results of your changes. You can now click on Computer and Documents to select an item several levels down.

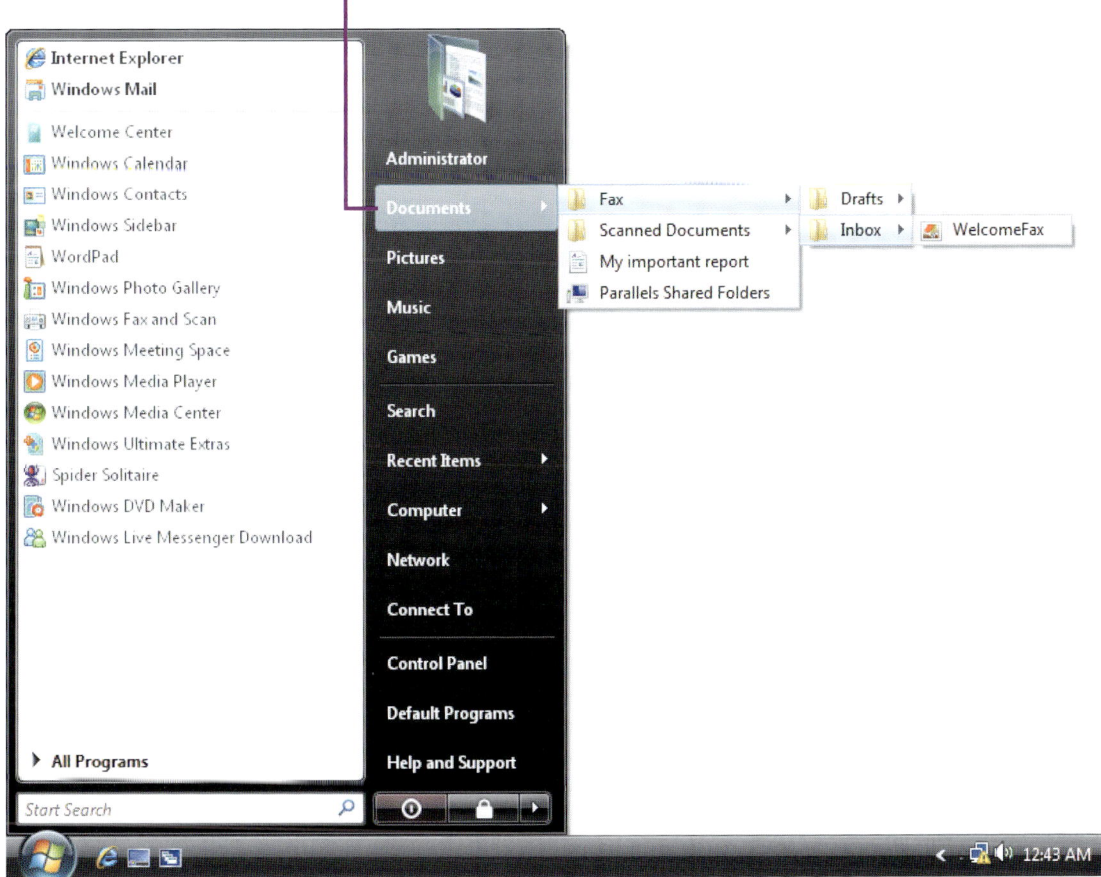

8 If you are satisfied with the results, click OK in the Properties dialog to close it.

Note that once converted to a menu, the item no longer acts as a link. For instance, clicking Documents no longer opens the Document window. From these menus you can only open a file; you can't open a folder.

pin a program

The left side of the Start menu is handy for opening programs with a single click. The icons on the upper left are always there for your use, while the icons below are shortcuts to programs you recently opened. To get to other programs, you have to first click the All Programs link.

If you want to make one of your programs always available in the Start menu, you can add it to the top left area of the menu. Windows calls this pinning a program to the Start menu. There are two ways to do this.

If the program is already in the recently opened portion of the Start menu, simply drag it up to the top left area of the Start menu.

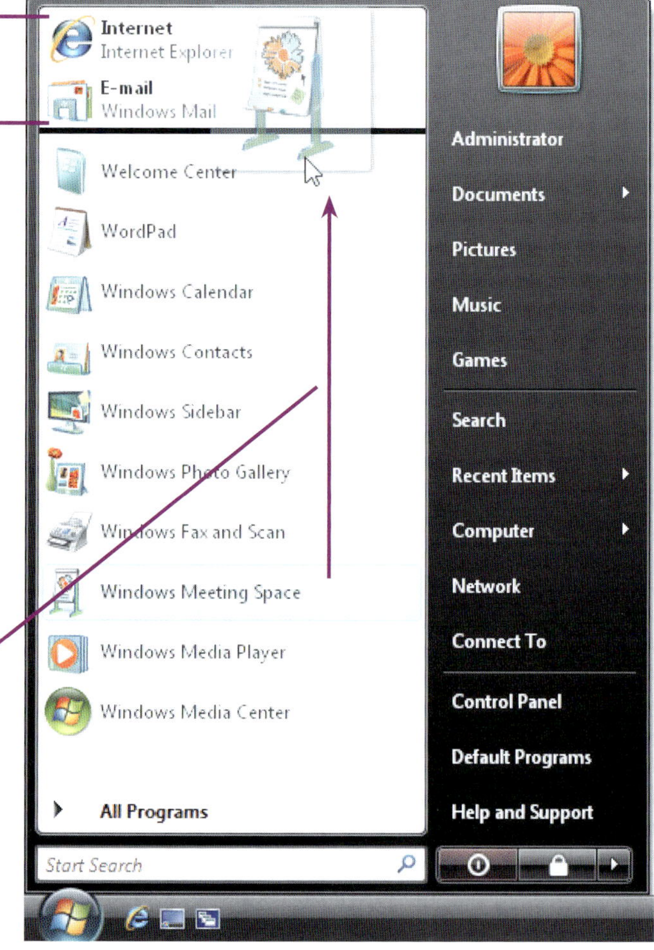

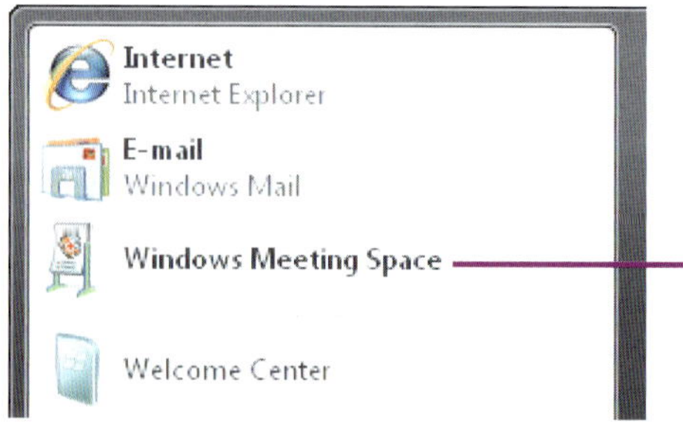

Your program is now pinned to the top of the Start menu.

If the program is not in the Start menu, you'll need to go to All Programs.

1 Open the Start menu, and click All Programs.

In Windows XP, a menu would pop up at this point. Windows Visa changes the left side of the Start menu to a view of all your programs.

2 If you don't see your program, it may be in a folder. Click a folder to expand it.

3 Right-click your program.

4 In the shortcut menu, select Pin to Start Menu.

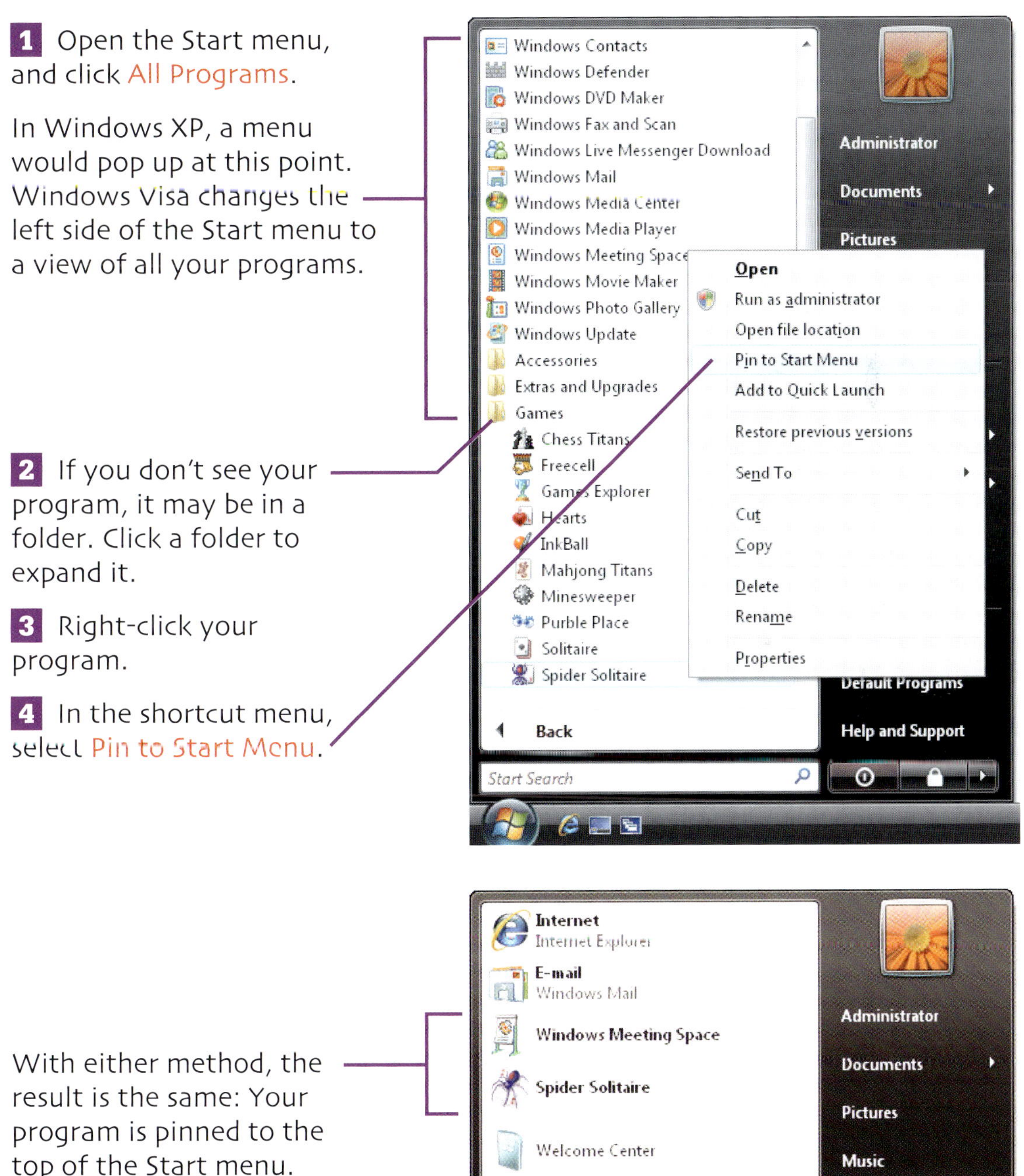

With either method, the result is the same: Your program is pinned to the top of the Start menu.

add a file or folder

Programs aren't the only items you can pin to the left side of the Start menu. You can add a shortcut to a file or folder for easy access.

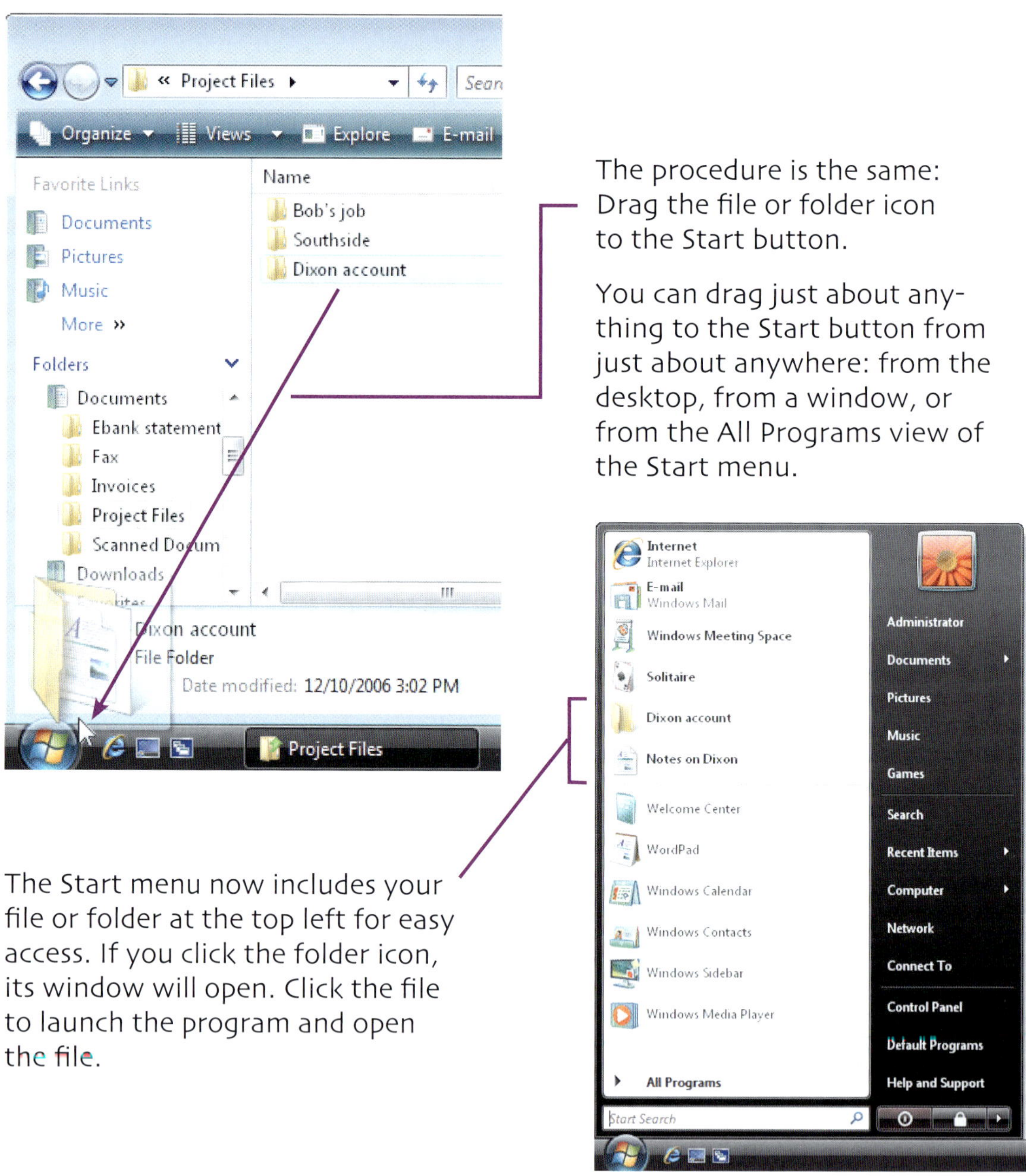

The procedure is the same: Drag the file or folder icon to the Start button.

You can drag just about anything to the Start button from just about anywhere: from the desktop, from a window, or from the All Programs view of the Start menu.

The Start menu now includes your file or folder at the top left for easy access. If you click the folder icon, its window will open. Click the file to launch the program and open the file.

delete a menu item

Of course, nothing is forever, including decisions you make in Windows Vista. If you no longer need an item pinned to the top left part of the Start menu, you can remove it.

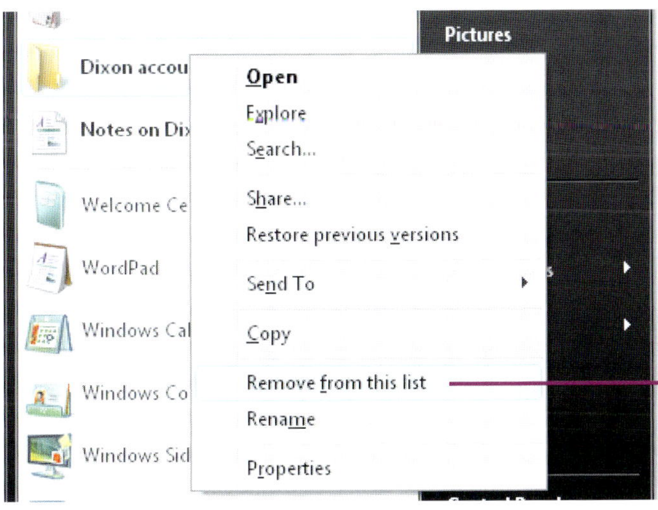

Right-click a file or folder in the Start menu and select Remove from this list. The item will disappear from the Start menu, but the original file, folder, or program is still in your PC.

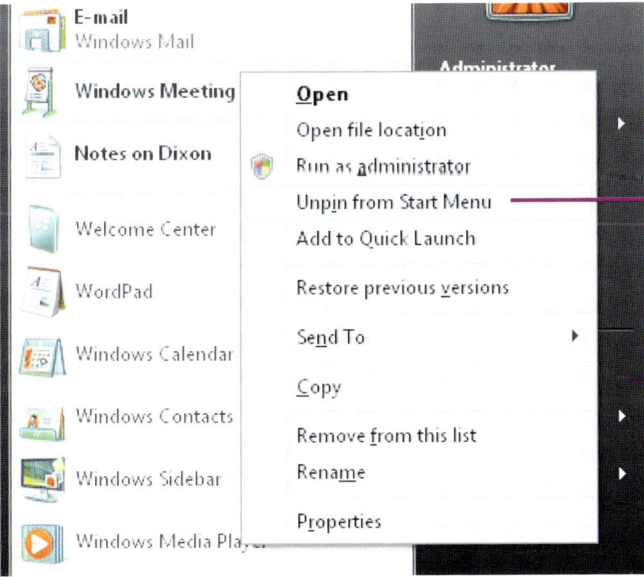

When you right-click a program at the top left of the Start menu, you get an additional choice, Unpin from Start Menu. When you select this, the program icon will move to the list of recent programs below the line.

make shutdown easier

Unlike the Turn Off Computer button in Windows XP, the Vista power button puts Windows into sleep mode.

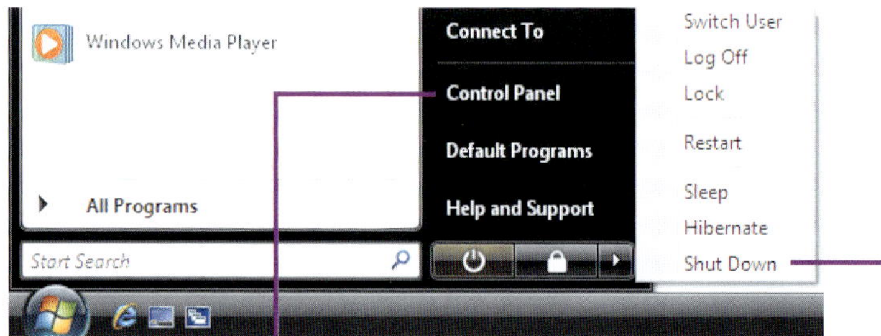

To shut down the computer, move the mouse pointer to the arrow and select Shut Down from the shortcut menu.

If you prefer the one-click shutdown of Windows XP, you can change Vista's power button into a shut-down button.

1 Select Control Panel from the Start menu.

2 Click Classic View in the upper left of the window.

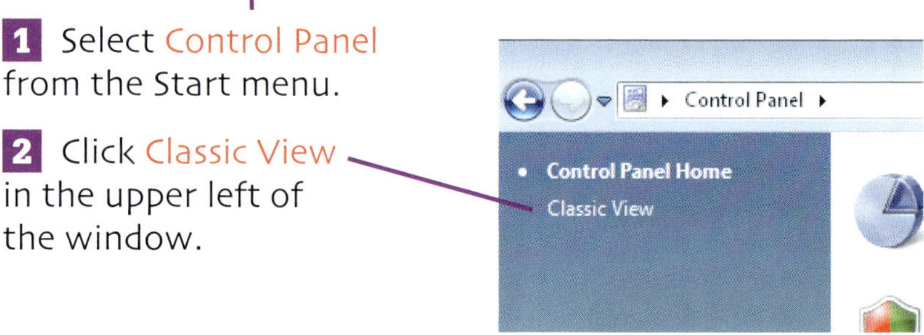

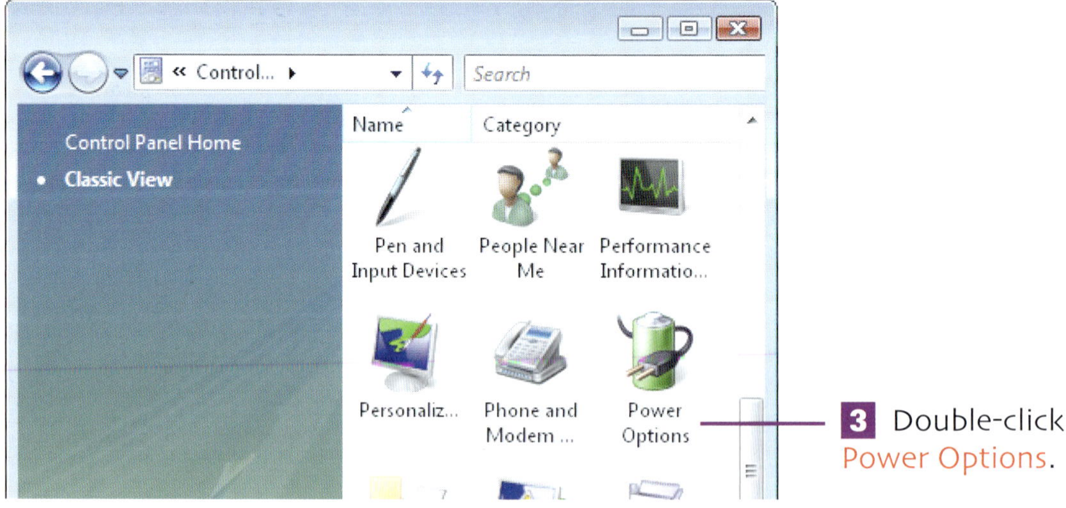

3 Double-click Power Options.

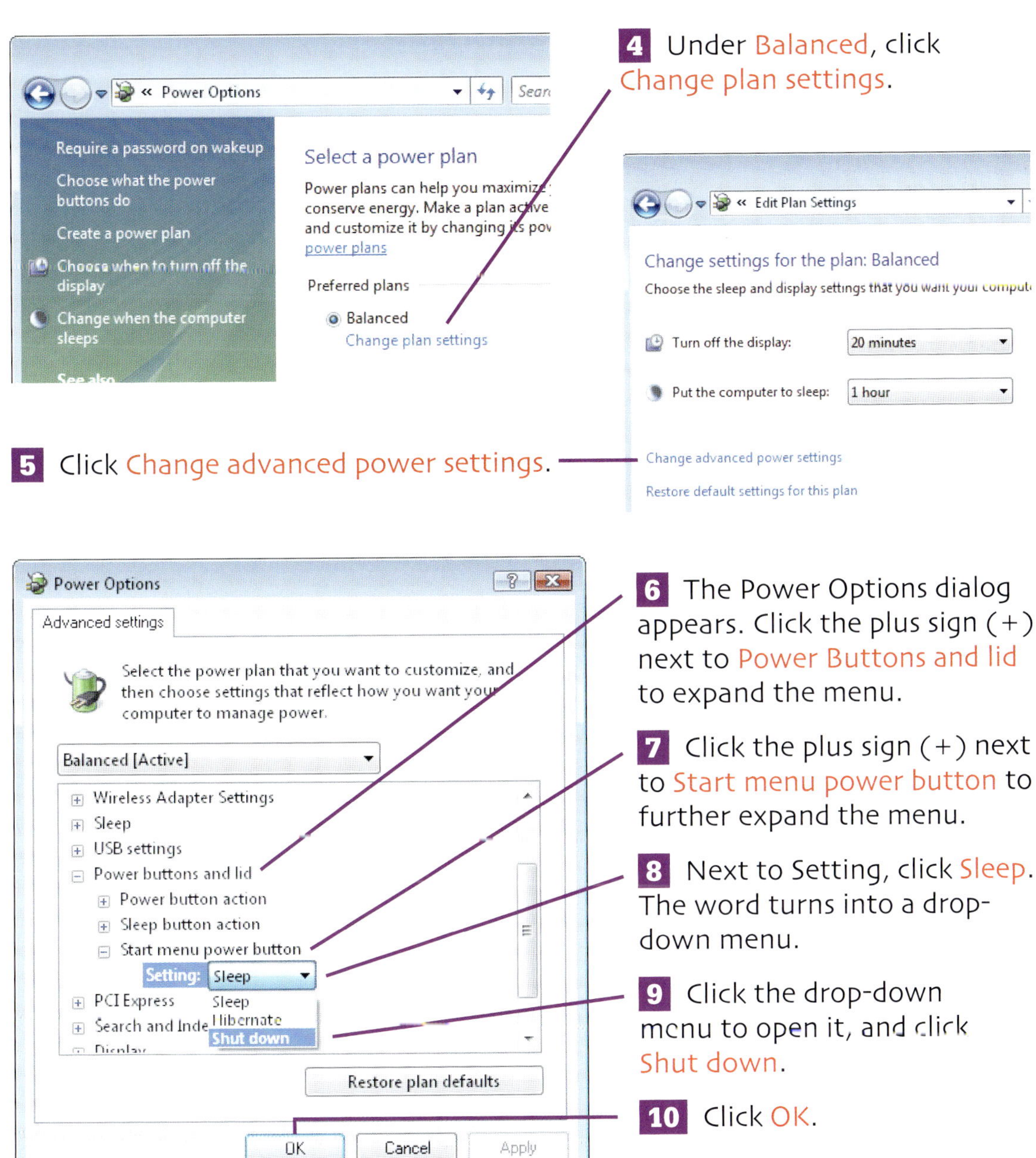

4 Under Balanced, click Change plan settings.

5 Click Change advanced power settings.

6 The Power Options dialog appears. Click the plus sign (+) next to Power Buttons and lid to expand the menu.

7 Click the plus sign (+) next to Start menu power button to further expand the menu.

8 Next to Setting, click Sleep. The word turns into a drop-down menu.

9 Click the drop-down menu to open it, and click Shut down.

10 Click OK.

Back at the Start menu, the power button is now red (instead of yellow) when you move the cursor over it. Clicking it now shuts down the computer.

extra bits

display more programs p. 60

- You may have noticed that the Start menu's Properties dialog gives you a Classic Windows Start menu option.

  This option provides a Start menu similar to those before Windows XP. It's a streamlined version that takes less screen space than the standard Vista Start menu.
- The classic Start menu has its own customization dialog box with options that are different from those of the standard Start menu.

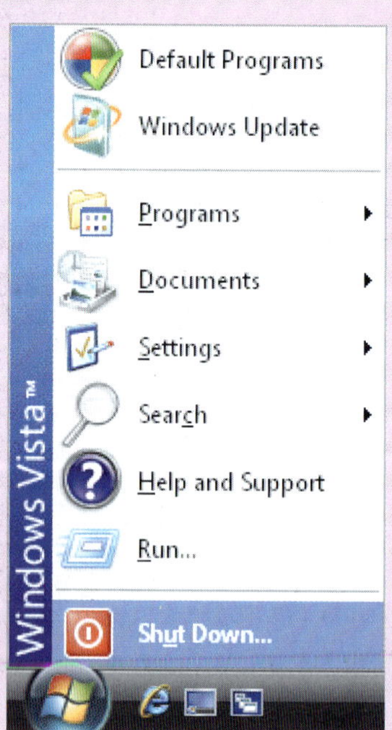

- When you switch to the Classic Start menu, you'll notice that an Internet Explorer shortcut icon appears on the Desktop. If you switch back to the standard Start menu, the Internet Explorer shortcut icon will disappear. This is because the Windows Vista Start menu includes a permanent Internet Explorer item, while the Classic Start menu does not.

display more programs p. 60

- Wondering where the Run box went to? Vista's search box also acts as a Run box. If you'd rather have the old Run command, you can add it to the Start menu.
- Right-click the taskbar and select Properties from the shortcut menu.

  Under the Start menu tab, click the Customize button.

  In the list of options, check Run command and click OK.
- Run now appears under Help and Support on the bottom right side of the Start menu.

7. take charge of the taskbar

The taskbar is a jumping-off point for opening folders and files. It includes the Start button and the Quick Launch toolbar area, which contains icons that open programs. You can add more icons for one-click access to the programs you need. There are also toolbars hidden away in the taskbar that let you get to even more of your files and folders. You can even move the taskbar around and change the way it looks.

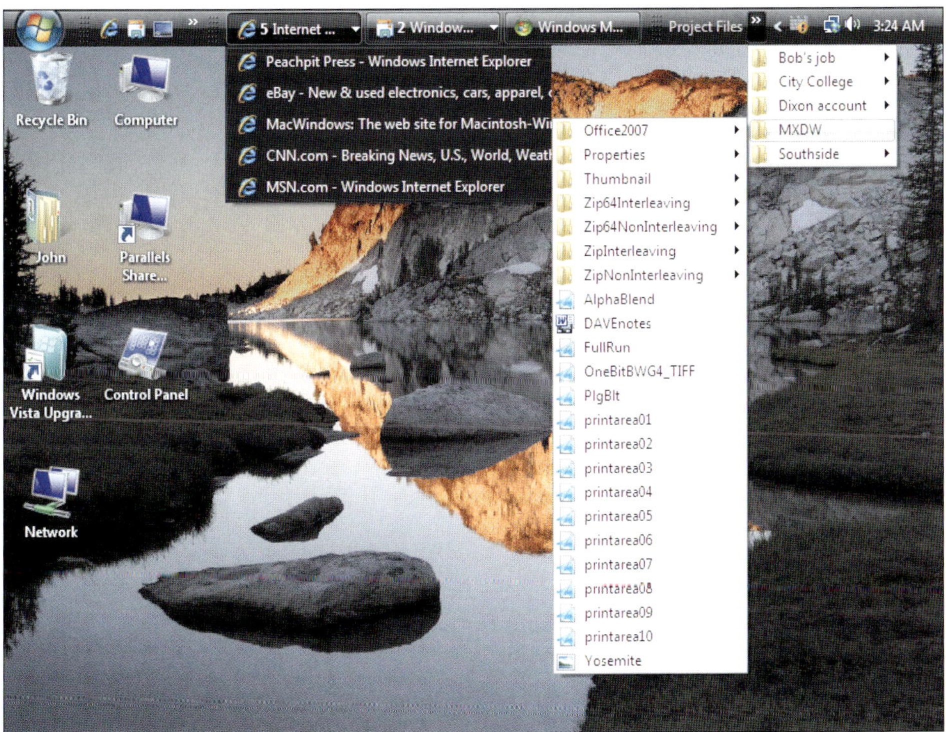

view minimized buttons

The main function of the taskbar is to hold buttons for minimized windows, but the buttons can be so small they don't show the windows' complete names. Windows Vista gets around this by giving you several ways to identify the button before you click it.

When Windows is using the Vista Basic theme, moving the cursor over a taskbar button brings up a balloon with the name of the file and the program that is displaying it.

In the Vista Aero theme, Windows presents a live taskbar thumbnail when you move the cursor over a button. The thumbnail displays the contents of a document and can even play a movie.

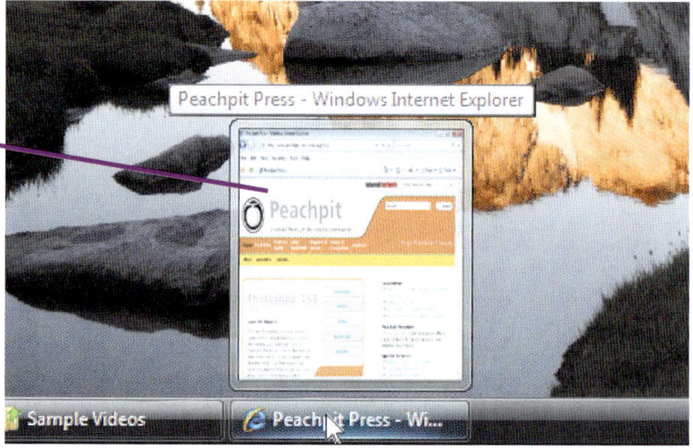

You won't be able to see live thumbnails if you don't have the hardware required to support the Aero theme, are running Vista Home Basic, or have Windows set to the Vista Basic theme. (See Chapter 4 for more on themes.)

Like Windows XP, Windows Vista automatically groups similar minimized window buttons when there are too many to fit on the taskbar. In this example, the group of buttons labeled Windows Explorer includes minimized folder windows and organizational windows such as the Control Panel.

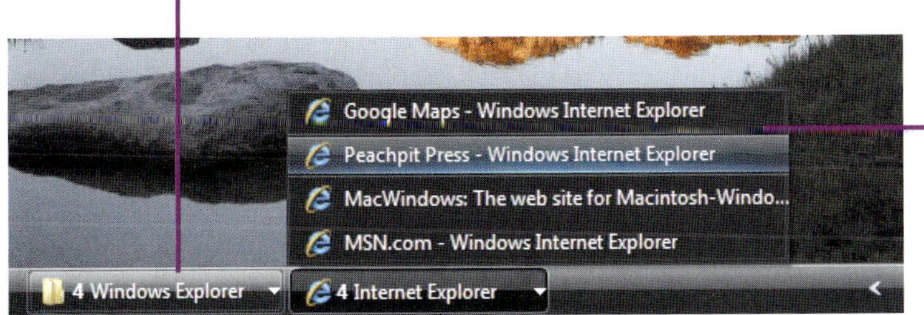

Click a grouped button, and a menu shows what's in the group. This group contains Web pages in open Internet Explorer windows. Open a window by clicking it in the list.

In the Aero theme, a grouped button still produces a live taskbar thumbnail when you move the mouse over an item in the list.

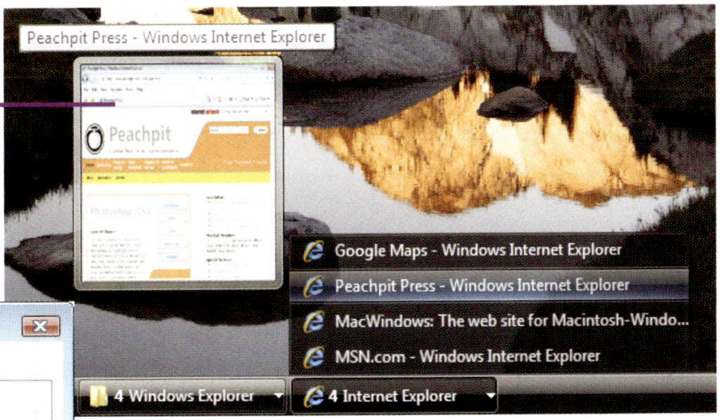

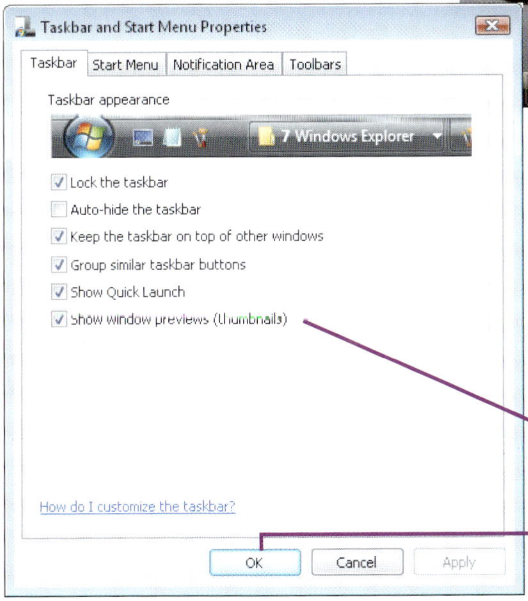

If live taskbar thumbnails are slowing you down, you can turn them off while still retaining the Aero theme.

1. Right-click an empty area of the taskbar.
2. Choose Properties.
3. Uncheck Show window previews (thumbnails).
4. Click OK.

add program icons

Directly to the right of the Start button, the taskbar holds icons that open certain programs when you click them. This area is called the Quick Launch toolbar.

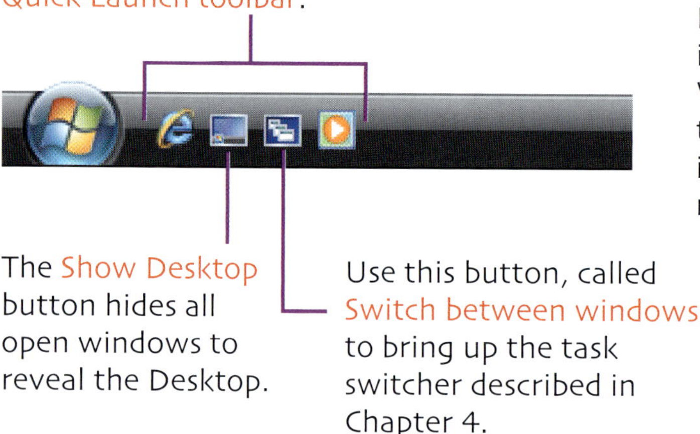

Here you see icons for opening Internet Explorer and Windows Media Player. To this, Windows Vista adds two icons that Windows XP does not have.

The Show Desktop button hides all open windows to reveal the Desktop.

Use this button, called Switch between windows, to bring up the task switcher described in Chapter 4.

You can easily create a button for another program by dragging it to the Quick Launch toolbar. In this example, we'll add Windows Mail.

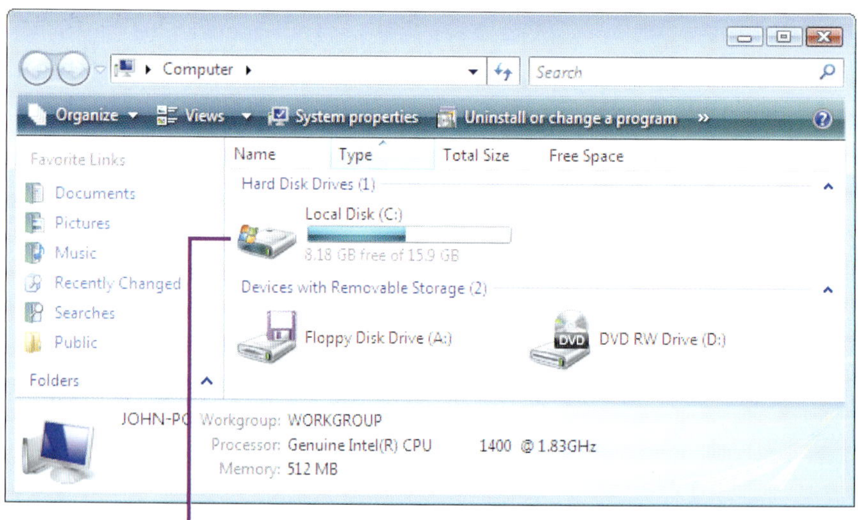

1 To find your program, open Computer and double-click your hard drive, usually called Local Disk (C:).

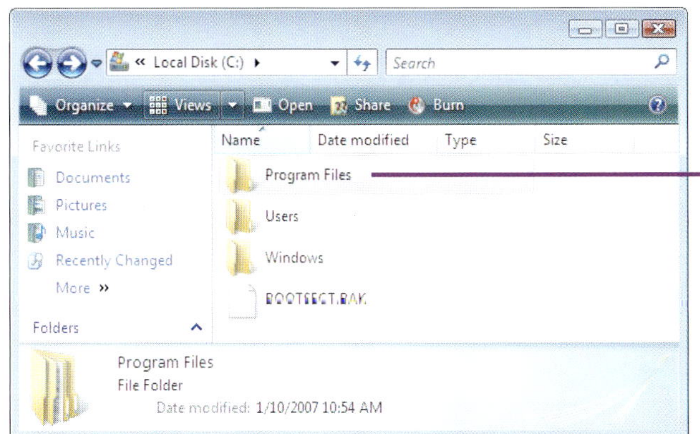

2 Double-click Program Files.

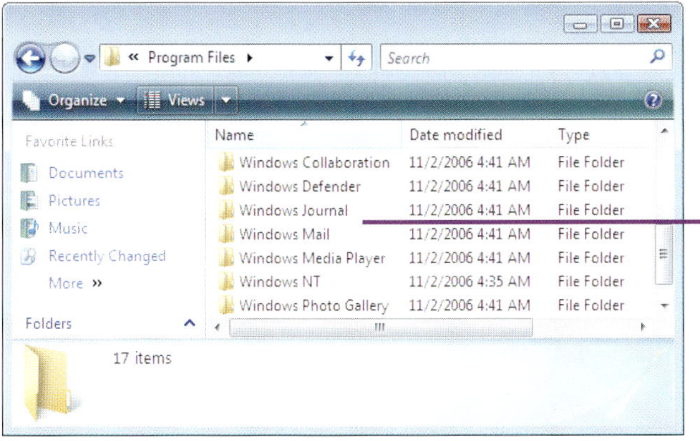

3 Scroll through the list of programs, find the folder with your program, and open it.

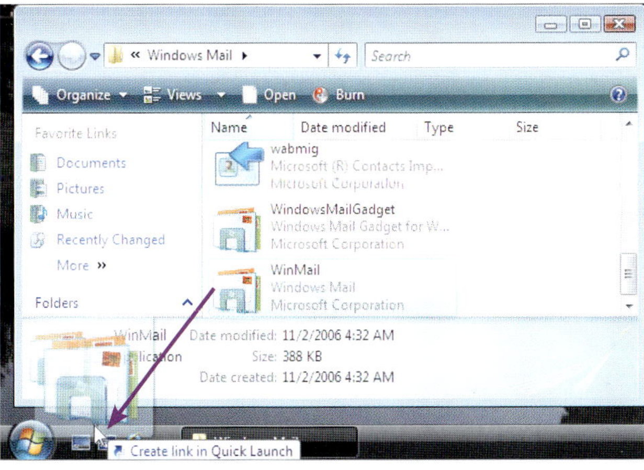

4 Drag the program file to the middle of the Quick Launch toolbar on the taskbar.

add program icons (cont.)

The program's icon is now on the taskbar. You can click it to open your program whenever you need it.

As you add items to the Quick Launch toolbar, you may find that Windows Media Player has been pushed off the taskbar. You'll find it in the pop-up menu if you click the double arrow.

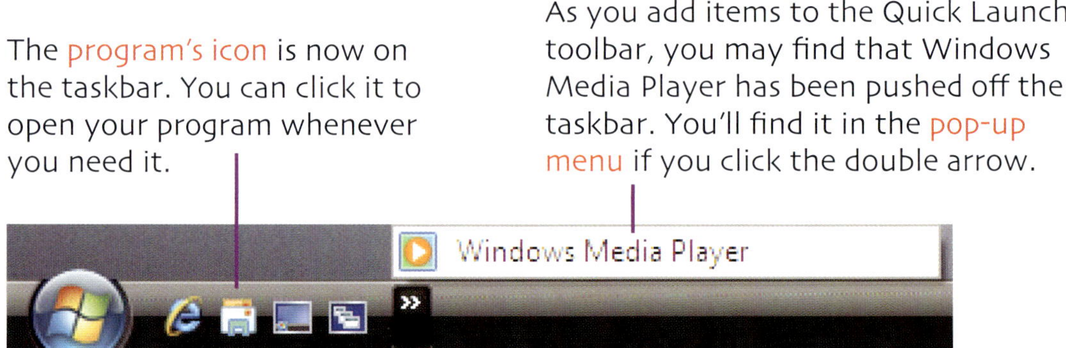

Fortunately, you can put the Windows Media Player icon back on the taskbar by widening the Quick Launch area.

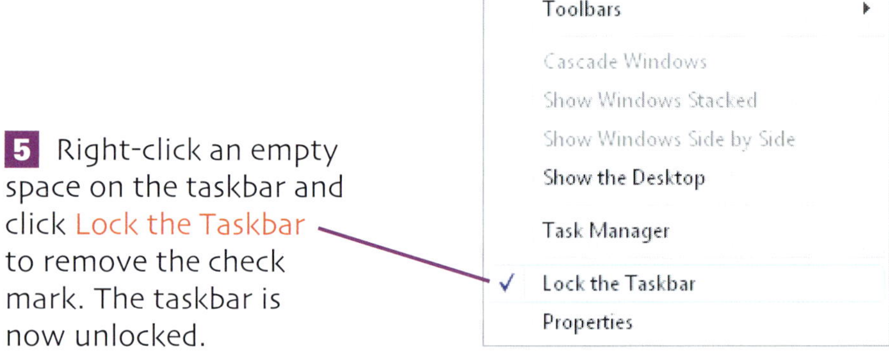

5 Right-click an empty space on the taskbar and click Lock the Taskbar to remove the check mark. The taskbar is now unlocked.

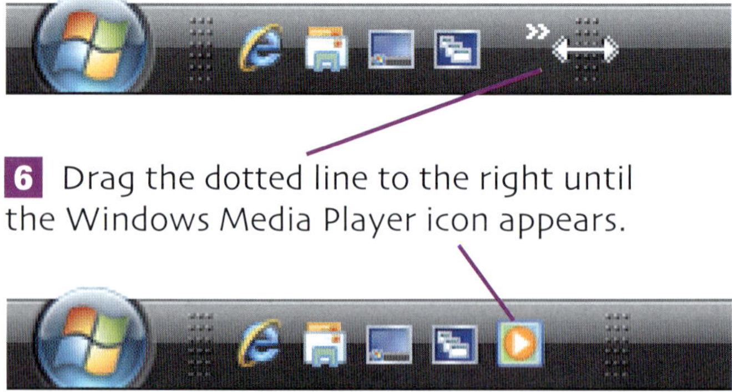

6 Drag the dotted line to the right until the Windows Media Player icon appears.

add folder icons

The Quick Launch toolbar shown on the previous page accepts more than just programs. You can also drag folders here. However, folders in the Quick Launch toolbar are links; one click opens the folder. You can't browse the folder from the toolbar.

In another area of the taskbar, near the right end, you can add folders that act as flyout menus, allowing you to see and select all the subfolders and files inside. Windows refers to these taskbar folders as toolbars, even though they look and act like menus.

1 Right-click the taskbar to bring up the shortcut menu (as on the previous page).

2 If there is a check next to Lock the Taskbar, click the check mark to remove it and unlock the taskbar.

This is a locked taskbar. There's no way to grab a toolbar and resize it.

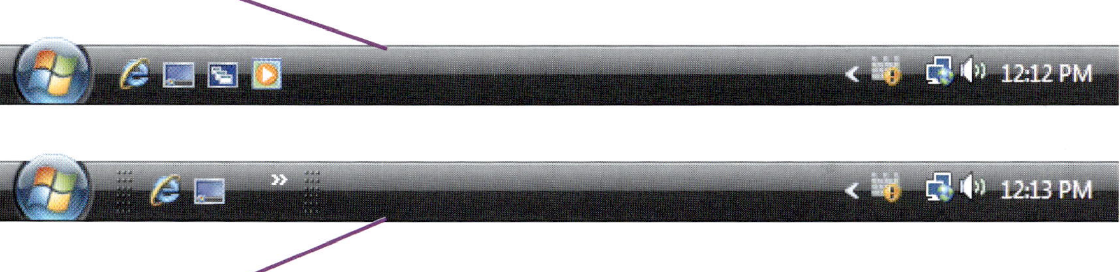

This is an unlocked taskbar, which sports two sets of 3D dots. These are dividers that you can grab to resize toolbars.

add folder icons (cont.)

3 Reopen the shortcut menu that you just opened and move the cursor to Toolbars at the top of the menu.

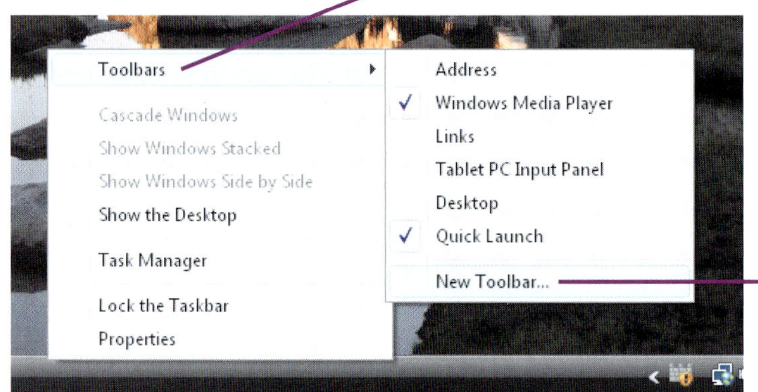

4 In the submenu that opens, click New Toolbar.

5 In the New Toolbar – Choose a folder dialog, navigate to the folder that you would like to put in the toolbar. Here, we are choosing the folder called Project Files.

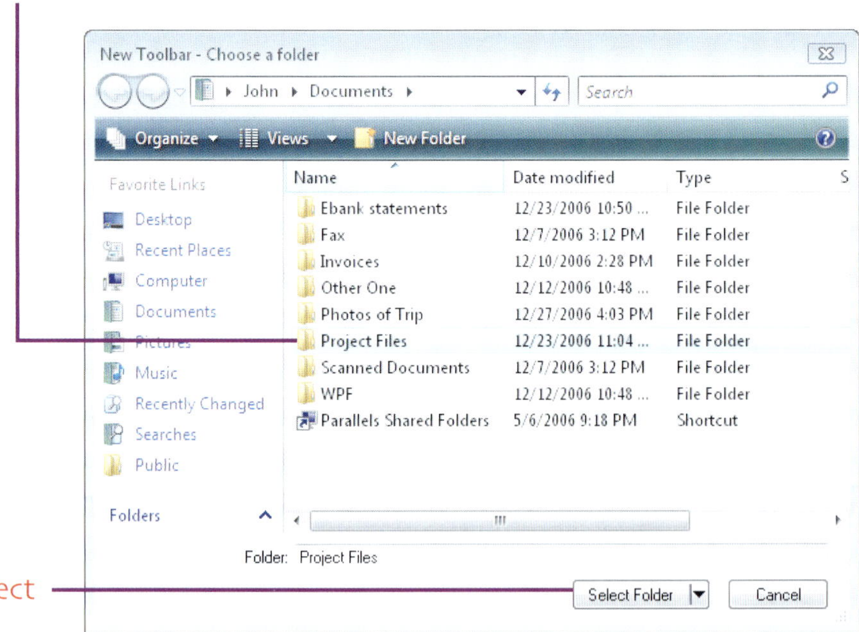

6 Click the Select Folder button.

7 A toolbar appears in the taskbar with the name of the folder you chose, which is Project Files in this example. Click the double arrows to open the toolbar's menu.

8 You can now navigate through the hierarchical menus to the folder or file you'd like to open.

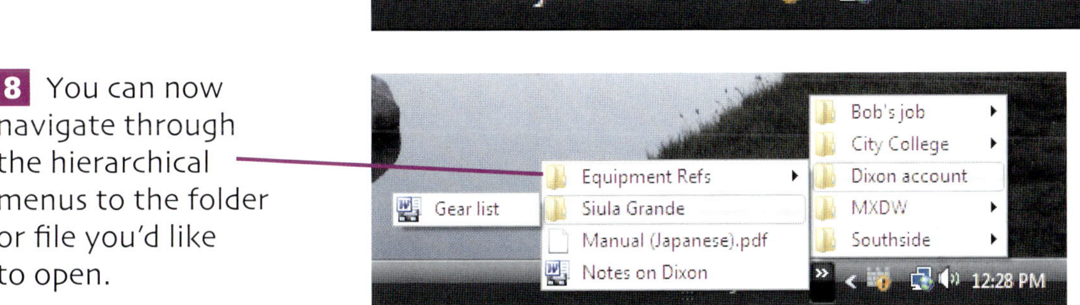

To remove the new toolbar from the taskbar, right-click it, move the cursor to Toolbars, then deselect the name of your folder.

move the taskbar

If having the taskbar at the bottom of your screen doesn't suit your style, you can move it to the top or sides of the screen.

The first thing to do is to unlock the taskbar as we did a few pages back: Right-click an empty space on the taskbar and select Lock the Taskbar to remove the check mark.

Now click an empty spot on the taskbar and drag it to the top or a side of the screen. Here's what it looks like on the right side.

On displays that are wider than they are tall, having the toolbar on the side can be an efficient use of screen space. But with this arrangement the taskbar button titles get truncated. You can fix this by widening the taskbar.

Grab the edge of the taskbar and drag outward.

You can now read the text in the buttons.

You can also widen the taskbar when it is located at the bottom of the screen by dragging the edge. Here's what it looks like after we widen it and lock it (right-click, then choose Lock the Taskbar). Notice that it can fit more buttons.

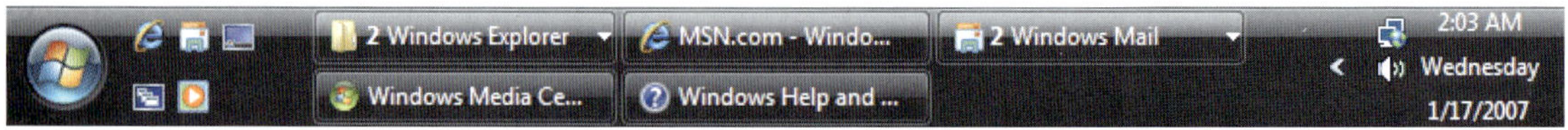

auto-hide the taskbar

If your screen real estate is valuable, you can hide the taskbar and have it automatically reappear when you need it.

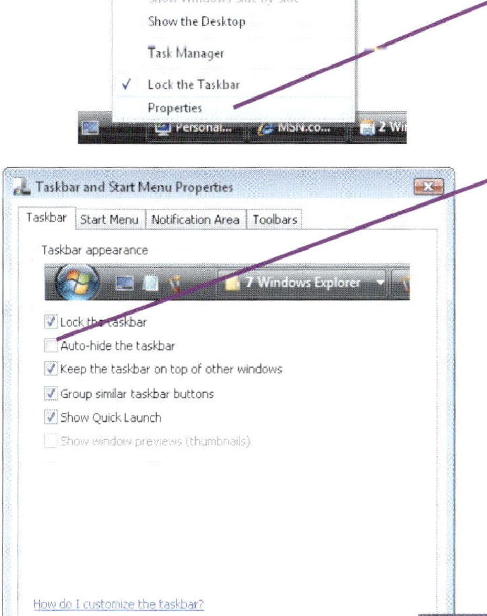

1 Right-click a blank spot on the taskbar and select Properties from the shortcut menu.

2 The Taskbar and Start Menu Properties dialog opens with the Taskbar tab selected. Click the check box next to Auto-hide the taskbar.

3 Click OK.

The taskbar immediately disappears.

To make the taskbar reappear, move the cursor to the edge of the screen where the taskbar is supposed to be. The taskbar slides up into view, letting you click whatever you need to. Move the cursor off the taskbar, and it once again slides off the edge of the screen.

extra bits

move the taskbar p. 82

- Windows XP has a trick up its sleeve that Vista doesn't. In XP, you can drag the Quick Launch toolbar or other toolbars off the taskbar to become floating palettes on the Desktop. Windows XP also lets you pin these toolbars to the top and sides of the screen.
- Windows Vista no longer lets you locate toolbars off the taskbar. You can move the entire taskbar, of course.
- Vista also doesn't let you increase the size of icons in the taskbar, another Windows XP trick.

8. navigate folder windows

Windows Vista makes some big changes to the way you navigate folder windows. It gives you new ways to move between different folders and to copy or move files. These are the main features.

The address bar displays paths in a different form than previous versions of Windows do, but you can use DOS-like paths as well.

This new drop-down menu presents links called breadcrumbs.

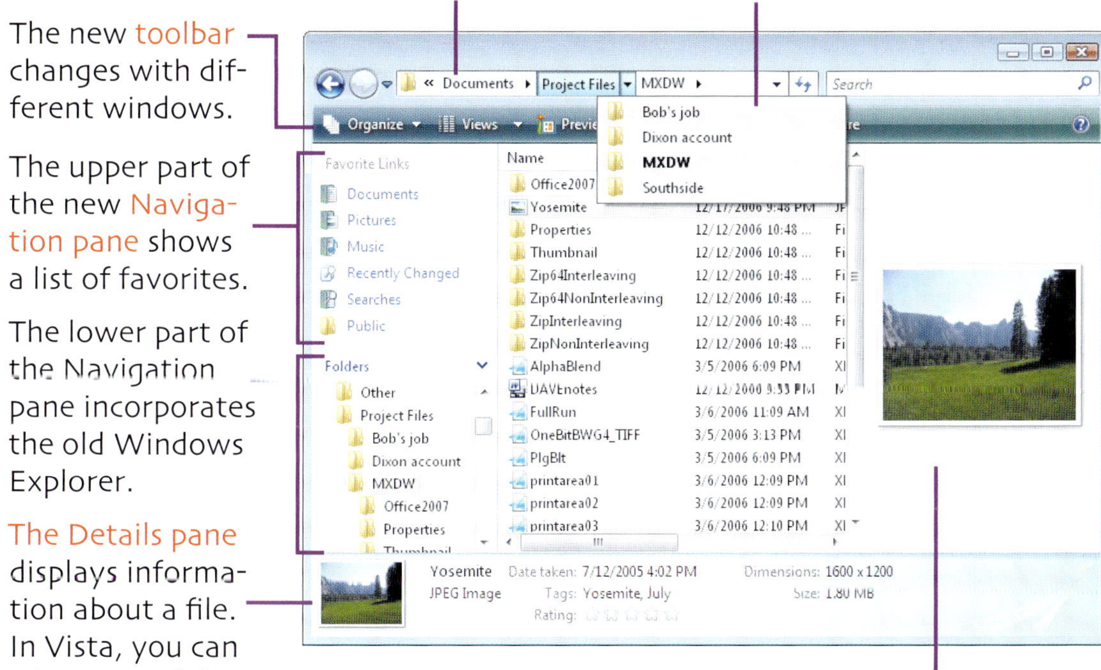

The Preview pane lets you see the contents of certain files without opening the file.

In this chapter, you'll work with all these features. We'll start with making them appear and disappear.

investigate the toolbars

The items on the toolbar change depending on which window is open. They can also change when you select an item in a window.

Organize and Views appear in every folder window. These will be the only two options showing in most folders if you don't have any items selected.

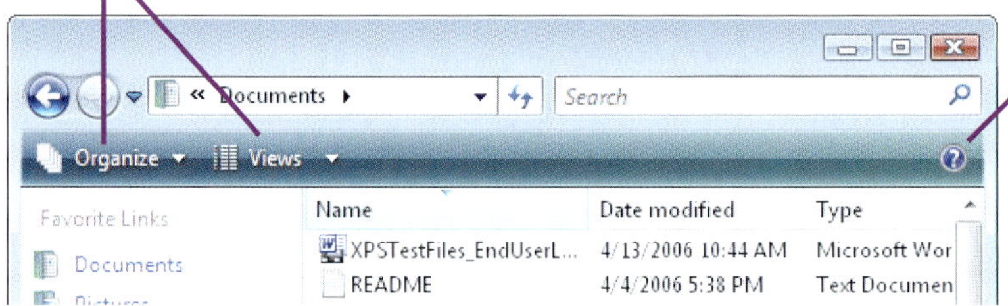

The Help button is also on every toolbar. It opens a Help and Support window with information related to the folder you have open.

When you select a folder, several more toolbar items appear. The Explore command opens the selected folder.

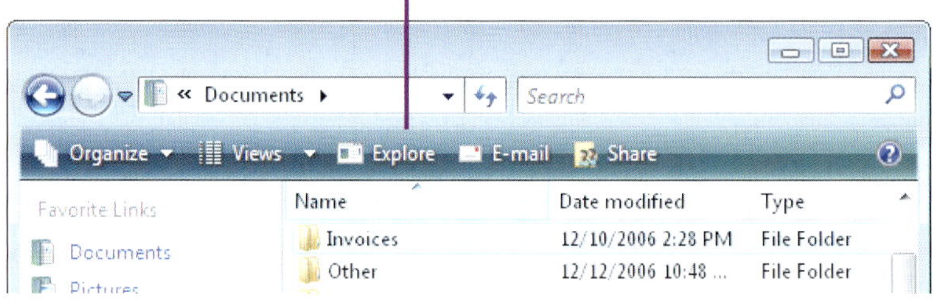

When you select a file, the toolbar looks slightly different. The arrow next to Open lists programs that will open the selected file.

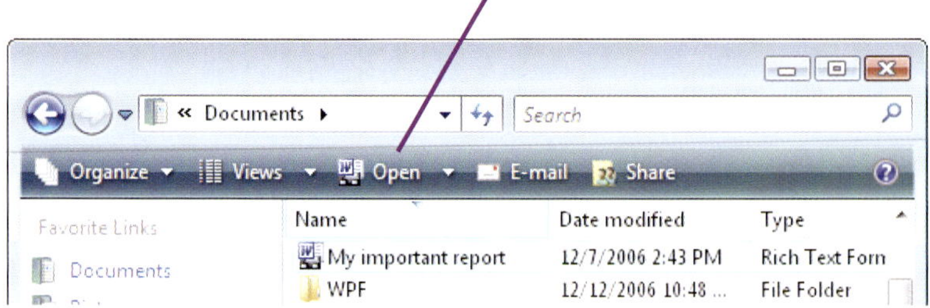

In some folders, such as Music, Pictures, and Movies, the toolbar may include Burn, for writing to a CD or DVD; Play all, for music; or Slide Show, for viewing pictures.

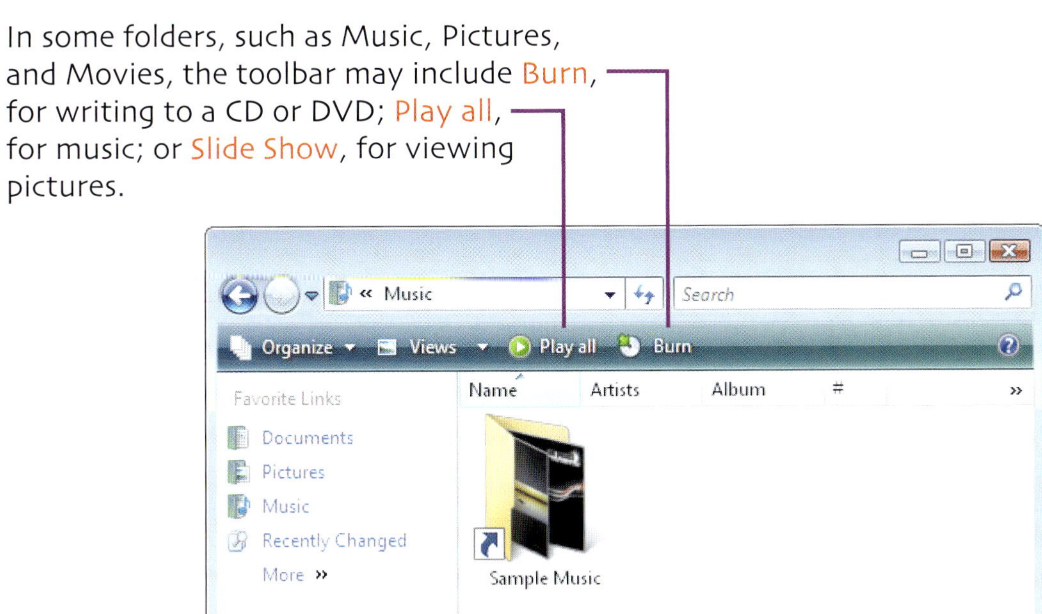

The Computer window has its own special toolbar elements, including the option to uninstall a program.

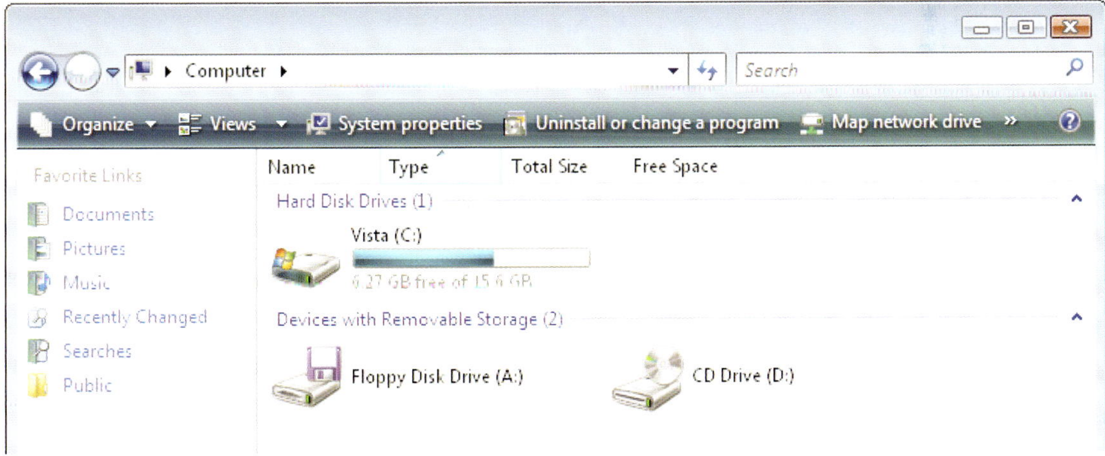

show and hide panes

Which of the window panes you see depends on which folder you open. Different folders default to displaying different panes. In any window, you can choose to display or hide any window pane.

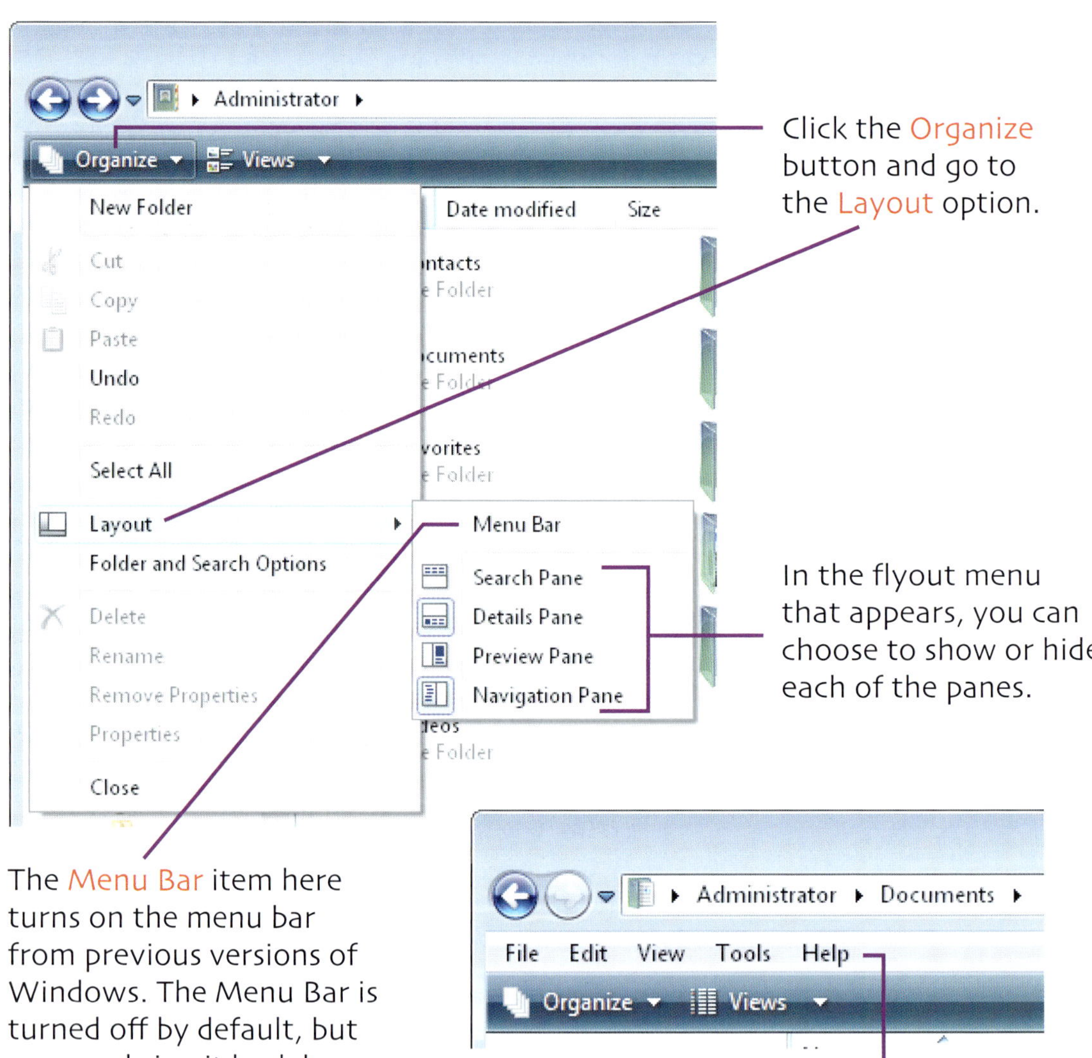

Click the Organize button and go to the Layout option.

In the flyout menu that appears, you can choose to show or hide each of the panes.

The Menu Bar item here turns on the menu bar from previous versions of Windows. The Menu Bar is turned off by default, but you can bring it back by selecting it here.

When turned on, the Menu Bar looks like this. It contains information that you can access in other ways, but it is handy to have if you are still getting used to the way Vista works.

add folders to favorites

The top of the Navigation pane contains links to common places. Click one, and the window takes you to that location.

You can also add your own folder as a link. For instance, you might have a folder for a special project that you open a lot. Adding it as a link in the Navigation pane means that you can access it from any folder window.

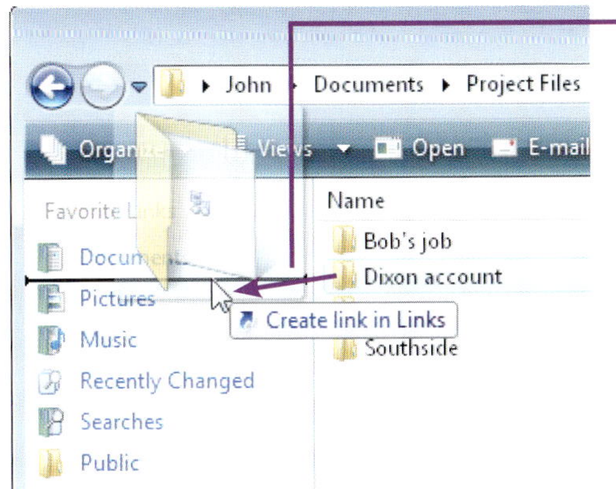

To create a link to a folder, drag it to the Favorite Links area in the Navigation pane. You can drag it in between any two existing links. A message will tell you that you are creating a link.

Be careful not to drop the folder on top of a link. If you do, your folder will be moved to that location instead of creating a link.

Your folder now appears in the Favorite Links list. You can move it to any location simply by dragging it up or down. You can drag any of the links to reorder them.

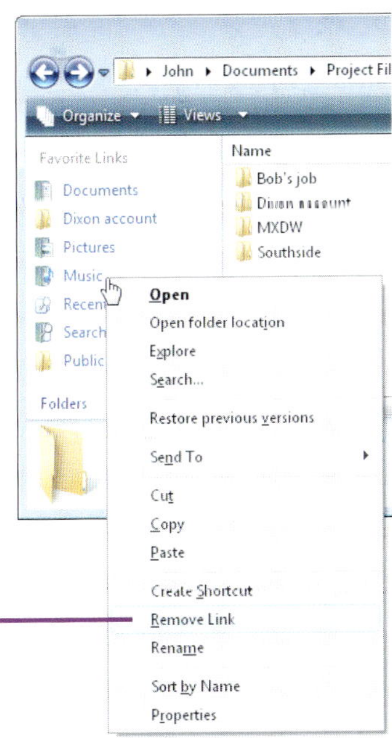

You can also remove links that you don't use. Right-click the link and choose Remove Link from the menu.

Any changes you make to Favorite Links will appear in the Navigation pane of every folder window.

use the explorer

With Vista, the old Windows Explorer is built into every folder window. In the bottom half of the Navigation pane is a section called Folders that displays the hierarchy of folders on your computer. In previous versions of Windows, this was called a folder tree. In Vista, this is called the Folders list. You can use this area to navigate and open folders. You can also use it to copy and move files.

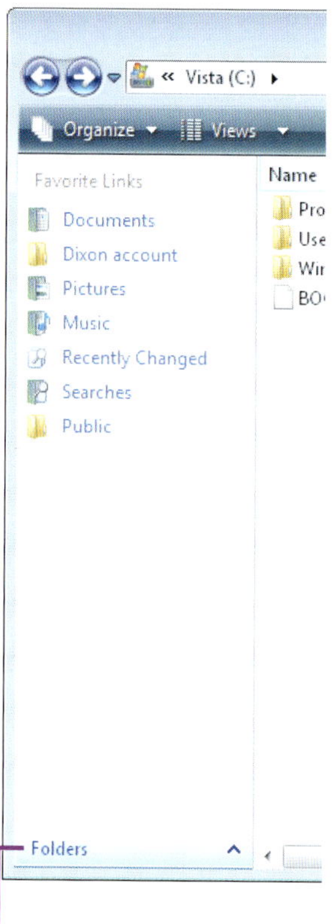

If you don't see the Folders list, it may be collapsed.

You can expand it by clicking the Folders title bar at the bottom of the Navigation pane.

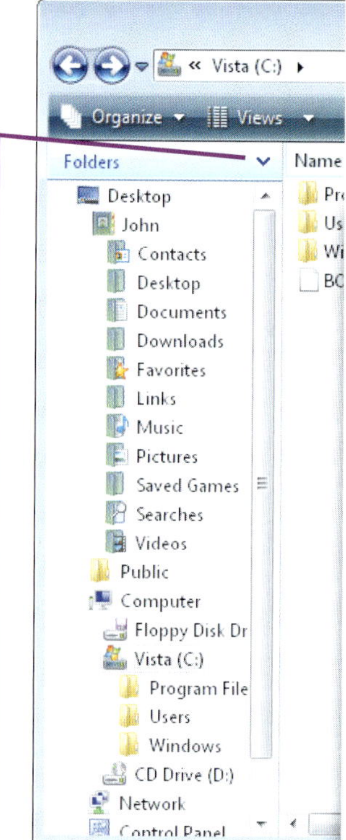

The Folders section expands to replace Favorite Links.

If you want both Folders and Favorite Links displayed, first click the arrow to collapse the Folders view.

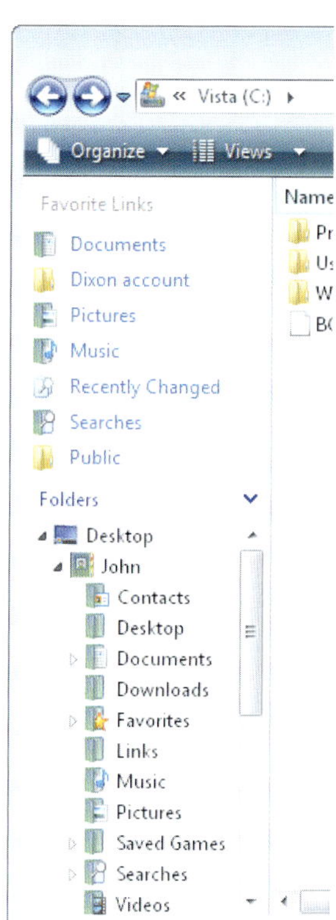

Then expand it by dragging the top edge of the Folders title bar up to the desired position.

Click a folder under the Folders list, and the main area will display what's inside that item.

When you move the mouse pointer over the Folders list or click in it, arrows appear to the left of some folders. (These were plus and minus signs in older versions of Windows.) They fade away when you click elsewhere.

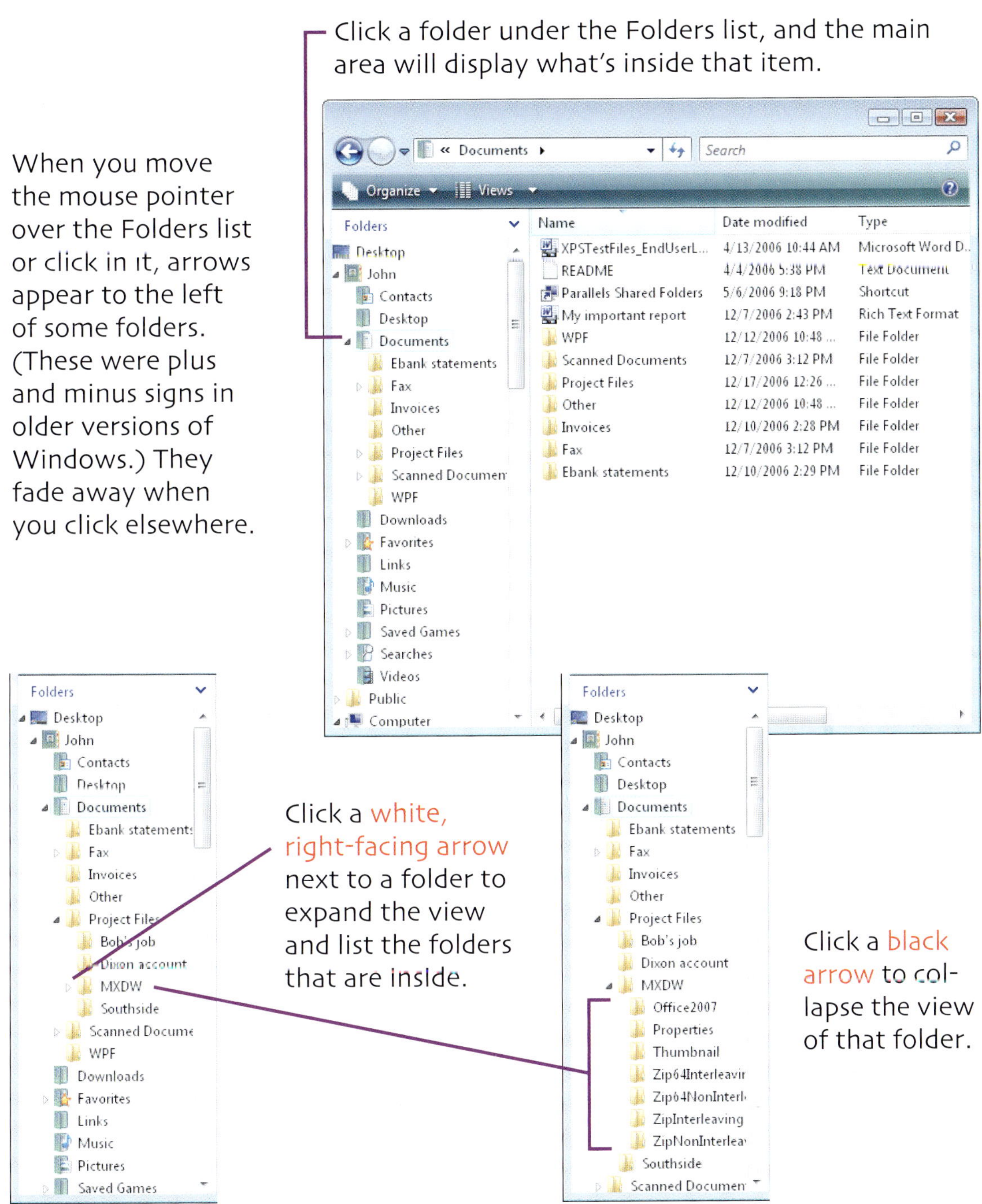

Click a white, right-facing arrow next to a folder to expand the view and list the folders that are inside.

Click a black arrow to collapse the view of that folder.

move or copy files

The built-in Explorer capability of Vista's folder windows also gives you a handy way of moving and copying files and folders.

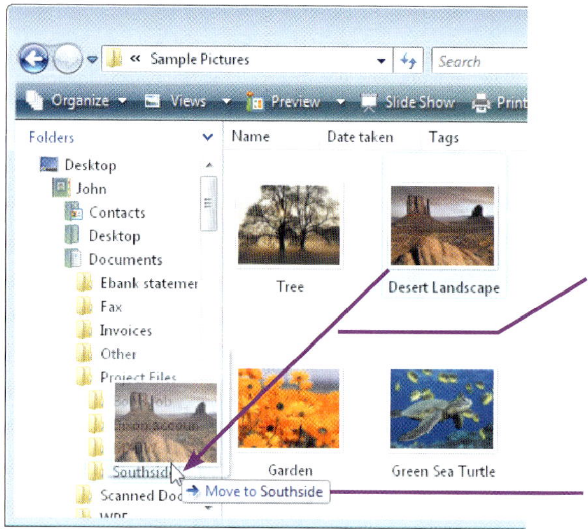

To move a file, drag it to a folder in the folders list.

To copy a file or folder instead of moving it, press the Ctrl key while you drag it.

Windows tells you whether you are moving or copying the file.

You can also use the copy-and-paste method using shortcut menus and the Folders list.

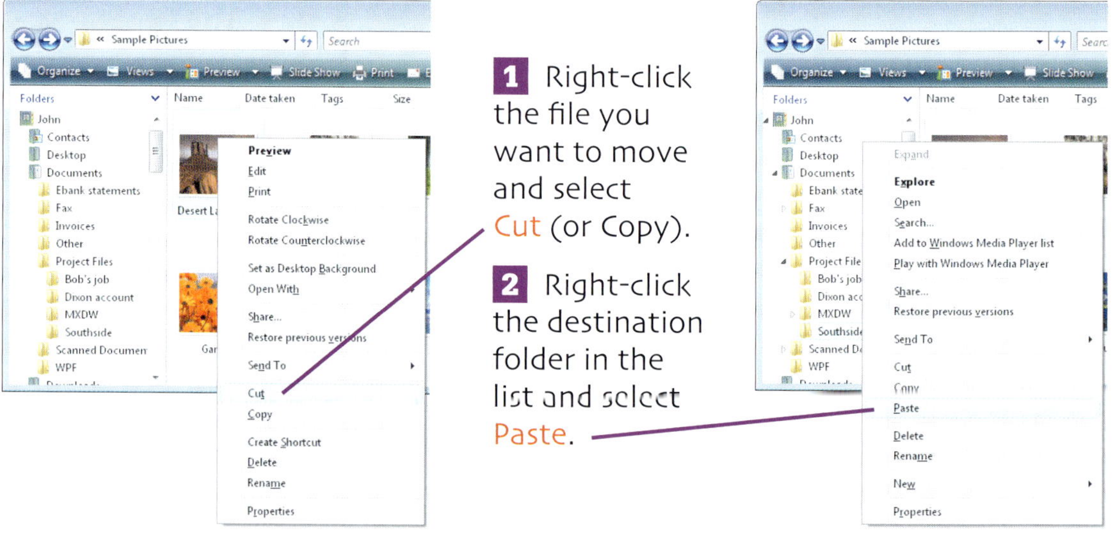

1 Right-click the file you want to move and select Cut (or Copy).

2 Right-click the destination folder in the list and select Paste.

use the address bar

The Windows Vista address bar is a versatile tool that offers several new ways to quickly get to folders. The most striking change from previous versions of Windows is that Vista displays the path using a method called breadcrumbing. (The name refers to Hansel and Gretel, who left a trail of breadcrumbs to find the path back home.) The name on the right is the open folder. The names to the left are the parent folders.

This bread-crumbing view doesn't just tell you where you are; it's also interactive. To go to one of the parent folders, click its name in the address bar.

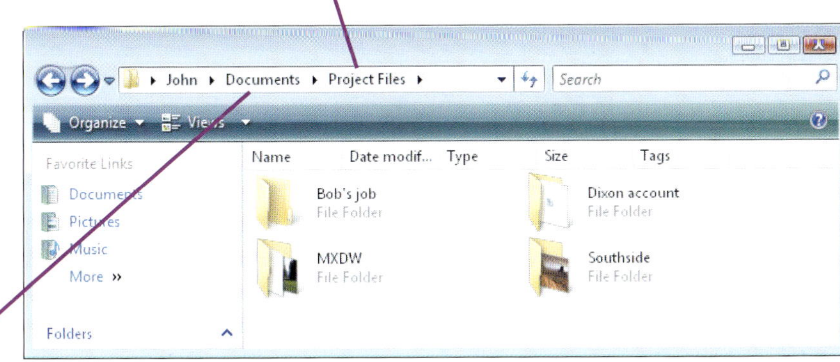

The address bar can also tell you what folders the parent folders contain and lets you navigate to other subfolders with a just a couple of clicks.

Click an arrow to the right of a folder name in the address bar. A drop-down menu shows the folders contained inside it. You can choose one to jump to that folder.

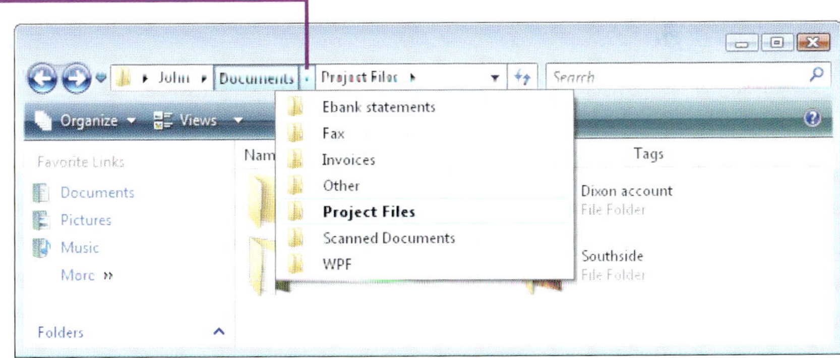

If you click the arrow to the right of your parent folder (in this case, Documents), you'll see a list of its subfolders, including the current open folder. The name in bold is the folder you are currently in. Click one of the not-bold folder names to go to that folder.

use the address bar (cont.)

You can also use the address bar to view and type a traditional folder path.

1 Click the folder icon.

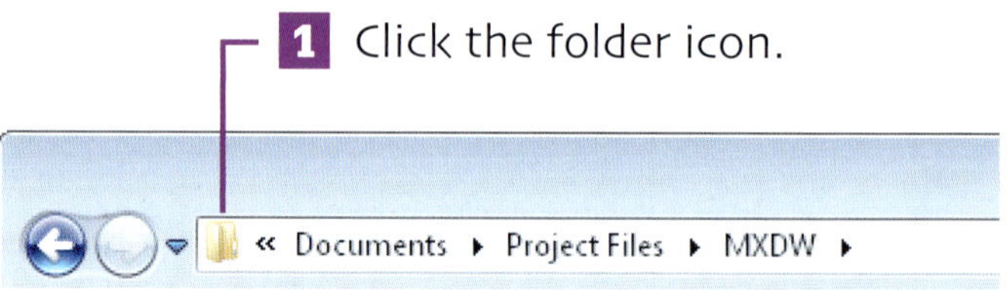

2 The address bar switches from the breadcrumb view to a traditional folder path. You can type a path to go to any directory on your computer.

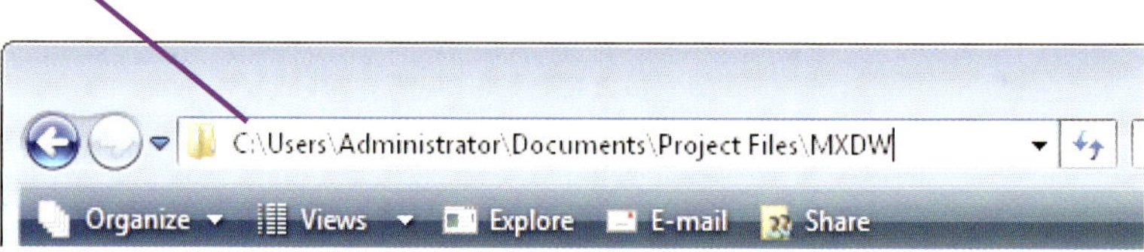

You can also type in the address of a Web site here. Press Enter to bring up Internet Explorer with the Web page you specified.

To the right of the address bar is the search bar. Type in a term here to search for items within the current folder. The results of your search are presented in the same window.

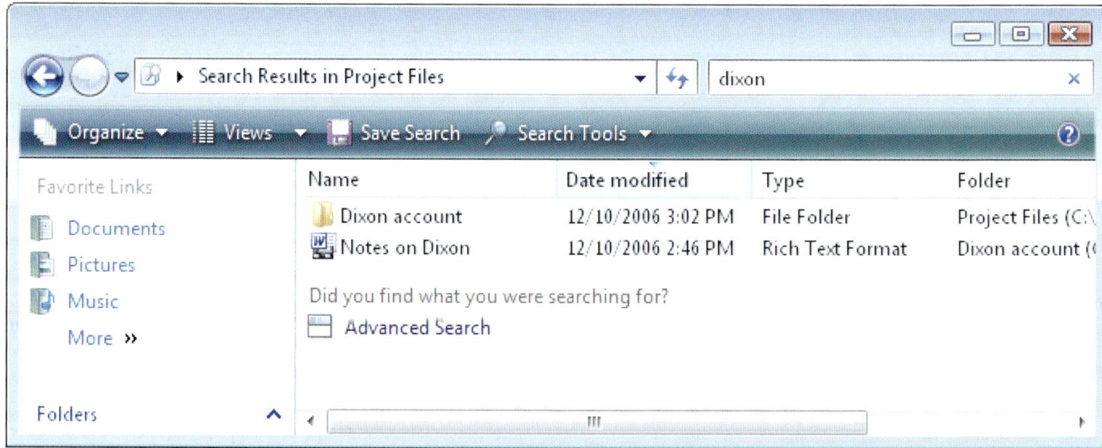

view and edit file info

The Details pane displays information about a file, such as its filename, date modified, and size. The Details pane also presents other information that you can edit on the spot. The type of information displayed depends on the type of file selected.

Here, we've selected a Word document in a folder window. The Details pane is displaying a title, author, and tags. Some of this information comes directly from the Word document, and some of it was typed in here.

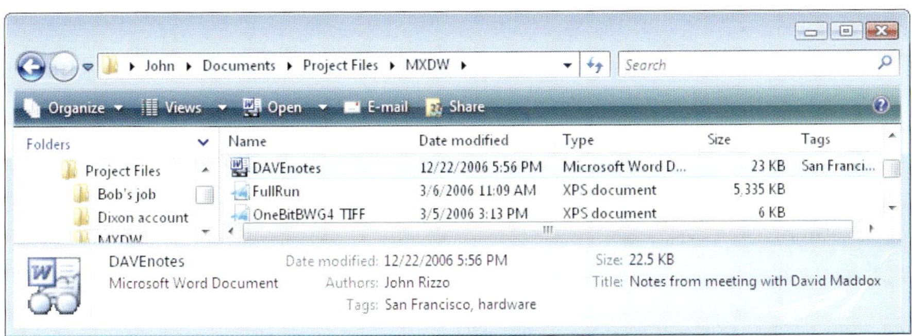

For music files, the Details pane can display album art and related information contained in the file. You can use the Details pane to edit (or add) the artist, album, and genre and add a rating.

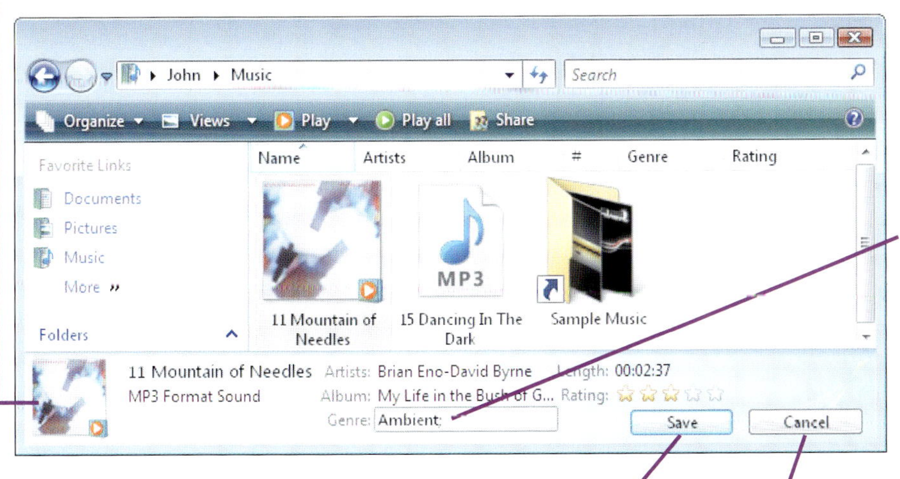

1 To edit the information, click the text in the Details pane. The text will turn into a field.

2 The Save and Cancel buttons will appear. Type the new text and click Save.

preview your files

The Preview pane lets you peek inside certain word processing files, pictures, audio files, contacts, and other file types, without having to open the file.

The Preview pane shows up automatically in some folders, such as the Pictures folder. If you don't see it, you can turn it on by going to the Organize menu and choosing Layout (as described earlier in this chapter).

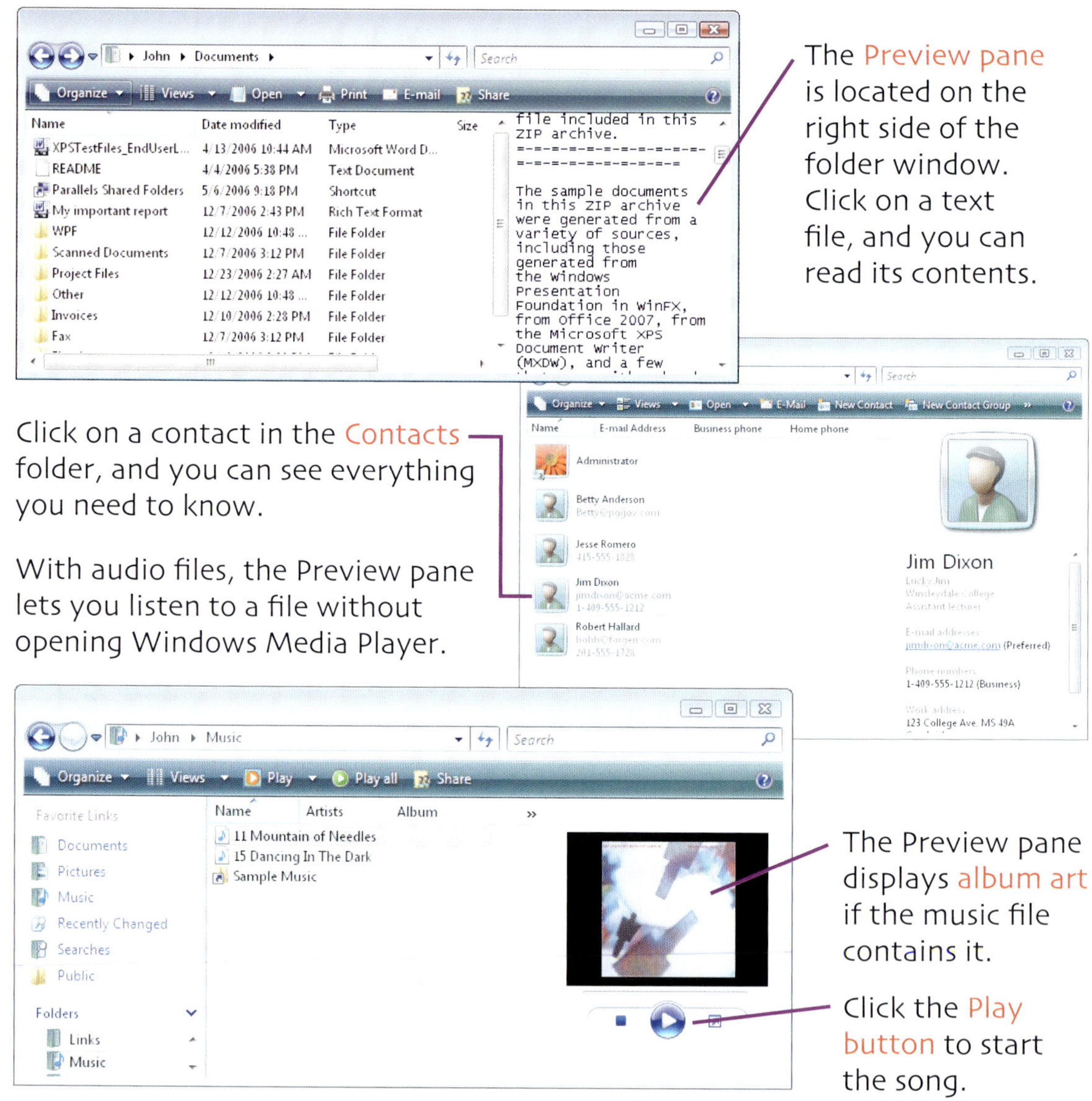

The Preview pane is located on the right side of the folder window. Click on a text file, and you can read its contents.

Click on a contact in the Contacts folder, and you can see everything you need to know.

With audio files, the Preview pane lets you listen to a file without opening Windows Media Player.

The Preview pane displays album art if the music file contains it.

Click the Play button to start the song.

change folder views

In any folder window, you can change the way you view files and folders. Click Views on the toolbar to bring up a different view. Keep clicking to cycle between four different views: List, Details, Tiles, and Large Icons.

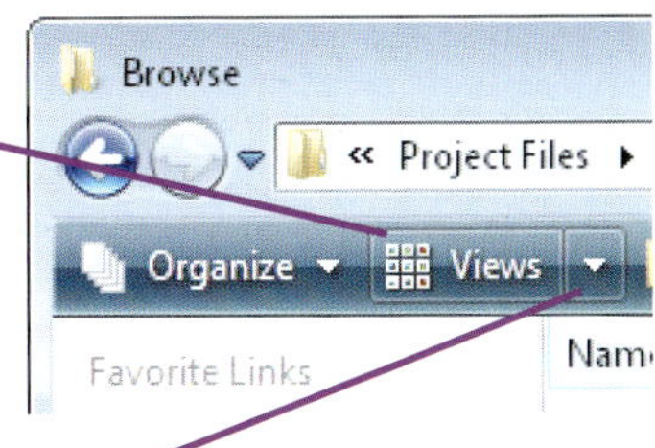

There is also a Views menu that lists seven different ways to see the file and folder icons inside. To open the Views menu, click the arrow on the right side of Views in the toolbar.

The four Icons views—Small, Medium, Large, and Extra Large—display only the filename and icon.

List view also displays the filename and icon, but items are smaller than in the small icons view, and more files can be displayed in a window.

Tiles view displays medium-size icons and filenames along with the type of document. Details view provides the most information, including date modified and file size.

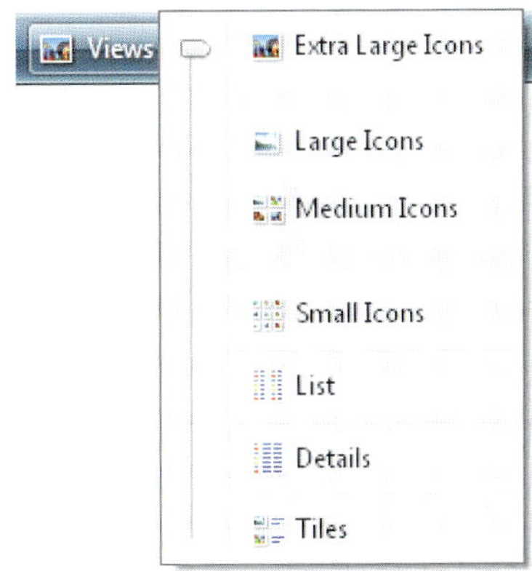

For folder icons, Windows Vista has a feature called Live Icons, which gives you a glimpse of what's inside the folder.

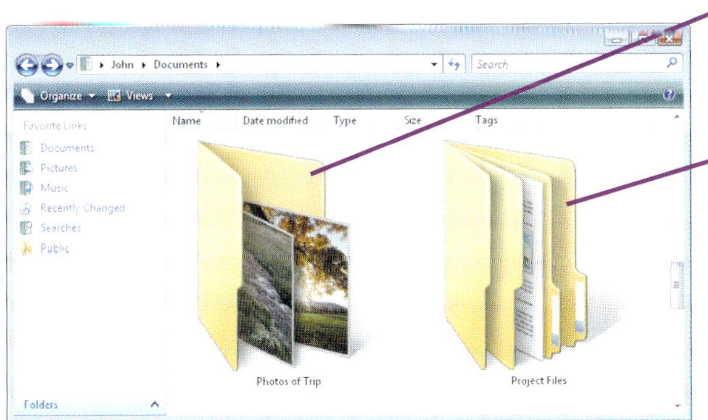

This Live Icon shows two of the actual picture files inside the folder.

If a folder contains other folders, its icon looks like this.

A folder containing music shows album art if it's available. If you have PowerPoint installed, the Live Icon will show the first few slides of the presentation.

Live Icons work with Tiles view, as well as the Medium, Large, and Extra Large (shown here) Icons views.

extra bits

show and hide panes p. 88

- Another way to display the classic Menu Bar in a folder window is to press the Alt key. You can press the Alt key again to hide the Menu Bar again.
- The Alt key won't hide the Menu Bar if you turned it on using the Organize menu. In that case, you have to use the Organize menu again to hide the Menu Bar.

use the explorer p. 90

- Another way to display the Folders list in the Navigation pane is to right-click the Start button and choose Explore. A new window will open with both the Favorite Links and Folders sections displayed.

change folder views p. 97

- You may have noticed that the Views menu has a slider bar. This isn't just for show. If you hold the left mouse button while you drag the slider between the Small and Extra Large settings, the icons in the folder will grow and shrink continuously. This allows you to set the size of icons in between the four standard sizes. So if Large is just a little too big, you can shrink it slightly without going down to Medium.

9. sort, group, & filter files

Windows Vista provides a number of ways to arrange folder contents. You can sort, group, stack, or filter files in a folder window with just a few clicks of the mouse. In previous versions of Windows, column heads were only available in Details view. In Vista, the column heads appear regardless of whether the files are arranged in columns or as icons. In any view, you click column heads to sort files.

Each column heading has a flyout menu that appears when you click an arrow to the right of the heading. The arrow only appears when you move the cursor over the column name.

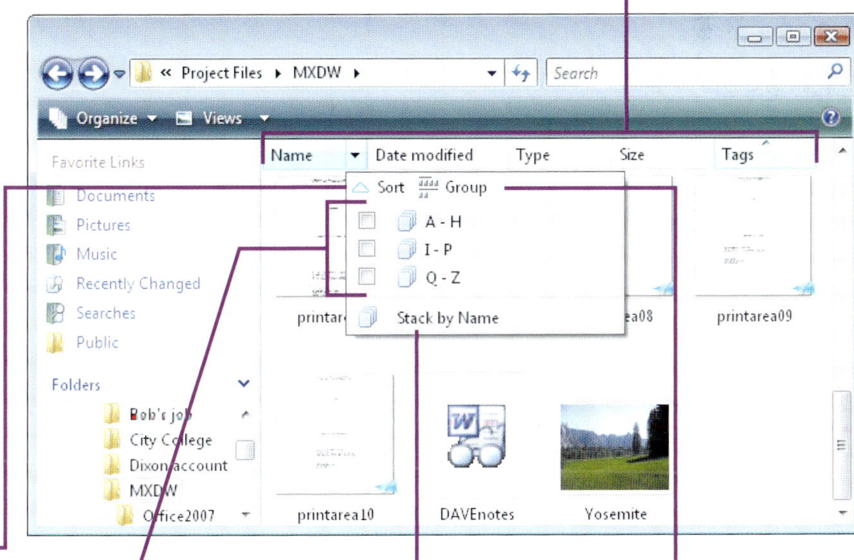

Sort arranges files and folders by name, date, or other criteria.

This area lets you filter files, so that only certain files appear in the window.

Stack creates temporary subfolder-like objects.

Group arranges files in clusters based on certain characteristics to make it easier to find a particular file.

In this chapter, you'll use these features to manage your files.

sort files & folders

For icon views, sorting files is easier in Vista than in previous versions of Windows. Just click a column head to sort by name, date, type, or other criteria.

In an icon view, icons can get out of order as you move them around. To reorder them, click a column heading. Here we'll click Name to sort alphabetically.

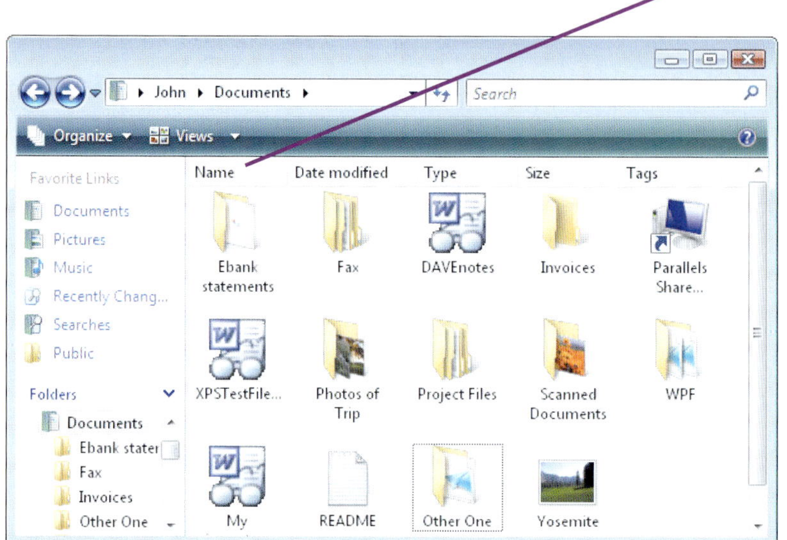

The icons are now arranged alphabetically; folders first, then files.

To reverse the order, click Name again. The window will sort in reverse alphabetical order, with the folders on the bottom.

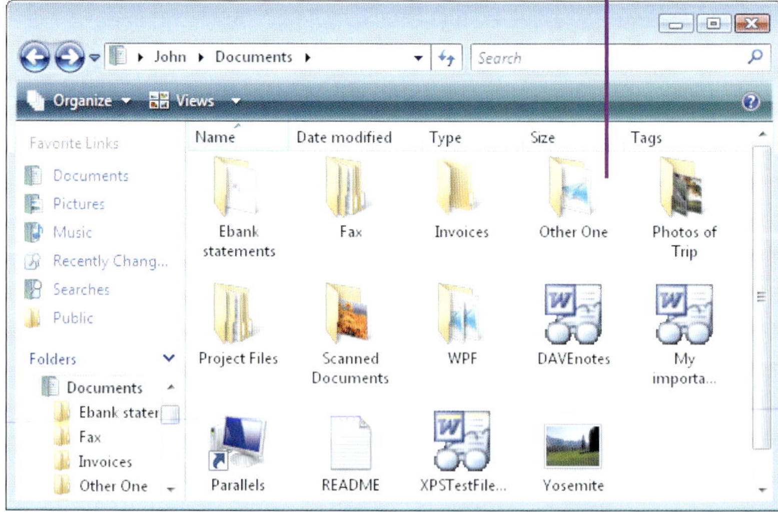

swap column heads

Not all folder windows are the same. The Music, Pictures, and Contacts folders have different column headings than do standard document folders.

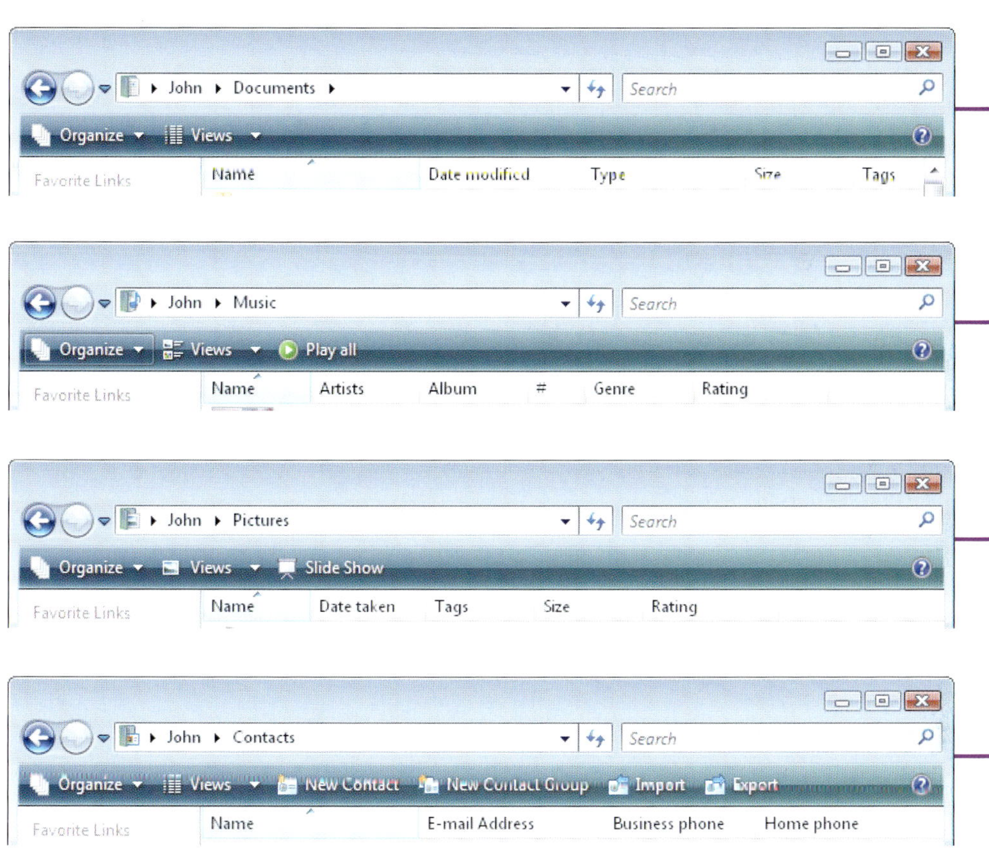

Each of these folders presents sorting criteria specific to the type of files kept inside. Several of the column heads let you sort by information that is contained inside the files, such as artist or album for music files, or phone number in contacts.

You can make any folder display these column heads. For instance, if you want to have your own music or pictures folder nested inside folders in some other location, you can tell Windows Vista what type of folder it is.

On the next page, you'll find out how.

swap column heads (cont.)

Here, we're going to change the column heads of an ordinary documents folder to those of a pictures folder.

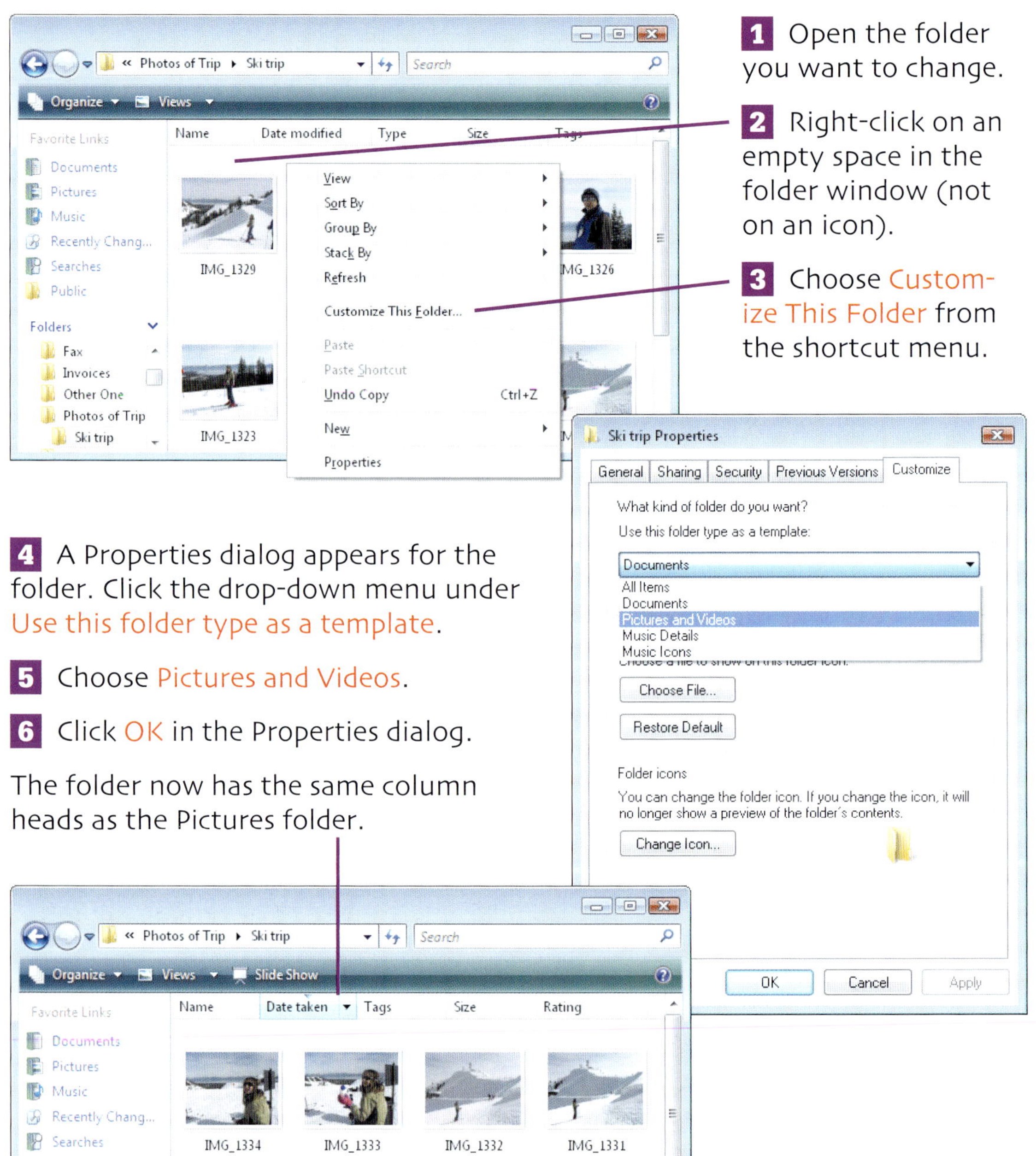

1 Open the folder you want to change.

2 Right-click on an empty space in the folder window (not on an icon).

3 Choose Customize This Folder from the shortcut menu.

4 A Properties dialog appears for the folder. Click the drop-down menu under Use this folder type as a template.

5 Choose Pictures and Videos.

6 Click OK in the Properties dialog.

The folder now has the same column heads as the Pictures folder.

add sort criteria

You don't have to be content with the sorting criteria that come with the various types of folders. There are actually dozens more to choose from, many of which look inside your files to sort.

You can add more sorting criteria by displaying more column heads. You can also remove column heads.

1 Right-click any column heading.

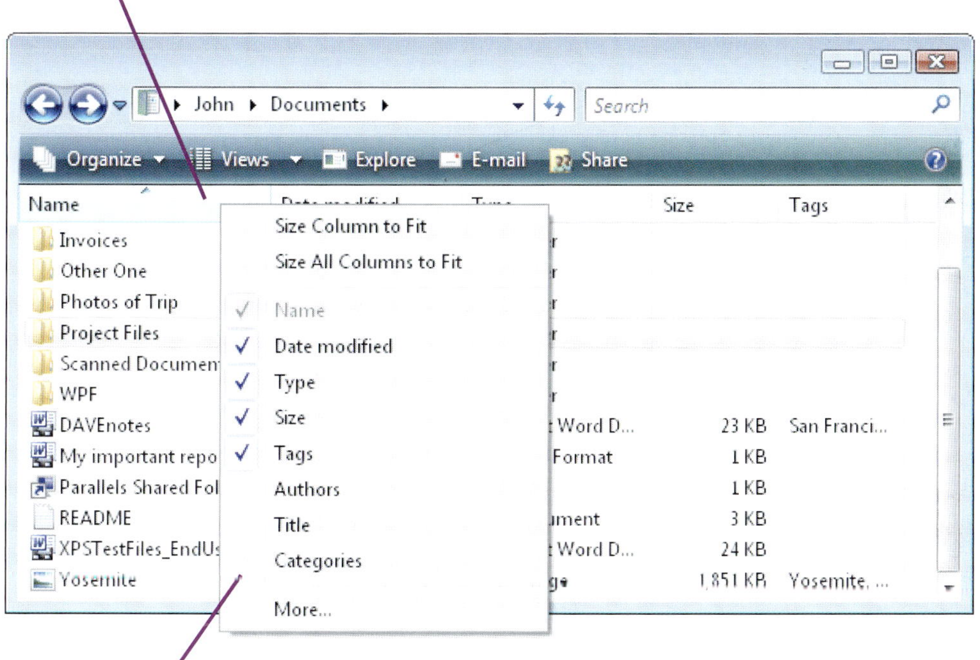

2 A shortcut menu appears with a partial list of possible column headings. The criteria that have check marks next to them are currently displayed as column heads. Clicking one of these to uncheck it would remove that column from the window.

The exact items appearing in the list depend on the type of folder. This is a documents folder, so the items in the menu are attributes found in Microsoft Office document files.

Clicking the More menu item brings up a complete list of dozens of criteria. Here, however, we'll click Authors to add it to the window.

add sort criteria (cont.)

3 Newly added columns always appear on the far right of the window, sometimes out of view. To make room for the new column, narrow the Name, Date Modified, and Size columns by dragging the lines to the right of the column headers.

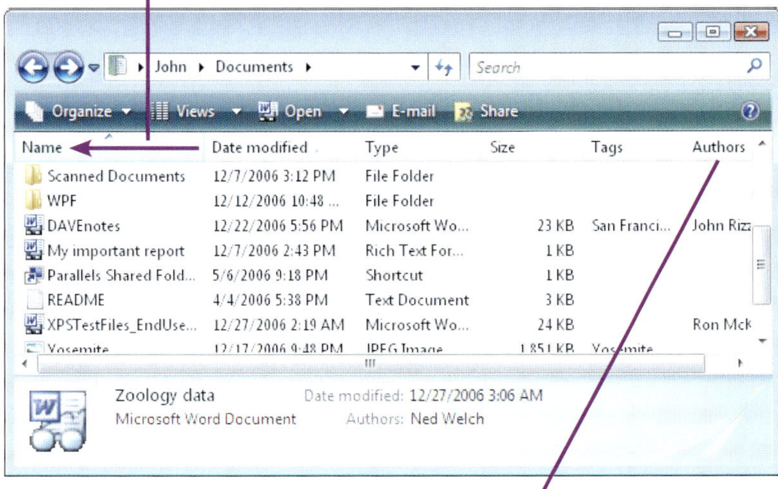

4 We now want to move the columns around. Grab the Authors column head and drag it to the left; let go when it's positioned next to Name.

5 Click Authors to sort by the new criterion. Click again to reverse the sort, putting the files with no author at the bottom. The result will look like this.

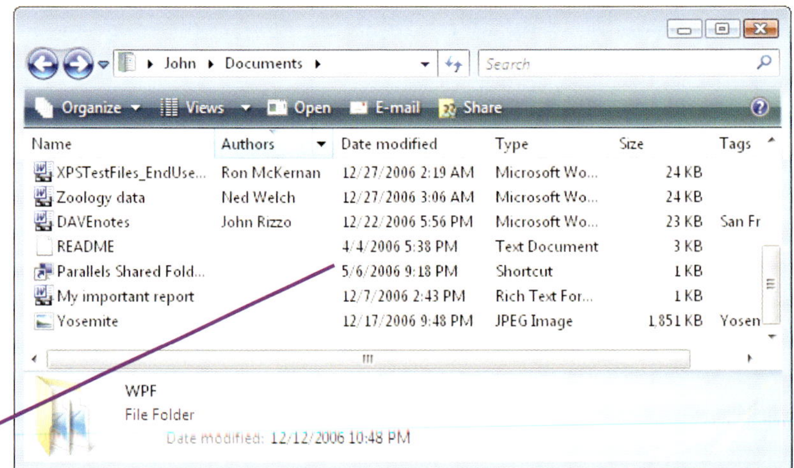

group files & folders

Another way to arrange files in folders is to group them. Grouping arranges files in categories. You can group by Name, Date Modified, Type, or any criteria that is a column head. Grouping is available in all views except the List view. We'll first group by name.

1 Move the cursor to the Name column head. An arrow appears to the right.

2 Click the arrow to the right of Name. A menu appears.

3 Click Group.

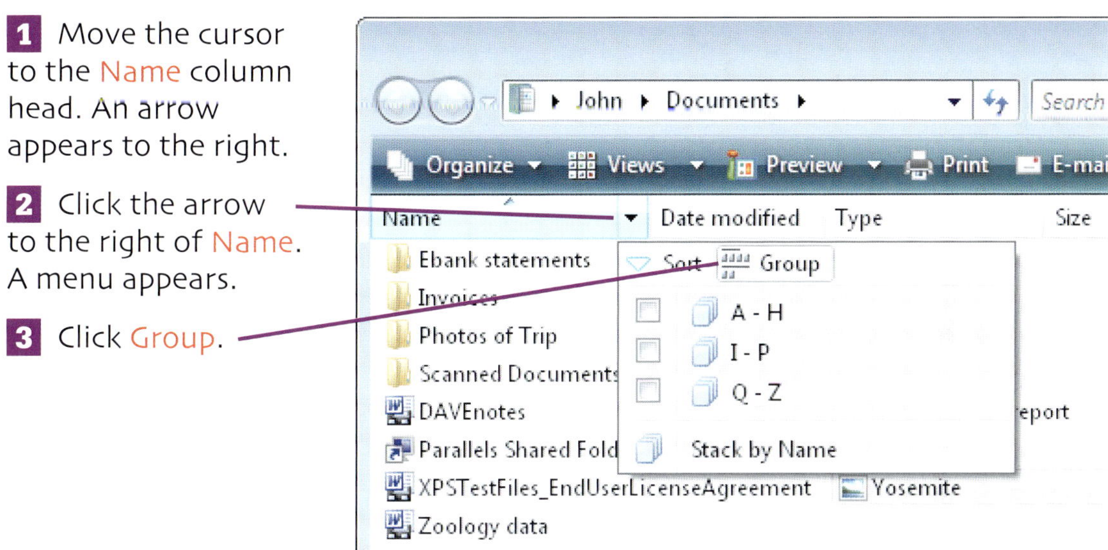

The objects in the window are now arranged in three alphabetical groups.

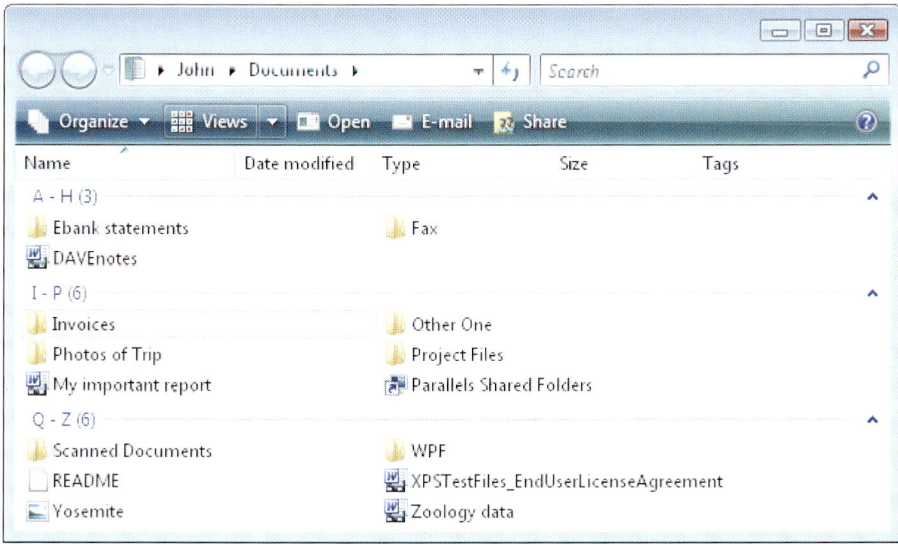

group files & folders (cont.)

Grouping by file type is often more useful than grouping by name. The procedure is similar: Click the arrow next to the Type column head, and select Group. Vista arranges similar files together like this.

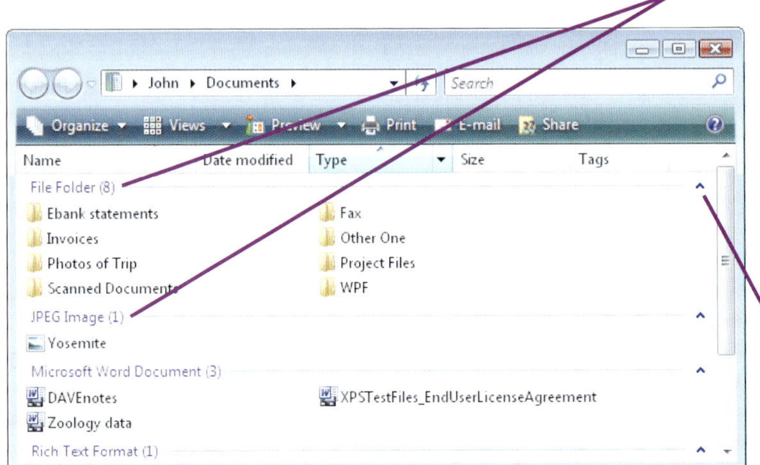

In this particular window, there are too many groups and files to be seen without scrolling. You can take care of that by collapsing one or more groups.

Click the arrow on the right side of File Folder and Shortcut.

The window no longer displays the icons in the collapsed groups.

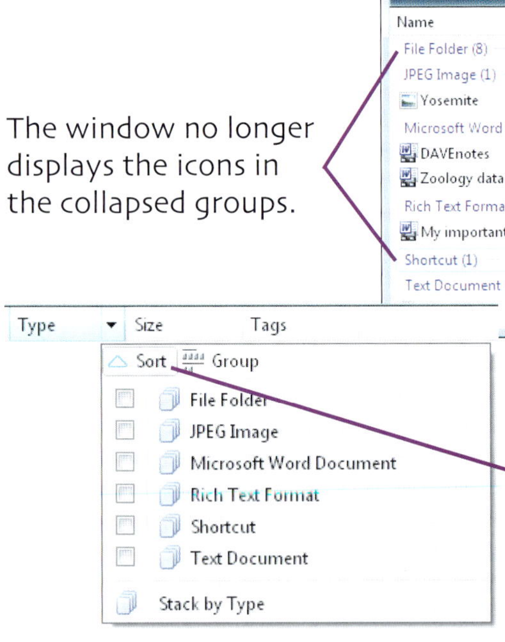

To turn off grouping and return to the default (ungrouped) view, click Sort in the column header's menu.

filter files & folders

When you have a lot of files to look through, you can filter them so that the window hides files you aren't interested in. As with sorting and grouping, you can filter using any criterion that is displayed as a column head. Filtering options are displayed as check boxes in the column head's menu. Here, you'll filter the files by a specific date.

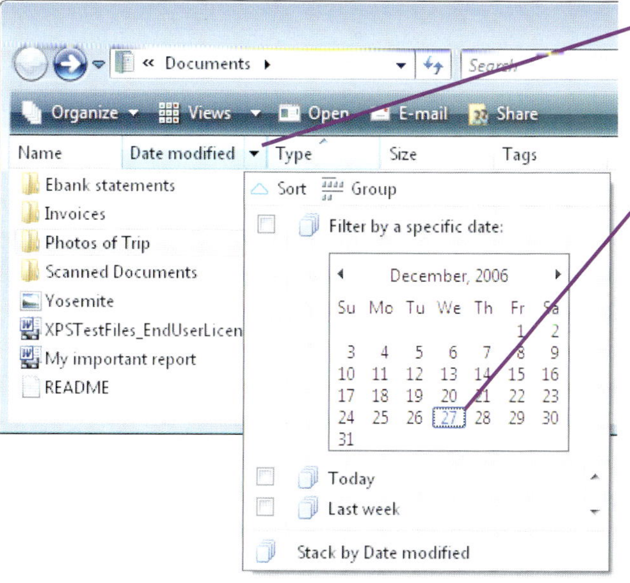

1 Move the cursor to the Date modified column head and click the arrow that appears to the right.

2 Find a date to use and click it. You can navigate to other months using the arrows to the left and right of the month.

3 Click the check box next to Filter by a specific date.

Many of the file and folder icons will disappear, leaving only those that were modified on the date you specified.

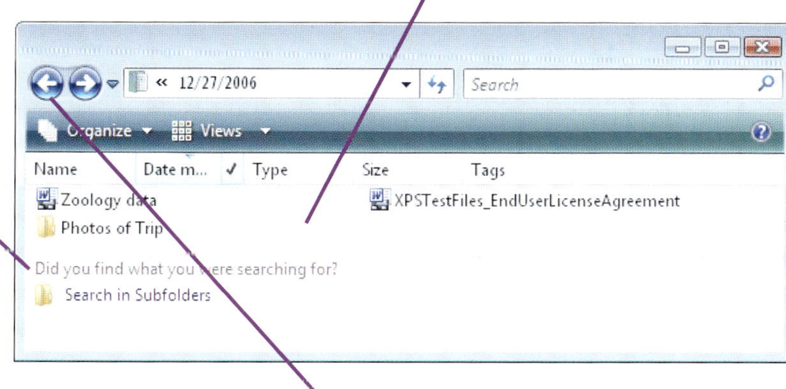

Windows will ask if you found what you were looking for and if you want to search inside subfolders. That's because filtering is actually a type of search that doesn't require typing. After a filter, the window displays the files and folders that were found.

To see all your files again, click the Back button.

stack files & folders

Stacking files is similar to grouping and filtering. Like grouping, it organizes files using criteria such as name, date, and file type. Like filtering, stacking reduces the number of icons in a window. It does this by creating groups of files called stacks, which act like subfolders. A stack can contain files and folders from multiple folders.

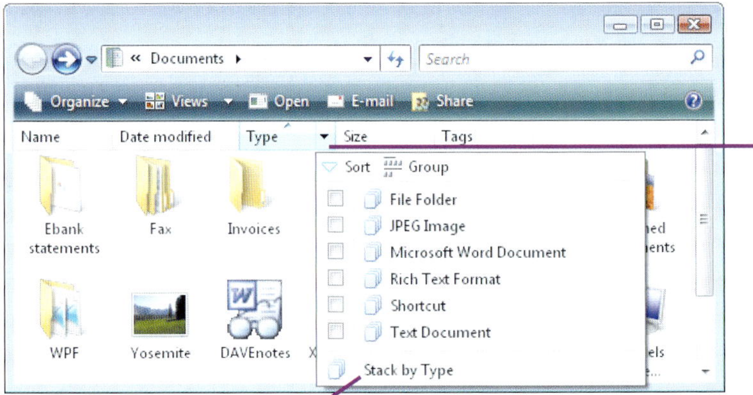

Here, you'll stack by type in the Documents folder.

1 Move the cursor to the Type column head and click the arrow that appears to the right.

2 Click Stack by Type at the bottom of the menu.

The window now shows stack icons, each with a name of a type of file.

3 Double-click a stack to open it. Here, we are opening the JPEG stack.

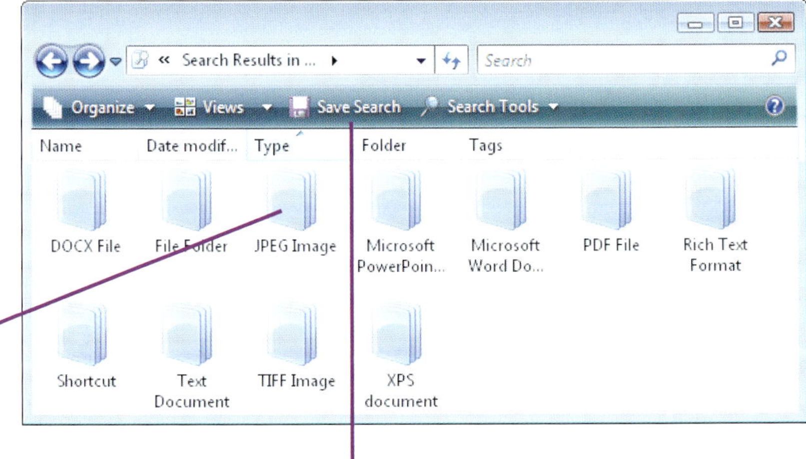

Stacking doesn't move or copy any files. Stacks are the results of a search, as stacking is actually a type of search. The Save Search button appears when you stack files.

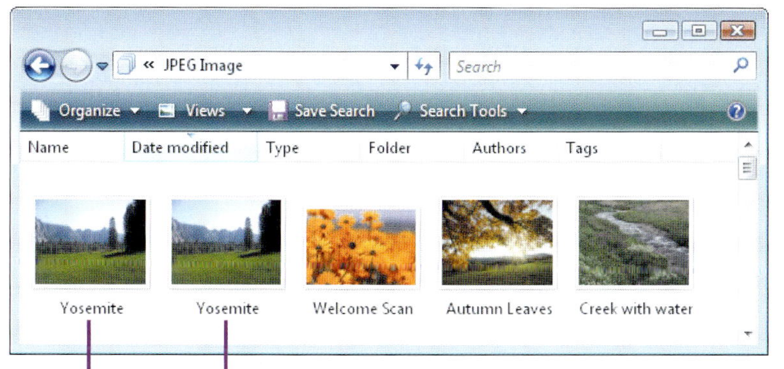

Our JPEG stack contains files and folders that reside in multiple folders inside our Documents folder. If copies of the same file are located in two different folders, the file will appear in the stack twice.

If you stack the Documents folder by date, you get stacks with names that refer to time frames: Today, Yesterday, Last week, and so on.

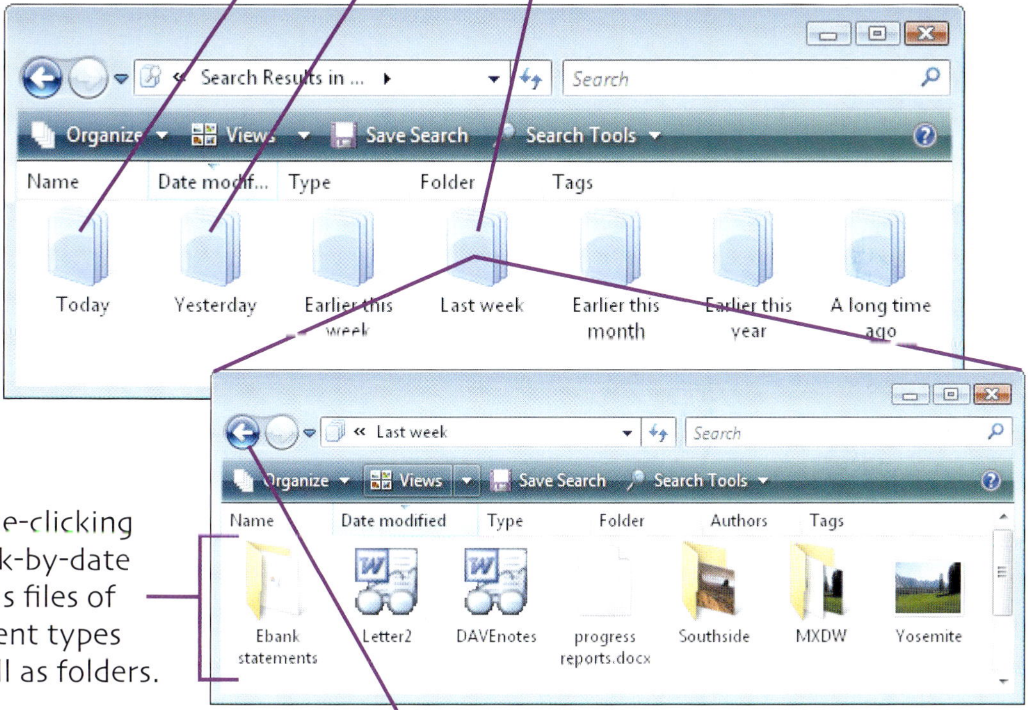

Double-clicking a stack-by-date reveals files of different types as well as folders.

To see all your files again, click the Back button twice.

extra bits

filter files & folders p. 107

- When you filter by date modified, the menu gives you two options to filter by: Today and Last week. If you click the down arrow to the right of these items, you get two more: Earlier this month and Earlier this year.
- We added an Authors column head in order to sort by the author information stored in Microsoft Office files. The flyout menu for this column also has a useful filtering feature. It provides a list of authors with check boxes next to each. Click one or more author names to retrieve files containing those authors.

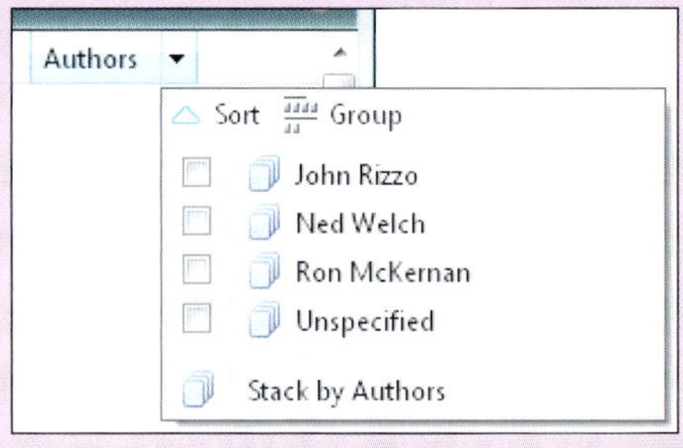

stack files & folders p. 108

- Stacks aren't really folders, but collections of search results. The files inside a stack might be located in different folders. So where are these folders really located? You can find out by right-clicking a file inside a stack. Choose Open File Location from the shortcut menu. Vista will open the actual folder that contains the original file.

10. secure your computer

One of the major advancements of Windows Vista over Windows XP is in security. Vista offers protection for your computer from malware, spyware, Trojan horses, phishing, and spam, as well as safeguards for your kids. Protection is turned on when you install Vista, but don't take it for granted. You should periodically run the checks that Windows provides.

The two main security features in Windows Vista are the Windows Security Center and Windows Defender. But Vista has much more—including Windows Firewall and Windows Update, which is important for getting the latest security patches.

For a bird's-eye view of Vista's security features, open Control Panel from the Start menu. Then click Control Panel Home, and then Security. You'll see a list of security features and links to configure, update, and run security software. This window will be the starting place for the descriptions in this chapter.

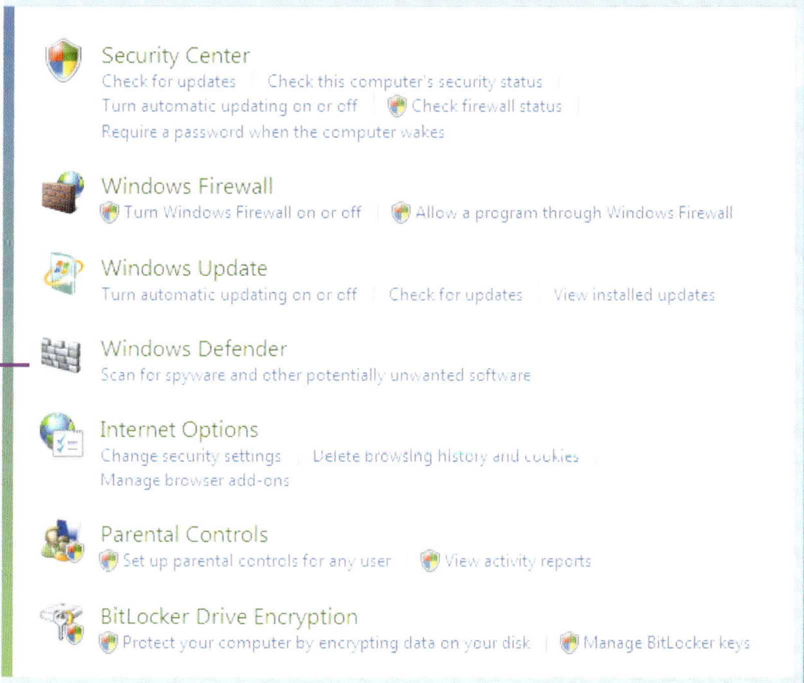

check security status

Windows Security Center presents the status of the most important security features of Windows Vista in one place.

While Windows XP also has a Security Center, the Vista version monitors more security measures, including some that are new to Vista. The Security Center tells you if the features are running or if you need to take some action to enable or update them.

One way to open the Security Center is to click its name in the Control Panel's list of security features, shown on the previous page. Here's another way:

1 Open Control Panel from the Start menu.

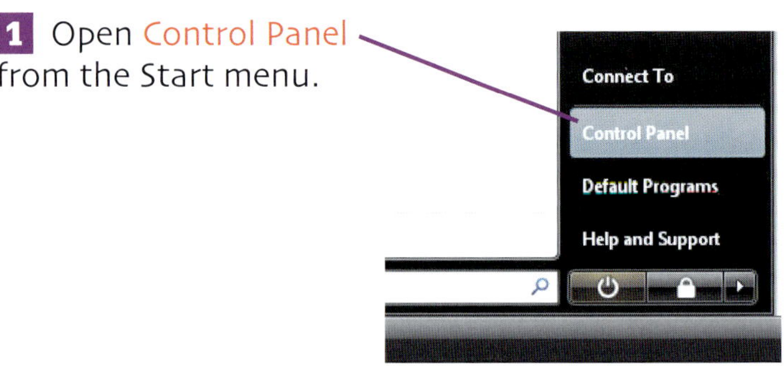

2 Make sure Control Panel Home is selected and click Check this computer's security status under Security.

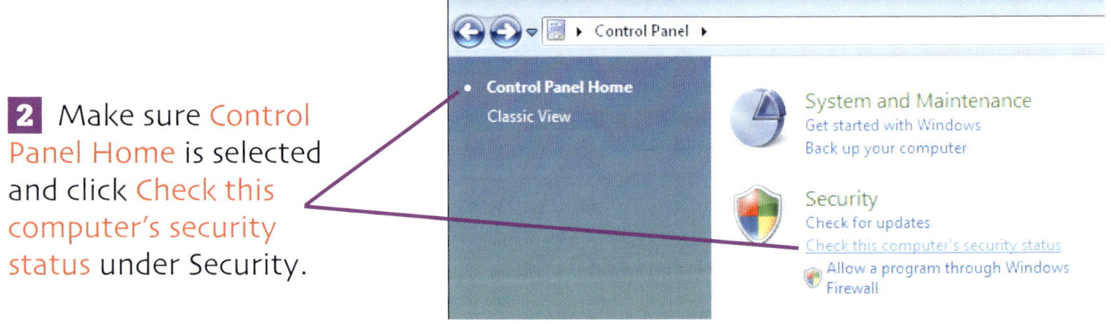

The Security Center monitors four sets of features. It provides brief reports for each, including their status, in the main part of the window.

The Firewall report tells you if your firewall is turned on. The firewall prevents certain types of network traffic from entering your computer.

Automatic updating checks to see if the latest Windows security patches from Microsoft are installed. Here, it tells us that there is a problem.

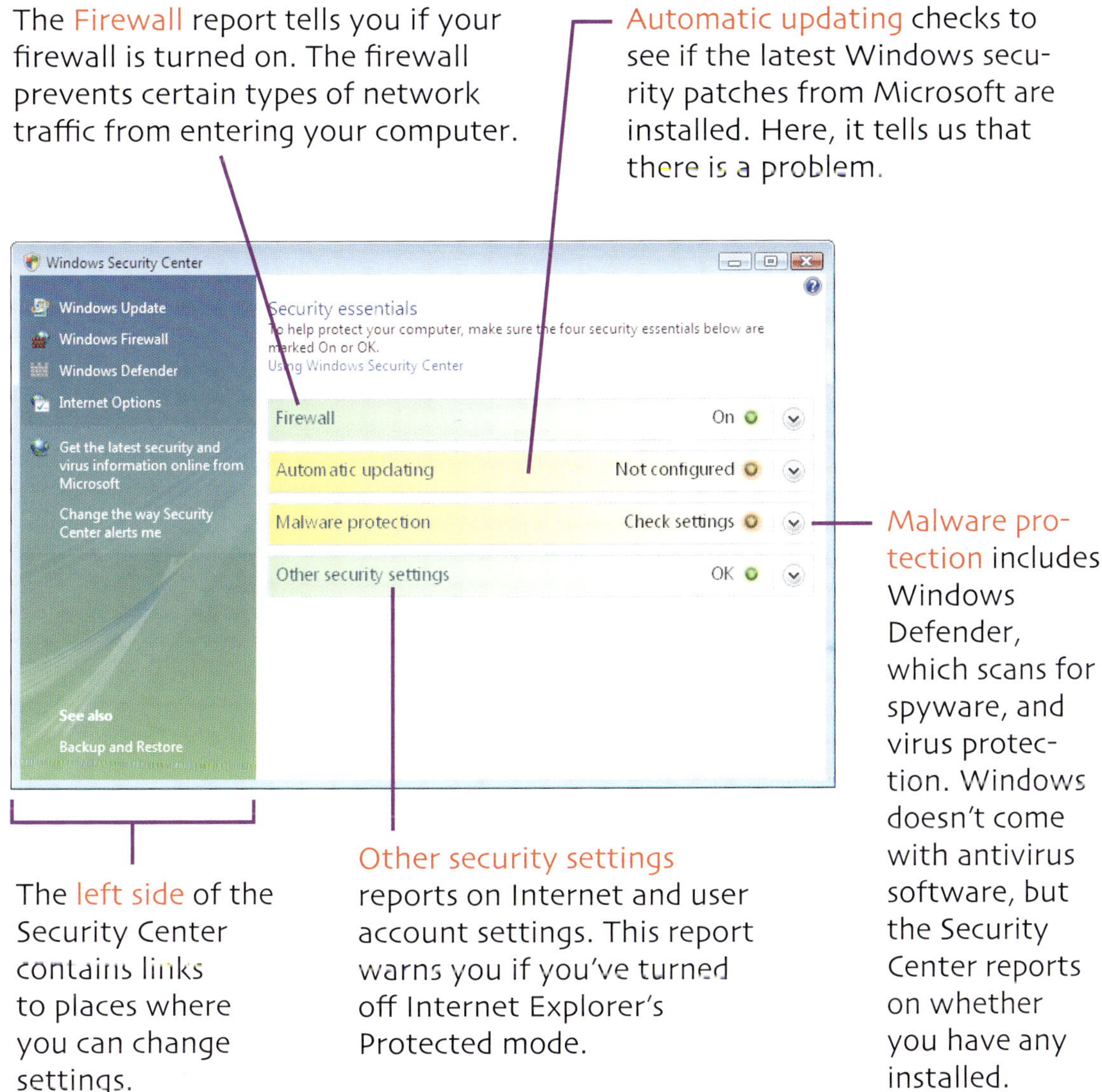

Malware protection includes Windows Defender, which scans for spyware, and virus protection. Windows doesn't come with antivirus software, but the Security Center reports on whether you have any installed.

The left side of the Security Center contains links to places where you can change settings.

Other security settings reports on Internet and user account settings. This report warns you if you've turned off Internet Explorer's Protected mode.

You can see more details about any of the four reports by clicking them. Here, we'll click the two reports that show problems, Automatic updating and Malware protection.

check security status (cont.)

By expanding the two areas, you can see the details of those security reports.

The Malware protection report warns that we don't have any antivirus software installed. Windows does not come with an antivirus program, but Microsoft recommends that you buy one.

The Find a program button is a link to a Microsoft Web page that lists antivirus programs.

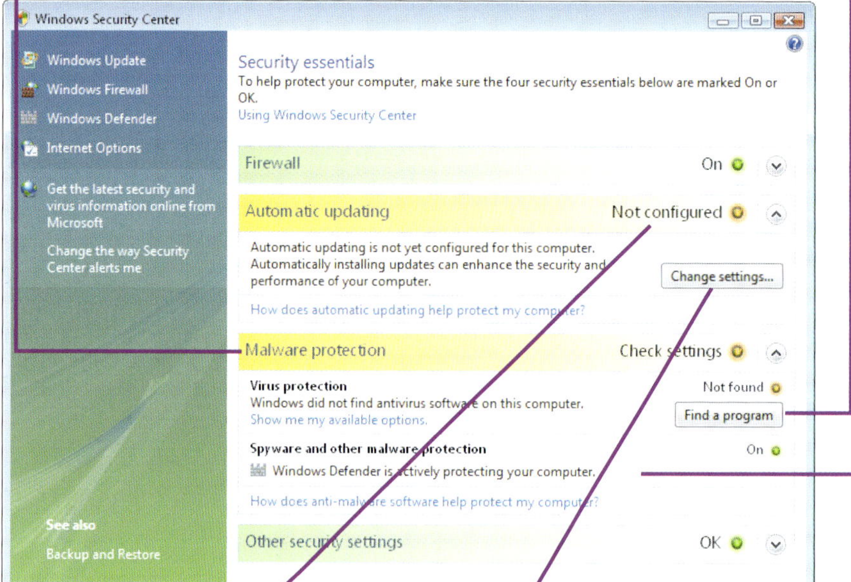

Windows comes with Windows Defender, which scans for spyware that may be hidden on your hard drive. Here, the report tells us that Windows Defender is set to automatically scan for spyware.

The Security Center also reports that Automatic updating is not turned on. This is important to have activated, as it will download and install the latest security updates to Windows.

You can activate it here by clicking the Change settings button.

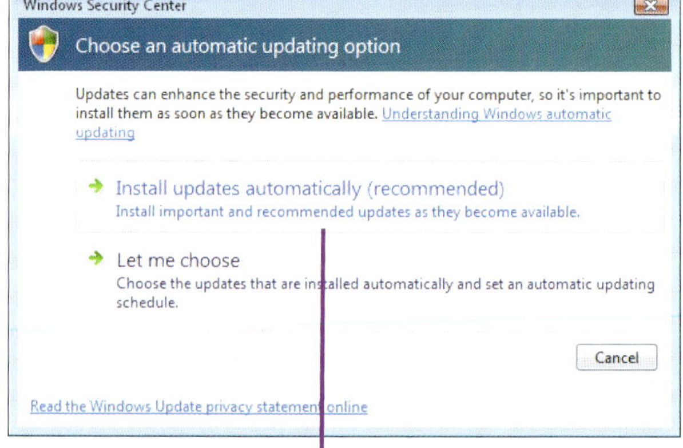

In the dialog that appears, click Install updates automatically.

customize the firewall

Windows Firewall helps keep malicious programs like worms (known as malware) off your computer by allowing only certain types of data through a network (typically the Internet). Vista's firewall is much more advanced than the one in Windows XP and has lots of tools for administrators. Fortunately, average users don't need to fiddle with them. You might, however, need to allow a network program through the firewall. Here, we'll allow Windows Media Player to receive content through the network.

1 Open the Control Panel's list of security features shown on the first page of this chapter.

2 Under Windows Firewall, click Allow a program through Windows Firewall.

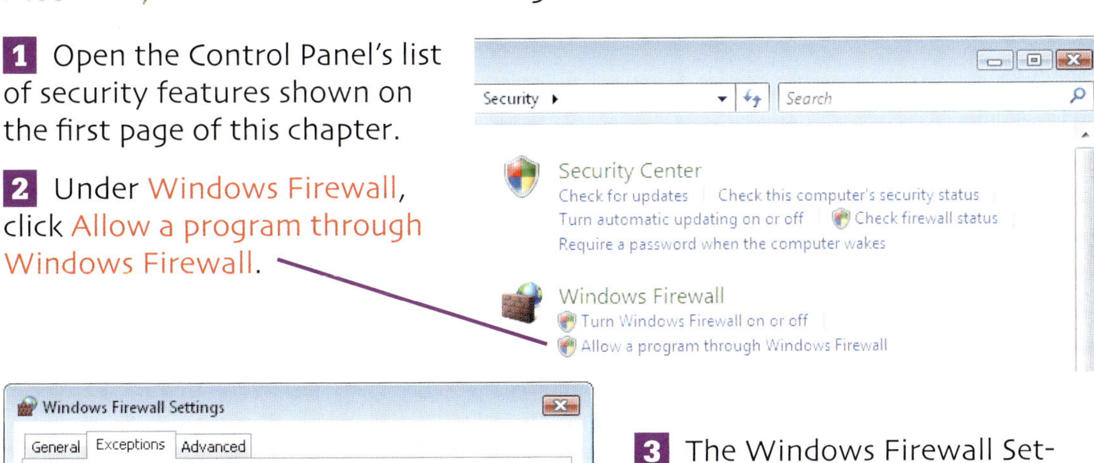

Windows Firewall Settings

General | Exceptions | Advanced

Exceptions control how programs communicate through Windows Firewall. Add a program or port exception to allow communications through the firewall.

Windows Firewall is currently using settings for the private network location.
What are the risks of unblocking a program?

To enable an exception, select its check box:

Program or port
- ☐ Remote Volume Management
- ☐ Routing and Remote Access
- ☐ SNMP Trap
- ☐ Windows Collaboration Computer Name Registration Service
- ☐ Windows Firewall Remote Management
- ☐ Windows Management Instrumentation (WMI)
- ☐ Windows Media Player
- ☐ Windows Media Player Network Sharing Service
- ☐ Windows Meeting Space
- ☐ Windows Peer to Peer Collaboration Foundation
- ☐ Windows Remote Management
- ☐ Wireless Portable Devices

Add program... | Add port... | Properties | Delete

☑ Notify me when Windows Firewall blocks a new program

OK | Cancel | Apply

3 The Windows Firewall Settings dialog appears. Under the Exceptions tab, scroll to Windows Media Player and click the box next to it.

4 Click OK.

On your own computer, you may find that Windows Media Player is already enabled. But if it, or another network program, isn't working, the Windows Firewall Settings dialog is a good place to check.

scan for spyware

Unfortunately, some malware can slip past firewalls, which also cannot stop viruses that are attached to e-mail. Software that you download can also be a source of spyware and Trojan horses. Spyware is malware that can secretly record your keystrokes (including credit card numbers that you type) and send the information to someone over the Internet. A Trojan horse can turn your PC into a zombie computer, which sends out spam without your knowledge.

To fight these threats, you can use Vista's Windows Defender to scan your computer for spyware and Trojan horses. It can perform a quick scan, which looks in the most likely places that spyware infects, or a full scan, which checks every file on the hard drive and all running programs. The full scan can take a half-hour or more, so use it only when you suspect an infection.

To perform a quick scan, do the following:

1 In the Start menu, click All Programs.

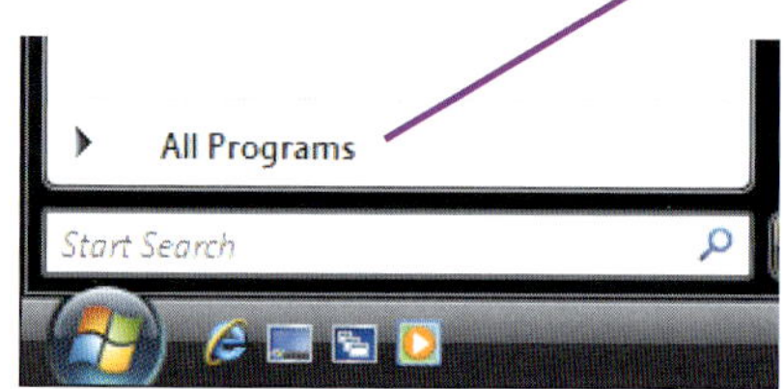

2 Click Windows Defender.

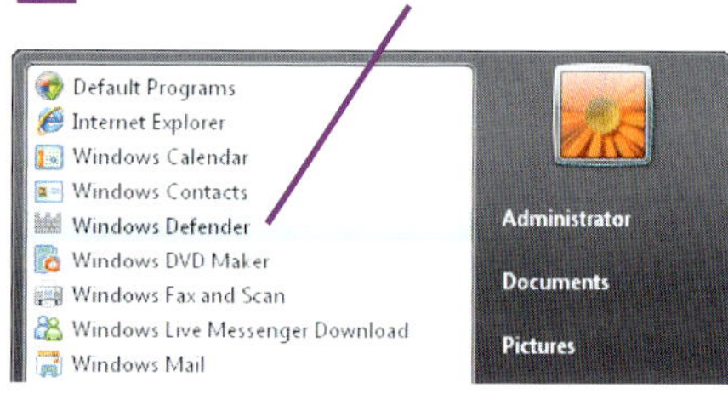

3 In the Windows Defender window that opens, click Scan.

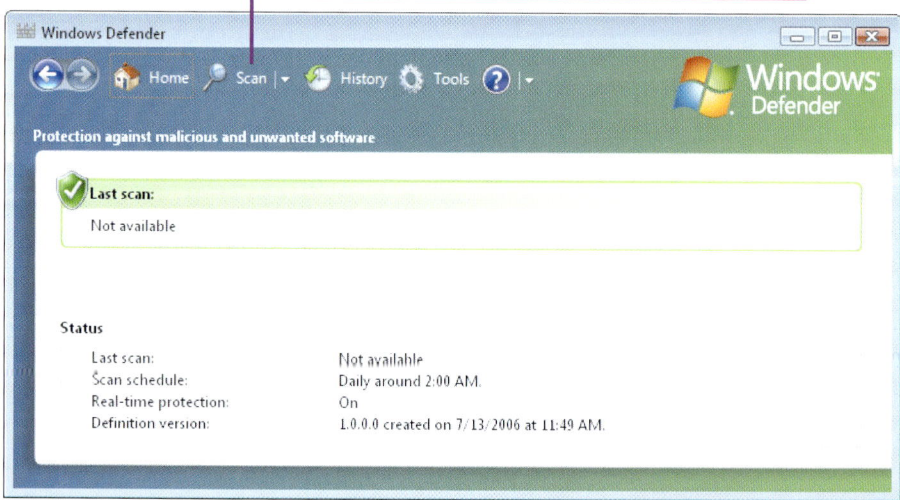

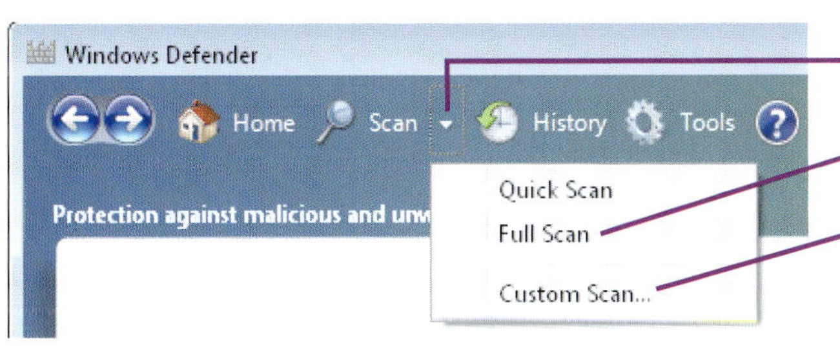

To conduct a full scan, click the arrow to the right of the word Scan to bring up a menu. Then select Full Scan.

The Custom Scan option here lets you pick specific files or folders to check.

After the scan, Windows Defender reports what it has found. Here, it reports that it hasn't found any suspicious software.

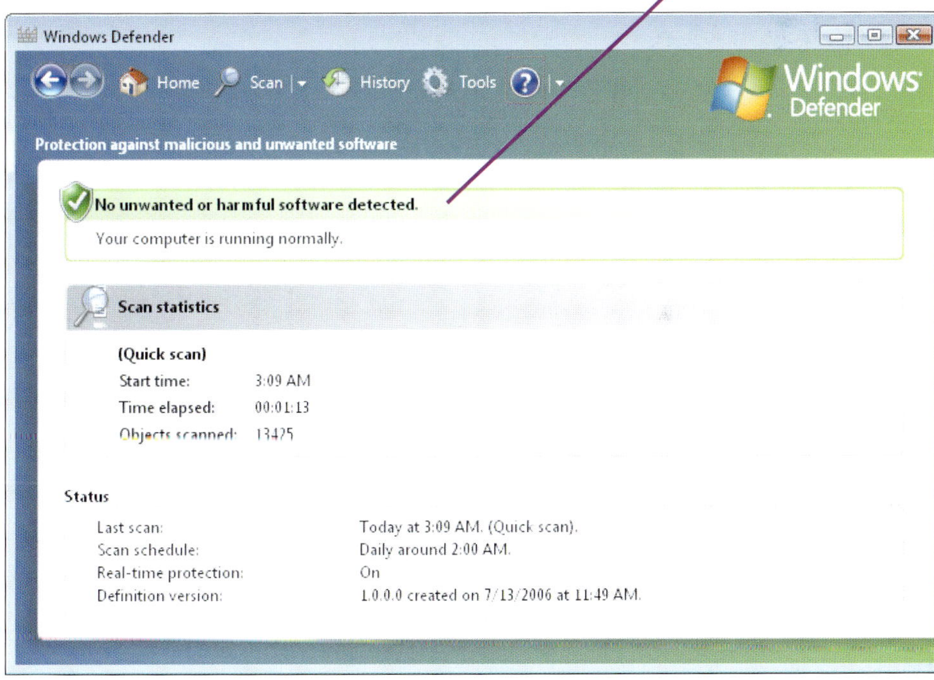

If it had found some potentially harmful programs, it would list them in this window and would give you the option of removing them, reviewing a report on what was found, or ignoring them. You would want to ignore a warning if Windows Defender erroneously flagged nonmalicious software, such as a driver that you have installed.

scan for spyware (cont.)

You can also set Windows Defender to do scans automatically. Even if it is set for daily scans, you may want to check on when they are scheduled for. If Windows Defender is set to scan at 2 a.m., and your computer is never on at that time, the scan won't run. To schedule automatic scanning, do the following:

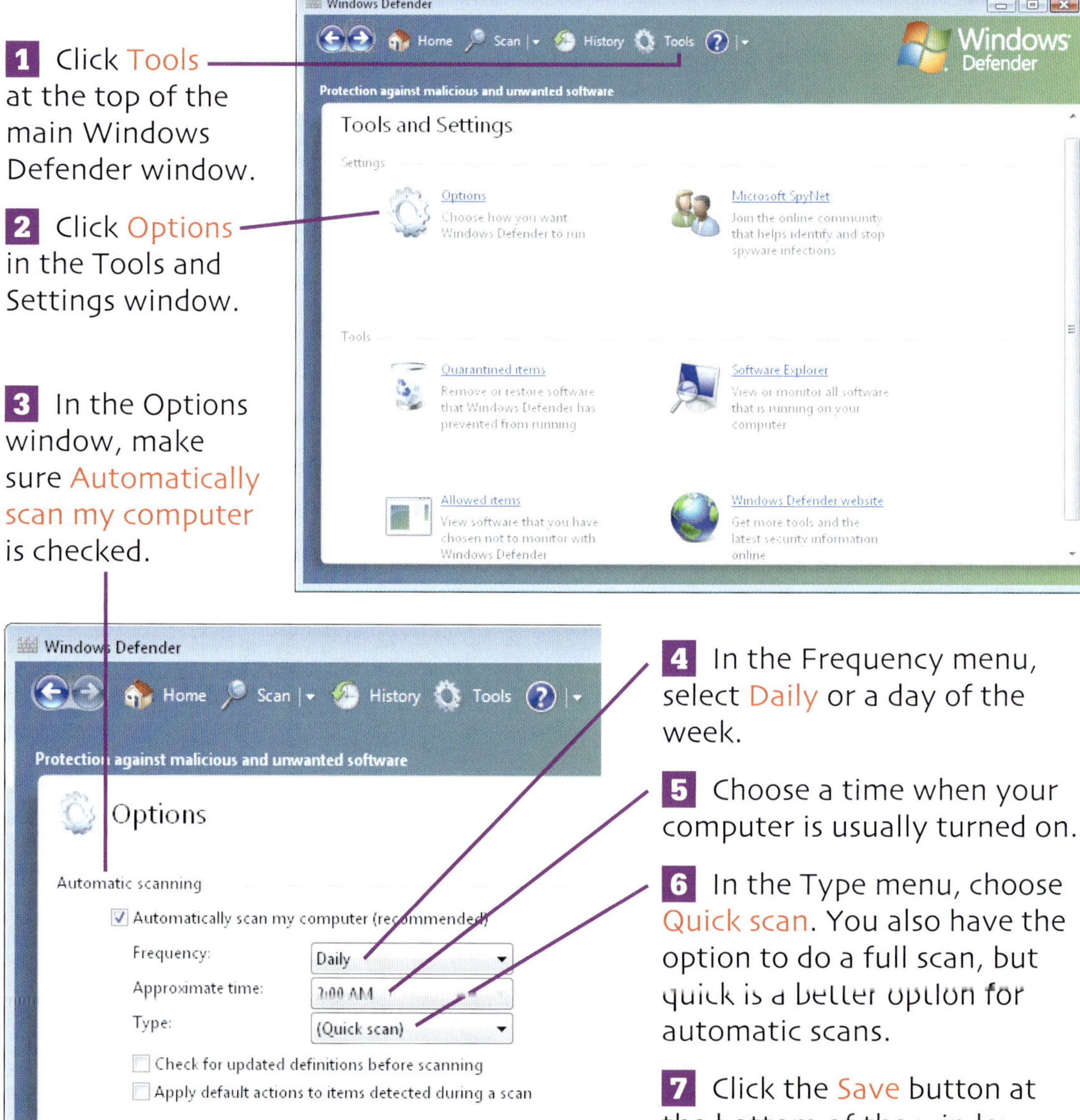

1 Click Tools at the top of the main Windows Defender window.

2 Click Options in the Tools and Settings window.

3 In the Options window, make sure Automatically scan my computer is checked.

4 In the Frequency menu, select Daily or a day of the week.

5 Choose a time when your computer is usually turned on.

6 In the Type menu, choose Quick scan. You also have the option to do a full scan, but quick is a better option for automatic scans.

7 Click the Save button at the bottom of the window.

secure web browsing

Phishing, one of the main security threats associated with Web browsing, is when someone creates a Web page that masquerades as a legitimate site to fool users into giving up passwords, financial information, or personal information. The phisher often attracts people to the fake page using e-mail.

Internet Explorer has a phishing filter that helps you determine whether a Web site is legitimate. The phishing filter analyzes the site you're visiting and compares the address to a list of addresses for known phishing sites.

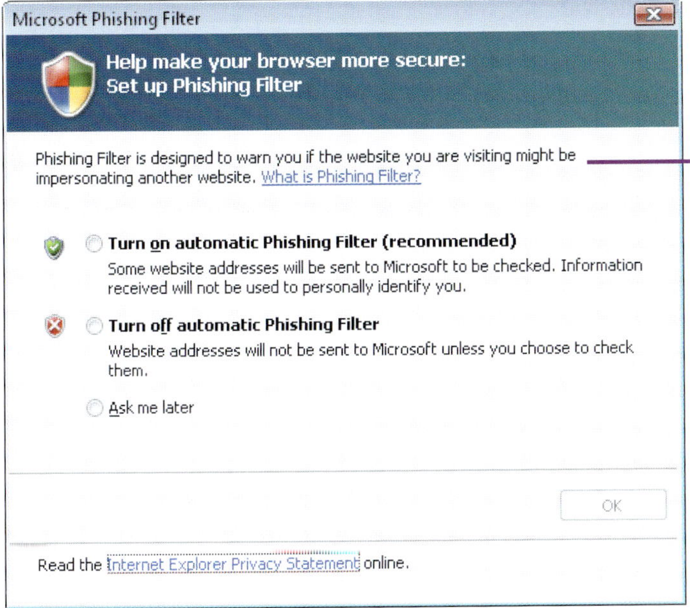

The first time you access a Web site that is not in Microsoft's list of legitimate sites, a dialog appears asking if you want to turn on the phishing filter. If you do, the filter will check every Web page you visit. When it finds a page that it suspects, it brings up a warning. You should not enter any information at such a site.

If you don't turn on the phishing filter, you can still run it manually for sites that you suspect of phishing. Go to Internet Explorer's Tools menu, select Phishing Filter, then Check This Website.

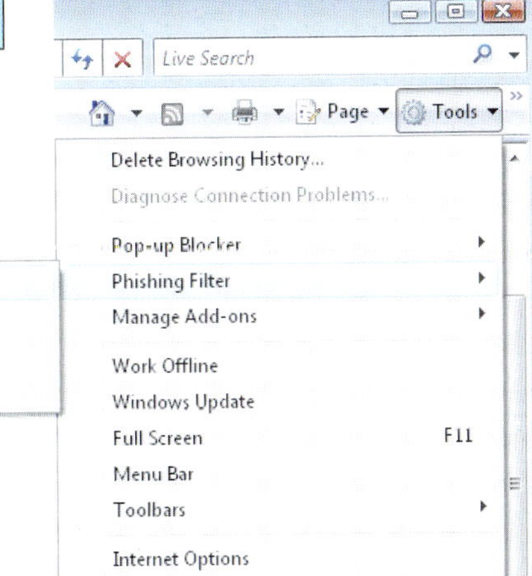

set spam filtering

The firewall cannot prevent e-mail viruses from getting through, so it is important to filter out spam (by far the most common way that e-mail viruses are spread). Windows Mail has spam filtering turned on by default, but you can adjust its settings.

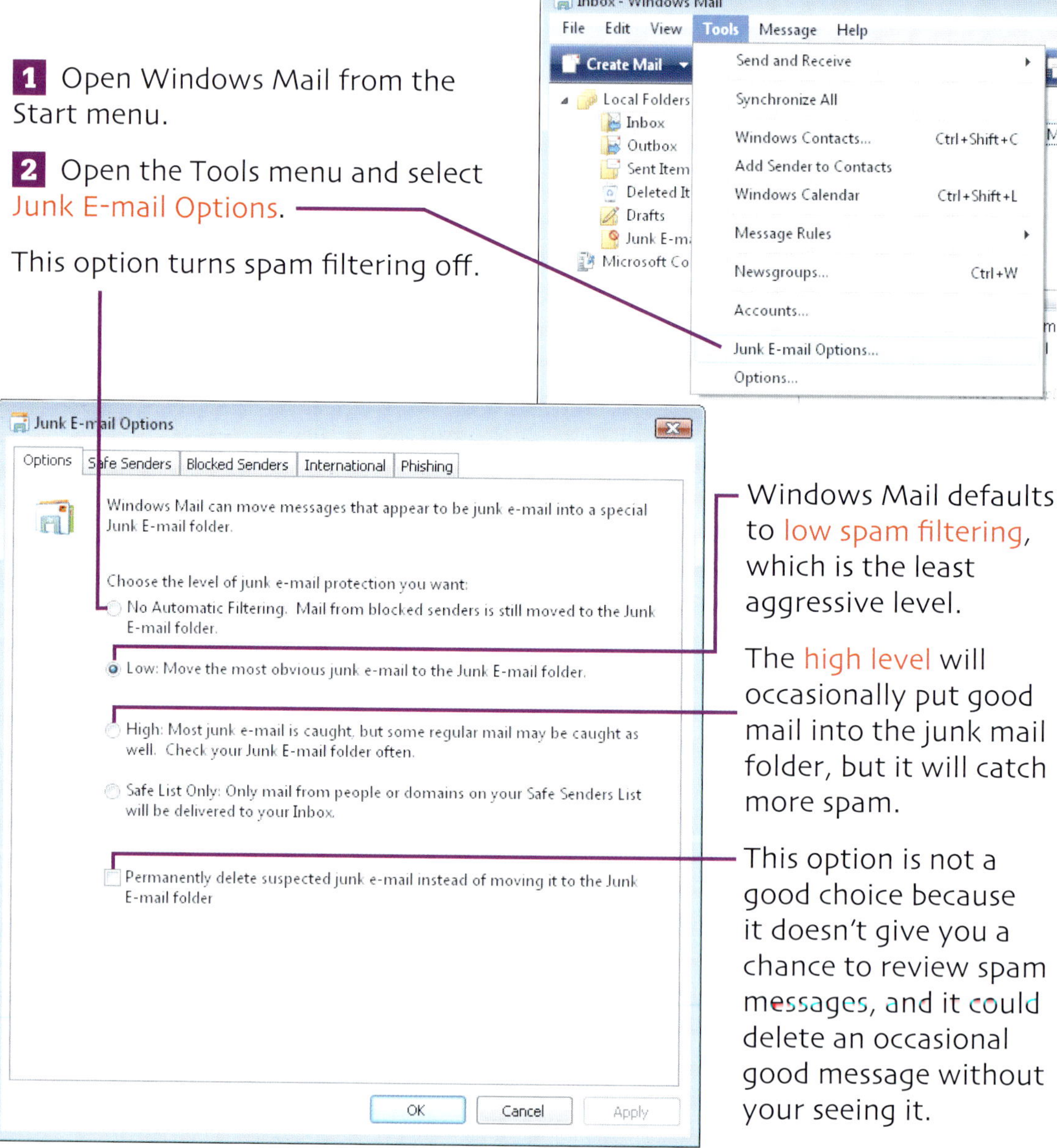

1 Open Windows Mail from the Start menu.

2 Open the Tools menu and select Junk E-mail Options.

This option turns spam filtering off.

Windows Mail defaults to low spam filtering, which is the least aggressive level.

The high level will occasionally put good mail into the junk mail folder, but it will catch more spam.

This option is not a good choice because it doesn't give you a chance to review spam messages, and it could delete an occasional good message without your seeing it.

set parental controls

Windows Vista has a set of controls to shield your kids from selected parts of the Internet and violent games, and to protect your information from your kids.

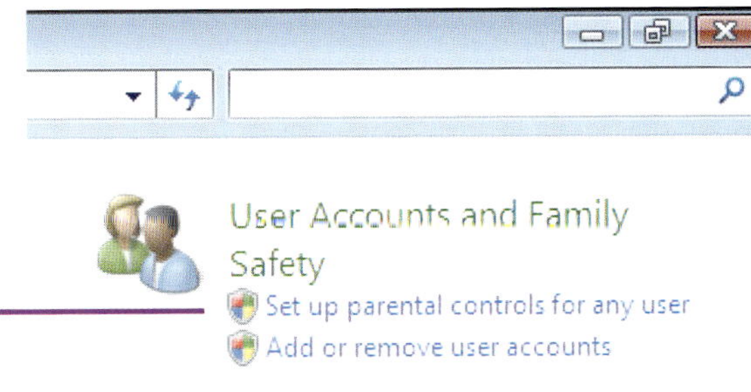

1 Open Control Panel from the Start menu.

2 In Control Panel Home, click Set up parental controls for any user.

3 You'll see a list of current user accounts.

If the only user account is for the administrator, you'll need to create a new user account for the kids.

If the administrator account doesn't have a password, you should add one to prevent your kids from turning off parental controls.

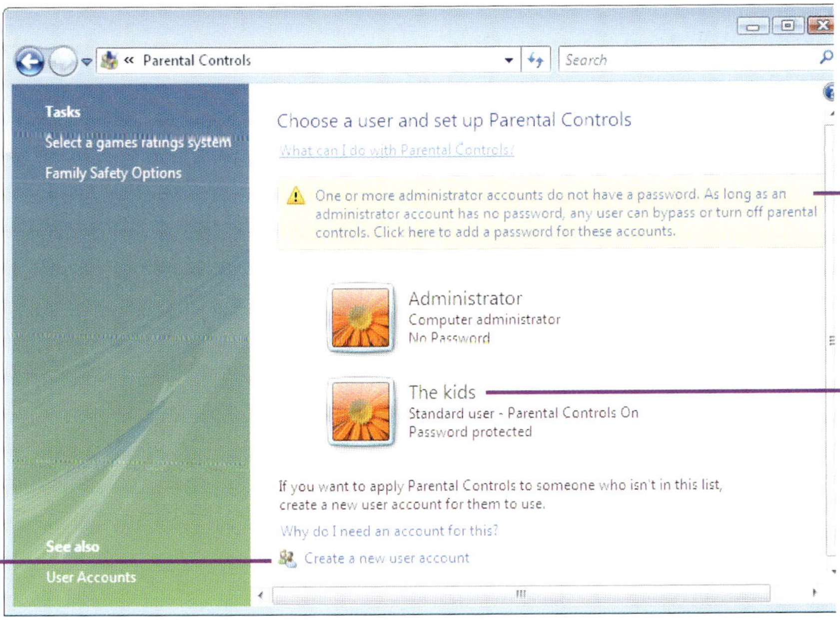

4 Click the user account you want to modify.

set parental controls (cont.)

5 The parental controls window appears. Click any blue link to create or change a setting.

Activity reports tell you what your kids have been up to. A report lists the top 10 Web sites visited and the top 10 blocked. It will tell you which games were played, what applications were run, and whether e-mail and text messaging were used.

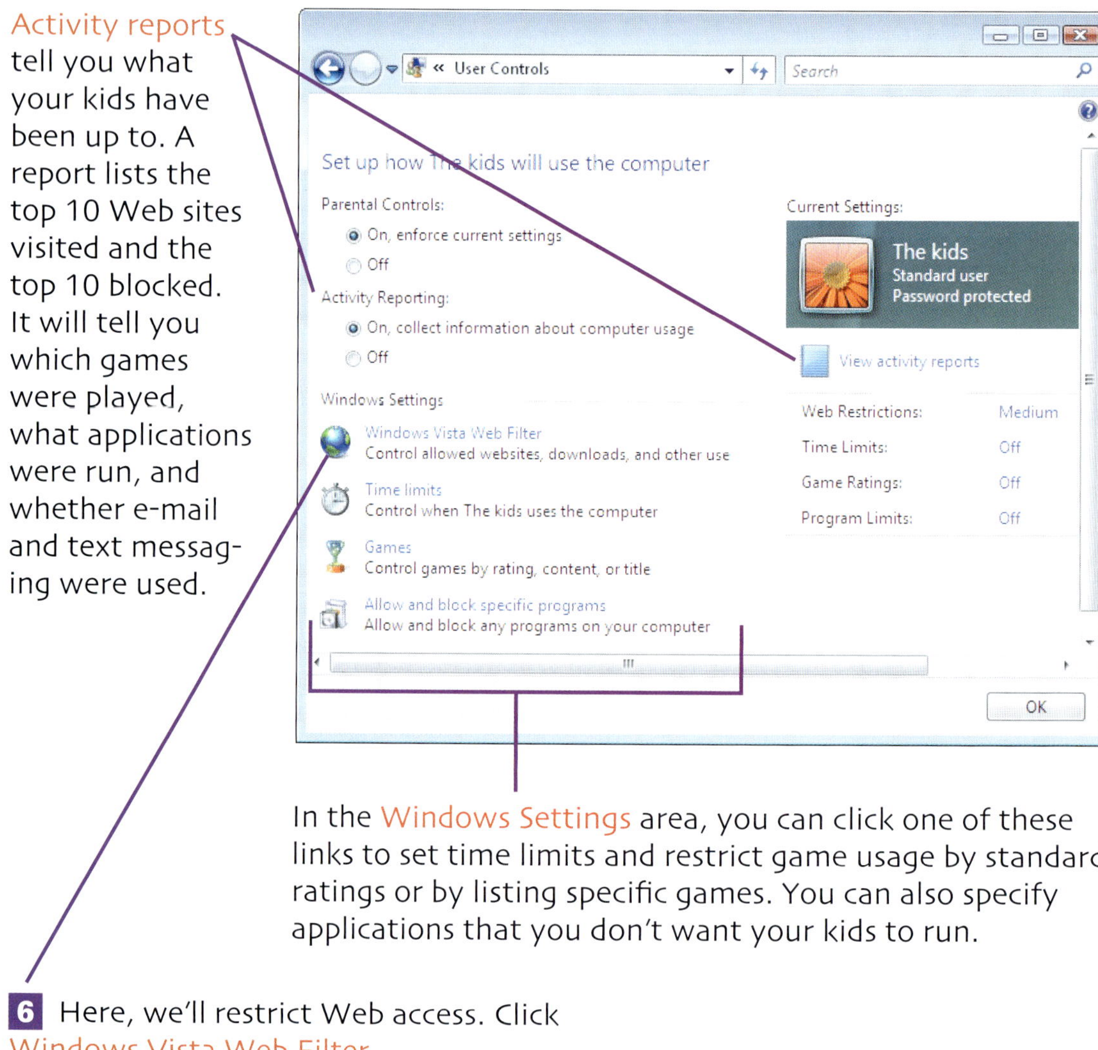

In the Windows Settings area, you can click one of these links to set time limits and restrict game usage by standard ratings or by listing specific games. You can also specify applications that you don't want your kids to run.

6 Here, we'll restrict Web access. Click Windows Vista Web Filter.

Click Edit the Allow and block list to type in specific addresses of Web sites you want to allow or block.

This check box turns off automatic Web filtering and permits access only to Web sites that you specify.

The area called Block web content automatically lets you set filters that block classes of Web sites. You can use automatic filtering in combination with blocking specific Web sites.

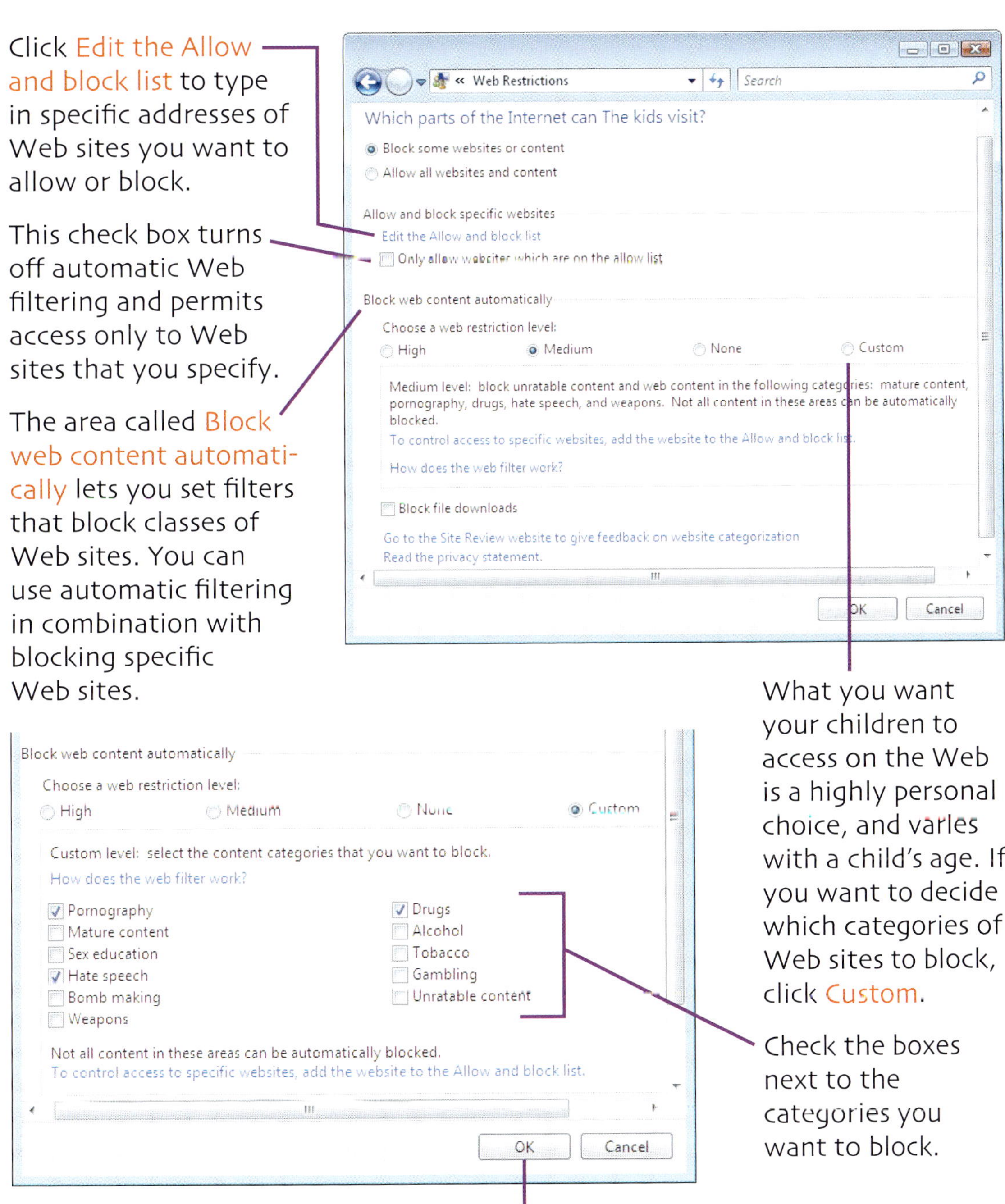

What you want your children to access on the Web is a highly personal choice, and varies with a child's age. If you want to decide which categories of Web sites to block, click Custom.

Check the boxes next to the categories you want to block.

Click OK when you are finished.

extra bits

check security status p. 112

- Windows Security Center and Windows Defender can send you alerts when they detect that some action is needed. They send alerts to the Notification area on the right end of the taskbar. Double-click an alert to open the appropriate dialog, where you can take the needed action.

customize the firewall p. 115

- If you are network savvy and want to use the advanced features of Vista's firewall, go to the Start menu and type Windows Firewall with Advanced Security in the Search box. Here you'll have access to more exceptions, monitoring, and rules for what can and can't get through the firewall.
- One interesting discovery that you'll make in the Advanced Security settings is that the Vista firewall also blocks outbound traffic. This prevents your infected computer from infecting others on your network. The bidirectional firewall feature is always turned on when the firewall is running, but you can't see it from the standard firewall dialog.

secure web browsing p. 119

- In Windows Vista, Internet Explorer runs by default in a new security mode called protected mode. This prevents Web-based software from modifying user settings or files, or downloading anything without your knowledge. Internet Explorer asks you to approve any download as it starts. If you don't know what the download is, you should not approve it.
- You can turn off protected mode by double-clicking the words Protected Mode: On at the bottom of the Internet Explorer window. This brings up a dialog where you can disable it. Doing this puts your computer at risk, however. You should have a very good reason before you turn off protected mode.

set spam filtering p. 120

- To prevent useful e-mail from being labeled as spam, you can specify users or domains as Safe Senders in Windows Mail.
- In the Junk E-Mail Options window, select the Safe Senders tab. You can type in individual e-mail addresses or specify a domain name, such as @company.com.

index

index

J

L

M

N

O

P

index

U

V

W

GET UP AND RUNNING QUICKLY!

For more than 15 years, the practical approach to the best-selling *Visual QuickStart Guide* series from Peachpit Press has helped millions of readers—from developers to designers to systems administrators and more—get up to speed on all sorts of computer programs. Now with select titles in full color, *Visual QuickStart Guide* books provide an even easier and more enjoyable way for readers to learn about new technology through task-based instruction, friendly prose, and visual explanations.

Task-Based
Information is broken down into concise, one- and two-page tasks to help you get right to work.

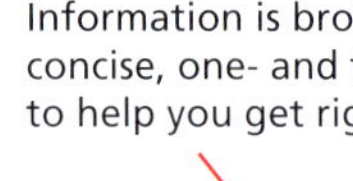

Visual
Hundreds of screen shots illustrate the steps and show you the best way to do them.

Step by Step
Numbered, easy-to-follow instructions guide you through each task.

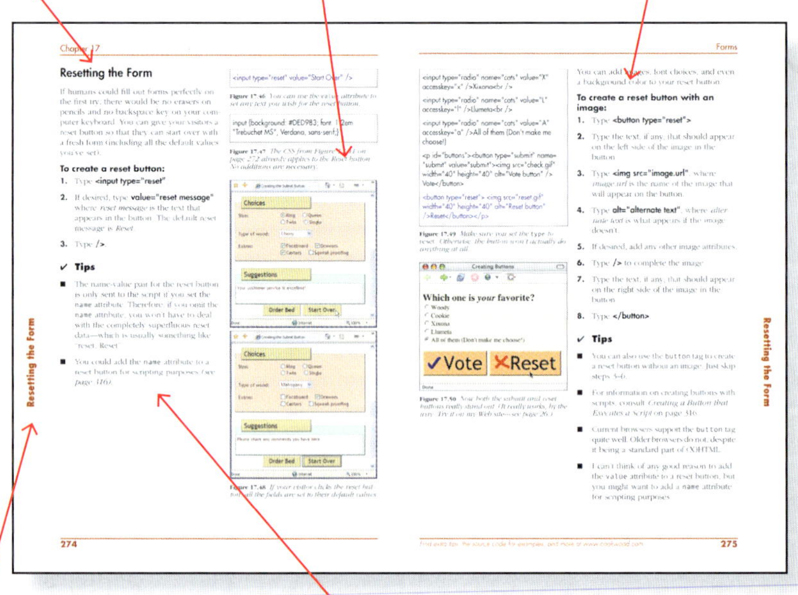

Quick Reference
Tabs on each page identify the task, making it easy to find what you're looking for.

Tips
Lots of helpful tips are featured throughout the book.